The World of the Russian Peasant:

Post-Emancipation Culture and Society

Edited by

Ben Eklof and Stephen Frank

D0062736

Boston
UNWIN HYMAN
London   Sydney   Wellington

Unwin Hyman, Inc.
8 Winchester Place, Winchester, Mass. 01890, USA

Published by the Academic Division of
Unwin Hyman Ltd
15/17 Broadwick Street, London W1V 1FP, UK

Allen & Unwin (Australia) Ltd,
8 Napier Street, North Sydney, NSW 2060, Australia

Allen & Unwin (New Zealand) Ltd in association with the
Port Nicholson Press Ltd,
Compusales Building, 75 Ghuznee Street, Wellington 1, New Zealand

First published in 1990

Library of Congress Cataloging-in-Publication Data

The World of the Russian peasant ; post-emancipation culture and
   society / edited by Ben Eklof and Stephen Frank.
     p.   cm.
   Includes bibliographical references.
   ISBN 0-04-445478-3
   1. Peasantry—Soviet Union—19th century. 2. Soviet Union—Rural
conditions. I. Eklof, Ben, 1946– . II. Frank, Stephen, 1955–
HD1536.S65W67 1990
305.5′633′0947—dc20   89-22637
                                                   CIP

British Library Cataloguing in Publication Data

The world of the Russian peasant : post-emancipation culture
   and society.
1. Russia. Peasants. Social conditions history
I. Eklof, Ben, *1946–* II. Frank, Stephen, *1955–*
305.5′63
ISBN 0-04-445478-3

Typeset in 10 on 12 point Garamond
and printed in Great Britain by The University Press, Cambridge

Contents

Acknowledgments   *page* v

Introduction   1

1   The Russian Peasant Commune after the Reforms of the 1860s
     Boris Mironov   7
2   Peasant Women and Their Work
     Rose Glickman   45
3   The Woman's Side: Male Outmigration and the Family
     Economy in Kostroma Province
     Barbara Engel   65
4   Peasant and Proletariat: Migration, Family Patterns, and
     Regional Loyalties
     Robert E. Johnson   81
5   Peasants in Uniform: The Tsarist Army as a Peasant Society
     John Bushnell   101
6   Peasants and Schools
     Ben Eklof   115
7   Popular Justice, Community, and Culture among the Russian
     Peasantry, 1870–1900
     Stephen P. Frank   133
8   Popular Religion in Twentieth-Century Russia
     Moshe Lewin   155
9   Images and Ideas in Russian Peasant Art
     Anthony Netting   169
10   The Russian Peasant Movement of 1905–7: Its Social
     Composition and Revolutionary Significance
     Maureen Perrie   193

Bibliography   219

About the Contributors   227

Index   229

Acknowledgments

The chapters in this book have been reprinted and revised with the permission of the authors and of the publishers. The editors wish to acknowledge the following sources:

Chapter 1, Boris Mironov, "The Russian Peasant Commune After the Reforms of the 1860s," from *Slavic Review* 44, 3 (Fall 1985): 438–67.

Chapter 2, Rose Glickman, "Peasant Women and Their Work," from Rose Glickman, *Russian Factory Women: Workplace and Society, 1880–1914*, 48–68 (Berkeley: University of California Press, 1984). Copyright © 1984 The Regents of the University of California.

Chapter 3, Barbara Engel, "The Woman's Side: Male Outmigration and the Family Economy in Kostroma Province," from *Slavic Review* 45, 2 (Summer 1986): 257–71.

Chapter 4, Robert Johnson, "Peasant and Proletariat: Migration, Family Patterns and Regional Loyalty," from *Peasant and Proletarian: The Working Class of Moscow in the Late Nineteenth Century* by Robert Eugene Johnson. Copyright © 1979 by Rutgers, The State University of New Jersey. Reprinted with permission of Rutgers University Press.

Chapter 5, John Bushnell, "Peasants in Uniform: The Tsarist Army and Peasant Society," reprinted from *Journal of Social History* 13, 4 (Summer 1980): 565–76, by permission of the editor.

Chapter 6, Ben Eklof, "Peasants and Schools," from "The Myth of the Zemstvo School," *History of Education Quarterly* 24, 4 (Winter 1984): 561–84 and "The Adequacy of Basic Schooling in Russia," *History of Education Quarterly* 26, 2 (Summer 1986): 199–224..

Chapter 7, Stephen P. Frank, "Popular Justice, Community, and Culture Among the Russian Peasantry, 1870–1900," from *Russian Review* 46, 3 (July 1987): 239–65.

Chapter 8, Moshe Lewin, "Popular Religion in Twentieth Century Russia," from *The Making of the Soviet System* by Moshe Lewin. Copyright © 1985 by Moshe Lewin. Reprinted by permission of Metheun & Co. in the U.K. and by Pantheon Books, a Division of Random House, Inc. elsewhere.

Chapter 9, Anthony Netting, "Images and Ideas in Russian Peasant Art," from *Slavic Review* 35, 1 (March 1976): 48–68.

Chapter 10, Maureen Perrie, "The Russian Peasant Movement of 1905–7: Its Social Composition and Revolutionary Significance." World Copyright: The Past and Present Society, 175 Banbury Road, Oxford. This article is reprinted with the permission of the author and the Society from *Past and Present: A Journal of Historical Studies*, no. 57 (November 1972), pp. 123–55.

Introduction

Ben Eklof
Stephen Frank

The study of the Russian peasantry has come of age during the last decade in both Western and Soviet scholarly communities. Fueled by the growing influence of social history and development studies in the sixties and seventies, building on theoretical controversies between neopopulists and Marxists at the turn of the century and during the NEP period, and utilizing the enormous storehouse of data collected by government and *zemstvo* statisticians, ethnographers, professionals, and peasant specialists in tsarist Russia, the field has made significant advances. Although older sources have been reevaluated and new material brought under scrutiny, these works largely represent an attempt to apply to Russia approaches successfully developed in the study of European and Third World peasantries by a new generation of historians, economists, anthropologists, and sociologists. To date no single monograph yet surpasses the seminal contribution made more than fifty years ago by G. T. Robinson, whose *Rural Russia under the Old Regime* remains the best study in English on the Russian peasantry. Cumulatively, however, research of the past decade has substantially altered or added depth to the portrait drawn by Robinson. Nowhere is this more evident than in recent scholarship concerned with the complexities of peasant culture and daily life in the late nineteenth century, the nature of Russia's pre- and postemancipation agrarian economy, and peasant politicization during the revolutions that shook the Russian Empire in 1905 and 1917.

The number of Western scholars pursuing the elusive Russian peasant has grown significantly, as has the scope of inquiry. To a large measure we owe these gains to earlier (and ongoing) work by Michael Confino, Peter Czap, Dan Field, Moshe Lewin, and Teodor Shanin. But enthusiasm has also been kindled, agendas set, and research methods honed by developments in the burgeoning field of peasant studies at the global level. We are learning, as Shanin and others have often pointed out, that many supposedly distinctive features of Russian peasant life are but regional variations of a global peasant culture. In his recent study, *Serfdom and Social Control in Russia*, for example, Steven Hoch argues that activities of communes in preemancipation rural Russia differed little from those of peasant communities throughout Europe in the modern era (a point that could be extended to South America or Asia as well). He further contends, as does Carol Leonard in her research on Iaroslavl province, that collective responsibility, strip farming, and periodic redistribution were variants of risk-avoidance techniques common to most peasantries. Thus though not losing sight of what was unique within the Russian experience, historians have ably demonstrated the value of a comparative approach in seeking to bring to life the aspirations and actions of Russia's peasantry. Anyone familiar with the achievements of social history, anthropology, and development studies will immediately recognize the collective debt owed to these fields by historians of Imperial Russia.

Methodologically, scholars have either examined the peasantry as a whole or focused on individual villages, estates, or districts; the one in search of broad commonalities and the other striving for rigor and precision. In these efforts both groups should be credited for wading through and making known the vast quantity of hitherto neglected yet extremely rich materials on peasant life in Russia. One major result of their research is a greatly expanded source base for further study, though such sources are not without problems. Because few peasants left written records about their lives, most sources used by social historians were produced by outsiders—that is, by nonpeasant observers of rural life. Large collections of material assembled by government committees or gathered by local organs of self-government (in particular, by the *zemstva*)—such as the Valuev Commission's investigation of agriculture and rural productivity, the Liuboshchinskii Commission's report on township (*volost*) courts, *zemstvo* budget studies and reports on health conditions and education, studies of rural handicraft industries, official reports on peasant disturbances, and Witte's special committee on the needs of agriculture, to name but a few—may all be viewed as inherently biased because of the social position, attitudes, and political perspectives of their authors. The same can be said of ethnographic material such as that found in numerous journals and monographs of the period or in tsarist archives. Contemporary descriptions of the commune, the peasant family, wedding rituals, holidays, religious practices, customary law, and other facets of rural life were written down by educated Russians, all of whom brought to their work their own views and assumptions and made clear choices (whether conscious or not) regarding which customs to record and which to ignore. Likewise, government censorship placed sharp limitations on the discussion of particular subjects in monographs or the press (sexual behavior, for instance, could rarely be discussed openly). Western scholars writing history "from the bottom up" have long been aware of such problems and the potential pitfalls they pose but have worked out strategies for reading and interpreting their sources. Here, too, historians of the Russian peasantry are learning from their counterparts in other fields, though the very newness of our material suggests that scholars continue to approach it with due caution.

The present reader brings together a representative selection of research that examines most directly specific aspects of peasant culture and daily life in late imperial Russia. Drawn from a much larger pool of possible contributions, it is the first such collection since the publication twenty-one years ago of *The Peasant in Nineteenth-Century Russia*, edited by Wayne S. Vucinich—a fact that alone reflects the need for making more readily available to students and specialists the findings of recent studies of the Russian peasantry. In 1968, writing in his concluding article to Vucinich's collection, Nicholas Riasanovsky noted the absence of scholarship on peasant culture and warned that "any discussion of the Russian peasantry in the nineteenth century omits reference to [peasant culture] at its own risk."[1] This volume is intended in part as a corrective designed to fill a serious gap in the field of Russian peasant studies. It demonstrates the significant progress made over the past two decades while at the same time indicating how much is yet to be done.

That the collection is limited almost exclusively to studies of culture and daily life is an indication of the quantity and range of current research, but this decision calls for some explanation. Although our own research interests played a part in the selection of material, the absence of single, representative studies on topics such as the rural economy and peasant politicization was far more important in determining the final structure and focus of the reader. Despite important work already published on these and other subjects, most are either specialized, regional studies or monographs. To treat each theme even partially would have entailed the inclusion of a far greater number of articles than space permitted and would still have resulted in a less than satisfactory diffusion of coverage. Availability and practical considerations of space, then, forced us to make the difficult choice between offering a highly limited sampling drawn from all areas of the field or a group of thematically connected articles. We have settled on the latter choice of a common theme, focusing on the material life, society, and culture of the late nineteenth-century Russian peasantry.

The collection begins with Boris Mironov's exceptional analysis of that most important institution in peasant life, the commune. The only Soviet contributor to this volume, Mironov draws from a wealth of sources to discuss the peasant commune's formal and informal structures, the range of functions that it performed (tax collection, road repair, mutual aid, social control), basic principles governing these functions, and the dual nature of the commune itself as both local agent of the state and protector of the interests of its members. He shows how the commune touched peasants in nearly all aspects of their daily lives, and provides fascinating examples of interaction among commune members. Finally, he addresses destabilizing factors within the postemancipation rural commune as well as those that led to its preservation into the twentieth century. Rose Glickman treats one important aspect of village labor in her examination of work performed by peasant women. Beginning with an overview of women's position in the peasant family, she first discusses their domestic chores and duties, then turns to the wide variety of jobs in which women were engaged (from fieldwork and other agricultural tasks to their crucial role in handicraft industries) and the significant contribution they made to the household economy.

The experience of peasants who journeyed outside the village for work or other purposes (such as military service), and of migrants to the empire's rapidly growing cities, is the focus of contributions by Barbara Engel, Robert Johnson, and John Bushnell. In her study of peasant women who remained in the village, Engel examines the impact of male outmigration on demography and the rural way of life and stresses the importance of family economy and family relations for the development of Russia's working class. Johnson treats such factors as patterns of peasant migration, the maintenance of village ties by migrant workers, life and labor in factories and cities, and the migrants' preservation of their culture within these new environments. Bushnell's article on the tsarist army demonstrates how powerful a force peasant culture could be even outside the village, transforming an institution whose purpose was to "civilize" the backward *muzhik* into a peasant society.

Articles by Ben Eklof, Stephen Frank, Moshe Lewin, and Anthony Netting offer a broad sample of work on peasant *mentalité* and popular culture. Examining the rapid spread of schooling among the postemancipation peasantry, Eklof questions the long-held assumption that the *zemstva* were primarily responsible for opening new schools in the countryside and shows that peasants themselves played an active, and at times dominant, role in this process by making decisions about the kind of education their children should have. Frank analyzes specific forms of popular justice practiced by Russian peasants (such as the *charivari*) and the beliefs that helped to sustain them. He argues that certain juridical practices in the village grew out of peasant culture and the conditions of rural life, and these practices often led to conflict with the state. Netting's study of peasant art seeks to demonstrate how symbols most commonly employed by villagers in their artwork were drawn directly from daily life and experience, expressing the collective character of peasant society noted by Mironov in his article on the commune.

Moshe Lewin provides a brief overview of popular religion and the supernatural in the Russian countryside, both of which played a major role in peasant thought as late as the 1920s. Though widely debated by contemporaries, this subject still awaits serious research. Finally, we include Maureen Perrie's article on the peasantry in the agrarian revolution of 1905. Taking a broad view at the national level, Perrie shows how the common interests and concerns of villagers overshadowed economic, intraclass distinctions to unite peasants in a wave of revolts that threatened the foundations of the autocratic state.

We should stress again that these articles represent only a small sample from a larger body of scholarship on the peasantry in Imperial Russia, much of which can be found in the bibliography at the end of this volume. By necessity much has been left out, including studies of the period before 1861. Nor was it possible (with one exception) for Soviet scholarship to be represented here, though students should be aware that major work has been done by historians, economists, and historical ethnographers in the USSR (Anfimov, Bernshtam, Fedorov, Gorlanov, Gromyko, Koval'chenko, Milov, Mironov, Minenko, Selunskaia, and Zorin, to name but a few). Excellent work has also been published in English on the peasantry under serfdom, as appears in the Bibliography (see Bohac, Czap, Hoch, Kolchin, and Melton). Even within the temporal boundaries we have imposed, however, only a limited number of topics could be covered. Those wishing to pursue the complexities of the peasant economy, for example, can consult studies by Baker, Gatrell, Gregory, Kahan, Munting, Pallott, Shanin, Simms and Wilbur. Robert Edelman and Scott Seregny have examined different aspects of peasants and politics. Important works by Timothy Mixter, Thomas Pearson and Christine Worobec, which are soon to appear in print, will greatly enhance our knowledge of peasant women, family, marriage, sexuality, village government, rural migrant labor, and peasant politicization.

Finally, in order to allow for as many selections as possible, most of the works included here have been edited and reduced, though we have taken care to preserve the fullness of each author's argument as well as the most interesting material presented in their studies. Readers wishing to pursue further research may thus wish to consult the original works or the monographs since published by these scholars in which each issue is given more complete treatment.

Note

1. Wayne S. Vucinich, ed., *The Peasant in Nineteenth-Century Russia* (Stanford, 1968), 265.

The Russian Peasant Commune after the Reforms of the 1860s

Boris Mironov

In the 1860s the Russian government carried out a series of major reforms that had important consequences for key dimensions of Russian society—its economy, judiciary, local administration, army, censorship, and education. Historians have generally agreed that the reforms exerted a profound influence on Russian historical development, but they have not arrived at an analogous consensus on *how* the reforms of the 1860s affected the general development of the country as a whole or the peasantry in particular.[1] In this article I seek to analyze the immediate effect of the reforms of the 1860s on the fundamental institution of the peasantry: the commune. I shall employ a sociological approach, a mode of analysis in which the specialized literature is both rich and diverse,[2] in an attempt to determine the underlying structural principles of the commune and to construct an analytical model for the functions and development of the repartitional land commune.[3]

The main focus of my study is the repartitional commune of the 1860s and 1870s.[4] An outstanding set of sources is available for these years: the descriptions (*opisaniia*) of 816 communes from a survey conducted between 1878 and 1880. The survey was based on a standardized questionnaire (with 143 and 155 question formats) devised by eminent scholars of the Free Economic Society and the Russian Geographical Society. The descriptions were obtained from people who lived and worked in the

7

countryside and were familiar with rural conditions: local administrative officials, landlords, priests, and peace arbitrators (*mirovye posredniki*).[5] The descriptions emanated from twenty Russian provinces, two Ukrainian provinces, and two Belorussian provinces. These communes may, moreover, be regarded as typical for their area, as the authors of the individual reports indicated that the particular communes they were describing were similar to dozens of other communes in that township (*volost*) and district (*uezd*).[6] For aspects of communal life not fully discussed in these descriptions, I also draw on a supplementary set of statistical, ethnographic, and legal sources as well as on folklore and belles lettres for a fuller account.

The Structure of Communal Life

As an analysis of the questionnaire shows, no two communes were identical. The most important differences derived from three main variables: (1) the form of economic activity, (2) the size of the population in a given commune, and (3) conformity of territorial boundaries—that is, whether commune and settlement boundaries coincided. The majority of villages can be assigned to the category of "agricultural village," a commune with a uniform peasant population engaged primarily in agriculture. Not all communes belonged to this category, however; there were also communes with a majority of members engaged in trade, artisan crafts, factory labor, innkeeping, and other forms of nonagricultural activity. Communes of these types developed a form of social and private life that differed fundamentally from that found in the ordinary agricultural commune. Most significant was the different social profile: nonagricultural communes had a far more complex, variegated social structure of estates and professions, and their populations often included several thousand people.[7]

In large agricultural communes of more than five hundred members, and especially in those with more than a thousand members, interpersonal relations took on a more formal character, and elected bodies—a kind of village bureaucracy—acquired particular significance in local governance.[8] In the middle-sized or small communes (up to five hundred people), the primary unit in local rule remained the village assembly (*skhod*), a gathering of all male heads of household; interpersonal relations here still tended to conform to the type of social relations found in small groups. "Composite communes" (*sostavnye obshchiny*) were those which united several sparsely populated villages; ordinarily they consisted of smaller units each comprising separate villages and virtually autonomous in operation. By contrast, the "fragmented commune" (*razdelnaia obshchina*), which existed wherever a settlement consisted of more than one commune, tended to merge into a large unit with common businesses, common responsibilities, and a common set of elected officials. In the 1860s and 1870s the larger communes (including the nonagrarian types) represented about 10 percent of all communes; composite communes formed 20 percent of all types, and fragmented communes about 4 percent.[9] Thus the typical agricultural commune, consisting of four to eighty peasant households/families and counting a population of 20 to 500 individuals (including children), and with territorial borders coinciding with those of the village, represented about 66 percent of all communes. The model commune consisted of eight to sixty households, 51 to 300 individuals; the mean in 1859 was forty-three households (254 persons), a figure that had risen to fifty-four households (290 persons) by 1877–78.[10] The model described in this article is that of the agricultural commune, which represented 66 percent of all Russian repartitional communes in the central provinces.[11]

The rural commune performed a broad range of functions, which can be divided into ten major categories:

(1) *Economic*: Regulation of land distribution and use, organization of production on communal lands.[12]

(2) *Taxation*: Apportionment and collection of monetary dues for the state, *zemstvo*, and commune; organization of peasant labor for obligatory tasks (the maintenance of roads, bridges, and ferries; convoy of prisoners and officials across the province; quartering of military units); responsibility for the collection and punctual delivery of payments due from each household; measures to collect arrears; keeping of accounts.

(3) *Legal*: Investigation of matters in civil law (disputes and litigation among peasants involving movable and immovable property within peasant allotments, or matters pertaining to loans, purchases, sales, and all sorts of transactions and legally binding commitments); compensation for losses and damages to peasant property; investigation and trial of criminal cases to be judged according to local custom (assault and battery, drunkenness, theft, but not including more serious offenses such as arson and murder).[13]

(4) *Administrative-police*: Maintenance of public order and the generally accepted norms of life and discipline within the commune; preservation of order and security of person and property; detention of vagrants, fugitives, and military deserters; enforcement of rules governing the registration, removal, and transfer of peasants from one commune to another; adoption of measures in the event of fire, flood, or other

emergencies; prevention of crime; adoption of measures to expose
and arrest the guilty, and preliminary inquest in such cases; punishment
of peasants for misdemeanors (fines, detention, and flogging); dispatch
of debtors (from tax arrears) to forced labor.

(5) *Integrative-defensive*: Unification of peasants into a cohesive body and
struggle for its interests vis-à-vis the state, landlord, other communes,
and institutions.

(6) *Cooperative-charity*: Mutual aid and assistance; food provisioning in
times of famine; poor relief; assistance to orphans, the ill, and old
people without kin; support of hospitals, welfare houses, public grain
reserves, and other social institutions.

(7) *Regulatory-educational*: Social control and socialization.

(8) *Cultural*: Management of public holidays, organization of recreation,
support of schools and libraries.

(9) *Religious*: Maintenance of churches and clergy; organization of religious
life; arrangement of religious holidays and agricultural rites during the
calendar year.

(10) *Communications*: Conduct of relations with local, township, district,
provincial authorities of the state and church.[14]

As this list suggests, the commune had to discharge a large and complex
set of functions. On one hand, the commune directed virtually all aspects
of the peasants' life, provided for their vital needs, and defended their
interests before the state; on the other hand, it was also an administrative
and policing body by means of which the government exacted taxes and
raised recruits from the peasantry and held them in obedience. Power
relationships in the commune were equally complex. The commune was
both an unofficial democratic organization (spontaneously formed on the
basis of neighborhood residence and the need for community among
peasants, it was used by peasants for their own benefit) and an officially
confirmed and recognized organization (which the government used in
its own interests). The goals of the government and of the peasants were
hardly identical. The result was a social and functional dualism based on the
contradictory tasks of the commune, and this dualism led to the formation
of a dual structure—a formal (official) and an informal (unofficial) one.

The formal structure of the commune was its external, visible organization: an official system of norms, values, roles, sanctions, prescriptions,
and institutions that were established by the state through formal legal
decrees. This formal structure was a necessary component of the general
state structure, its nuclear unit; as such it represented a direct link to the
official state apparatus, which both recognized and supported the commune.

The formal structure ensured that certain goals that the government set for the commune would be reached. The informal structure of the commune was its latent, internal organization composed of unofficial values, norms, roles, institutions, and sanctions that were transmitted by custom and tradition, derived spontaneously from daily work and relationships, and did not owe their existence to the state. This informal structure served the unofficial collective goals of the commune and did not intersect with the formal state administration. In other words, the formal structure enabled the state to extend its policies and its ideology to the peasants; to impose fiscal, administrative, and police functions on the commune; and hence to transform the commune into a state institution. The informal structure enabled the peasants to defend themselves against the state, performed essential functions in daily life, and preserved the commune as an institution of customary law.

Each structure contained three component elements: law and morality (behavioral norms), modes of action (which enabled the peasants to correlate behavior with law and morality), and leadership. Each of these components merits closer analysis.

The official law and the officially recognized morality of the state were limited primarily to the towns. As far as the peasantry was concerned, official law applied only in those relatively rare instances when the peasant dealt directly with the government: when dealing with matters outside the confines of the commune or when conducting business with state courts (voluntarily or involuntarily). Because most of the peasants' affairs involved members of the same commune or neighboring communes, matters governed by state law occupied an insignificant place in their lives. Most activities were regulated by unofficial norms, which jurists have termed "common law" or custom.

The origins of common law reached far into the past. In contrast to official law, common law lacked precision and uniformity, especially when applied to concrete issues. Matters were decided on an ad hoc basis—"according to justice," "according to the conviction of conscience," "according to the individual," and "according to the circumstances." Unofficial norms of law and morality were not codified (the first steps in this direction were not taken until the 1870s and 1880s), but they were often formulated as proverbs. These norms, invisible to the outsider, derived from the history of a given commune, the particular interpersonal relations in the commune, and the relationship of the commune to other social groups and the state. Most important, in relations among peasants, especially within a given commune, common law had far greater significance than official state law.[15] From the point of view of the state, custom and common law filled the gap that existed in the legal regulation of society.

Moreover, the differences between official and common law increased with the passage of time. Although this generated discrepancies, some of them serious, fundamental contradictions—which might have threatened the very existence of the contemporary social order—did not yet exist. The government was indeed at pains to ensure that discrepancies not grow into a major conflict, and sometimes it succeeded not only in eliminating the tension between formal and common law but even in using elements of common law to its own advantage. For example, according to official law the chief form of property was individual, private property. Nevertheless, until the early twentieth century the state recognized both familial and communal forms of property ownership, subject to regular redistribution; both forms were found in the common law of the peasantry. The state did so for the simple reason that this best guaranteed collective responsibility of the peasantry before the state and prevented the transfer of land to a prosperous elite and the formation of a landless peasantry incapable of fulfilling its obligations to the state. Similarly, official law was dominated by the principle of individual responsibility (fiscal and legal matters) before the state; yet in the case of the peasants the state recognized collective responsibility, a norm of common law. Again it did so because that approach facilitated the collection of taxes: by leaving it to the peasants to distribute this burden among themselves and to take the economic condition of each into account, the state did not have to control and evaluate the incomes of individual households.

The same dualism is found in the moral code that operated among the peasants. The communal conception of morality, which in many respects overlapped the official, recognized moral values, applied fully to interpersonal relations within the commune, extended to a lesser degree to peasants from other communes, and had only slight validity in dealings with the state, other classes, and other estates. The peasant deemed it "immoral" to deceive a neighbor or relative, but to deceive a government official or landlord was quite a different matter—indeed, that was a moral deed worthy of encouragement. Stealing something from a neighbor, violating the boundary markers dividing allotments, or cutting wood from the commune's forest without permission was immoral, but picking fruit from a squire's orchard, cutting wood in a forest belonging to a noble or the government, or putting some of a squire's land under plough—these were acts free from moral censure.[16] Thus the peasants had one morality when dealing with members of their own commune and quite another for outsiders, especially those who were not peasants. This accounts, at least in part, for the contradictory assessments of the peasants' morality. Representatives of the dominant class or the intelligentsia who did not have much opportunity to observe the behavior of the peasants within the commune gave a very low evaluation of their morality. By contrast, those members of the intelligentsia who nourished positive feelings toward the peasants and who knew them well rated their morality very highly.[17]

Leadership and Social Control

The formal and informal structures of the commune each had its own system of social control. Elements of formal control included fines, flogging, the confiscation and sale of property, detention, expulsion from the commune, consignment into the army as a recruit, exile, and imprisonment. Informal social control was exercised through caustic remarks, nicknames, disdainful treatment, scornful laughter, malicious gossip, and the like but could also include mob law. Public opinion as an instrument of informal control acted as the main regulator of peasant behavior.[18] Those who deviated from group standards, from the norms of common law, encountered at first ridicule, then open censure, and finally exclusion or expulsion from the commune (which could consist also of exile or forced recruitment into the army out of turn). Communal justice might even culminate in death (for instance, peasants not infrequently killed arsonists, robbers, and horse thieves).[19] Social control was so powerful that it was impossible for peasants to exist—physically or psychologically—if they found themselves in a hostile relationship with the commune.[20]

Both structures also had their own leadership. The formal structure had a regular hierarchy of officials: village and church elders; clerks; tax collectors; shepherds; and supervisors of grain stores, schools and hospitals, forests and fields. The informal structure, however, had its own leaders, whose influence derived from personal authority rather than official status. The formal structure was linked to the regular state apparatus, whereas the informal leadership was part of the unofficial governance in the commune.

The government did not risk appointing its own people, who would have been independent of the peasants, to official positions in the commune: that would have been too expensive and ineffective at the same time. It preferred to use leaders who had been selected by the peasants themselves. For this purpose the most important of the elected communal officials—the elder and the tax collector—were accorded official administrative powers and subordinated to the township and district administration of the state. In this way the government hoped to transform the elected officials into adjuncts of official authority and make them largely independent of the peasants. By law these elected officials were to be chosen at a meeting of the commune, but dismissal followed a different rule: removal from office of the most important elected official, the village elder, was a prerogative not of the commune but of the district state administration (subject to confirmation by the provincial governor).

The government not only gave a precise definition of the duties of the most important elective offices and their subordination to the superior state administration, but it also held their occupants responsible for "bad" (from the official perspective) performance of their duties (measures used in such cases included fines, brief incarceration, and judicial prosecution). The performance of administrative and police duties by elected officials was placed under the exclusive supervision of the district administration; only activities of elected officials in the economic and material spheres of village life were under the control of the commune.[21] Thus the government attempted to place the elected officials in a position of superiority, to sever the bond between those who elected and those who were elected, and to transform elected commune members into officials who would be independent of the commune.

If, however, one analyzes how these officials actually functioned, it is clear that the government did not reach its goal: elected officials did not stand above the commune but operated under its authority, and all administrative and police measures in the commune were taken only with the consent of the village assembly. Only very rarely did elected officials become a hostile authority standing above the peasantry: they had to be periodically reelected,[22] had no significant privileges, did not break their ties with the peasantry (elected officials were not freed from taxes and other obligations, except those in kind, and continued to perform all forms of peasant labor), remained under the control of public opinion in the village (and, in the event of malfeasance, faced the threat of retribution), and shared the common interests of the peasants, not the interests of the state. As a rule the elected officials acted as defenders of the commune, as its petitioners and organizers. Frequently they emerged as the leaders in peasant disorders despite the threat of harsh punishment.[23]

The position of the commune officials was, of course, an exceedingly difficult one. It was no accident that volunteers for these positions were rare, and the government had to compel people to serve by making it impossible to decline office; exceptions were made only for those over age sixty, those who had already served a full term, and those seriously ill.[24] Because many peasants had served or in the future would have to do so, they displayed sympathy and respect for these offices. Some of the peasants' proverbs expressed their sentiments: "No one applies to become elder, but you can't refuse the commune," or "You'll get kasha to eat if you become a priest, but just a slap in the face if you're made a village guard."[25]

Hence the elected officials emerged simultaneously as official overseers and as unofficial leaders in the commune. As formal officials they enjoyed power under state law by virtue of public election by the peasants themselves. But as leaders they were influential only to the degree that they represented the desires and goals of the informal group.

As a rule those elected to communal office were the "prosperous peasants," "the orderly," "the good," those neither old nor young (aged forty to sixty). It was expected that they run their household efficiently, have considerable life experience and authority, be energetic, and possess organizational skills. As a result, these positions ordinarily were in the hands of the more prosperous and respectable stratum of the peasantry.[26] Evidence for this is found, for instance, in data on the literacy of village elders. Whereas the literacy rate among the peasantry as a whole in the 1880s was no more than 8 to 9 percent, that among elders was twice as high—19 percent.[27] The influence of the elected officials, especially elders, depended entirely on their personal qualities.[28] But even influential elders could not act contrary to the village assembly and village opinion,[29] at least not for any extended period: a new election brought their removal, and sometimes mob law dealt with them as well.

The real "leaders" in the commune were the older peasants, the *stariki*, representatives of the older generation whose children were already adults. Ordinarily the peasant gave up his land allotment at the age of sixty, and the tax duties were removed from him; but he often remained fit for labor and did not cease to work. The older peasants preserved a clear mind, possessed much experience in life, and enjoyed a reputation as "right thinking" (honest and just); together they constituted a group and sometimes formed an informal "council of elders" (*sovet starikov*). They enjoyed considerable influence in the commune and they embodied its traditions, norms, and values. Every important matter in the commune was discussed first with the *stariki*, and in most cases their opinion was decisive: the village assembly made its decision only with the consent of the *stariki*.[30] The high prestige of the older peasants is explained by the fact that communal life was based on an oral tradition handed down from father to son. Older men emerged as most authoritative, for it was they who had the greatest professional and general knowledge; they were a living encyclopedia. The importance of their voice in all matters ensured the enormous influence of tradition in the daily life of the commune.

The elected officials constituted the executive power of the commune. By law they had to execute the will of central and local administrative authorities in the fiscal, administrative, and police spheres of communal life; at the same time, they had to carry out the will of the commune in economic and social matters. The will of the government was expressed in orders and directives; that of the commune was articulated in resolutions of the village assembly. Yet the elected officials could take no action without the consent and sanction of the assembly. Government directives had to be approved by the village assembly before they could be implemented, as the peasants acquiesced only in resolutions adopted by the assembly. Despite the intent of the state, the decisive element in the commune's government, its executive body, was therefore the assembly—a most democratic institution that had been forged by centuries of practical experience among the Russian peasantry. In the great majority of cases the assembly—again, contrary to the law—did not adopt a resolution by majority vote but attempted to reach unanimity; at any rate a decision was not made until the dissenting minority ceased to remonstrate (silent disagreement was regarded as agreement, in accord with the principle that silence is consent). Because the assembly had to make the decision in any matter that arose, it was precisely in the assembly that the contradictions between the formal and informal structures of the commune—as well as all other contradictions that existed within the commune—had to be resolved. Complex questions had to be discussed over a considerable period in the assembly repeatedly in heated debates. And the opinion of the assembly took shape under the strong influence of the *stariki*.

Not all government orders met with approval from the peasants, for in most cases they concerned new obligations, taxes, and duties for the commune. When especially important questions were being discussed, the representatives of the local administration therefore did not rely on the elected officials but attended the assembly sessions in person. At times local administrators had to make enormous efforts to convince the peasants that they must accept and implement a certain decree. These efforts involved persuasion and threats, demagoguery and coercion; the priest was also summoned to preach. In most cases the assembly displayed comprehension, if not approval, and passed the requisite resolution. But if the peasants deemed it impossible to implement the new order, they firmly stood their ground, resorting to passive resistance, and in extreme cases they did not shy away from active protests.[31] The Russian peasantry was by no means a "Kaluga dough" from which the government could bake any pretzel it wished, as some historians have asserted.[32]

Discussion of strictly internal communal affairs at the assembly had a more peaceful character, though situations of conflict often arose even here. First, sharp differences of interest frequently existed between individual peasants or groups of peasants, either for economic or for personal reasons. Second, and more important, decisions about internal communal matters could not be resolved within the informal structure but had to be reconciled with the demands of the formal structure. The elected officials bore responsibility for decisions of the assembly, and the state authorities held them criminally accountable for decisions that went beyond established law.

Thus the informal structure had an important place in the life of the commune; the formal structure was adapted and sometimes even subordinated to it. There was interaction and opposition between the two structures, but only rarely did all their elements fuse into a single whole. The government was able to draw the representatives of the communal administration into the system of state administration, to incorporate the *mir* into the state system as a nuclear unit of administration, and, with the assistance of elected officials and parish priests, to impress its policies and ideology on the rural population.[33] This process found its expression in the peasant proverb, "The commune is irreplaceable"—the authorities needed the commune to enhance their own power.[34] Nevertheless, the government could not transform the communal administration into a simple appendage of the state machinery or the commune into a purely formal official organization.[35] Because it lacked the requisite bureaucratic resources, the government could neither monitor the peasants' income nor establish a national income tax (and still less organize agricultural production in the commune): hence it was forced to allow the peasants considerable autonomy. Because elective offices changed frequently and positions were not associated with particular individuals or families for an extended period, and because the assembly functioned as the principal decision-making body, practically all men in the commune had to be concerned with community affairs. For that reason authority in the commune was not alienated from its rank-and-file members and bore a collective character, and progress up the service hierarchy of the formal structure depended less on loyalty to the state administration than on an individual's status in the informal structure, with personal charm, competence, friendship, kinship connections, and other factors playing a role. At the same time, common law did not allow some subgroups—women, youths, and men without an independent household—to participate in the assembly and hence excluded them from communal politics and power. This fact represented an important limitation on democracy within the commune.

Communal Cobesiveness

Interaction among commune members was extensive, even though it was marked by a certain formalism, especially in large communes. Human relations were of an intimate, personal character; they were based not on subordination but on affect or enmity, on kinship or neighborliness, on material or moral dependency. Moreover, interpersonal relations encompassed not merely a particular part of an individual's life but involved the whole person. This was reflected in the fact that all adults, and often the children too, had nicknames and addressed one another not by first names or surnames but by their nicknames—as "Clever," "Sandgrouse," "Calf," "Heart," "Tiger," "Wolf"—which often designated distinctive physical or character traits.[36]

Commune members interacted very intensively and were heavily dependent on one another. It is nearly impossible to find a single significant social act of the peasant (within the commune, to be sure) or a significant event in his life that was not influenced by the commune through either its formal or its informal structure. Land allotment and use of other communal resources, the performance of various duties and obligations imposed by the state, the division of property, departure for employment outside the commune, observation of religious rites, welfare for orphans, maintenance of schools, measures against cattle plague and fires, weddings and births, deaths and illnesses, family feuds—all were part of the life of the commune. For the peasant the commune was the most important reference group, even more important than such primary groups as the family and immediate neighbors.[37] It embraced not just a part of his life activity, not just certain parts of his personality, but his entire being and existence.[38]

There is yet another important characteristic of life in the commune: socialization was through direct experience, oral tradition, and living examples.[39] This kind of socialization (which arose from the fact that even in the 1880s, approximately 90 percent of the peasantry was illiterate)[40] minimized intergenerational conflict in the areas of culture and ideology. To be sure, significant material and psychological differences existed between generations.[41] But these were transitory differences that did not involve disagreement over fundamental principles and hence did not undermine the cultural continuity between generations. This form of socialization in the commune united fathers and children, placed the children in profound dependency on the fathers, raised the authority of the aged, and oriented the young toward tradition. All these are typical elements of a culture based exclusively on oral, direct transmission of experience from one generation to the next.

Although an individual peasant's role depended on his personal qualities and immediate circumstances, the socialization process and the strong social control exercised by the commune did not allow a distinction between the individual and the group: the peasant's "I" merged with the communal "we." The result, though imperceptible and unnoticed by the peasant himself, was a far-reaching regulation of the peasant's whole life and the observance (more often unconsciously than consciously) of those stereotypes and models existing in the commune.

It is important to note that the peasant did not perceive his fusion with the commune as a violation of his individual rights, that he did not feel enslaved by the commune. Because the feeling of "I" was only inadequately developed, the individual peasant voluntarily sought to immerse himself in the "we" of the commune.[42] The most striking example of this was the fact that decisions in the assembly were ordinarily expected to be unanimous, and if that unanimity was wanting, the commune made long, stubborn efforts to achieve it through compromise and suasion.[43] Although the fusion of the individual peasant with the commune could have meant the forcible subordination of the minority to the majority, this was rarely the case, at least in the period under examination, and the peasants regarded involuntary subordination as both extraordinary and undesirable. The relationship between peasant and commune may be called organic, voluntary conformism. This conformism was political, intellectual, moral, and social, and it made for standardization of the peasants' needs and interests.

Organic conformism found expression as well in the low degree of deviant behavior in the village. For the period 1860 to 1880, crime,[44] and suicide rates[45] were twice as high in the city. Divorce was also far less frequent among peasants than among urban residents.[46]

Ethnographic sources reveal an amazing homogeneity in material culture, customs, and habits among the peasantry, especially within the confines of a single commune.[47] Neither in clothing, hairstyles, nor household furnishings did the peasants pay heed to fashion. Changes in the peasants' material culture proceeded very slowly and derived from economic necessity or practical utility. According to Georg Simmel, indifference toward fashion demonstrates an absence of individualistic striving to differentiate oneself, to separate oneself from the larger group.[48] The uniformity of material culture and behavioral models, along with the absence of individualistic strivings, all reflect the organic conformism of the communal peasantry.

To be sure, the commune could not—anymore than serfdom in an earlier time—completely fetter and suppress the peasant. Total absorption of the peasant by the commune did not occur and, indeed, was hardly possible. The peasant did not become a robot, automatically responding to the orders of the commune; on the contrary, the commune left room for diversity and originality, even for open revolt by the individual. Manifestations of individualism were permissible both within the commune (in relations within the family, in work on one's own plot, and in one's own household economy) and beyond its confines (during trips to the market, to the city, or to work outside the commune). Only in those questions that concerned the common interest of the whole commune was the peasant's behavior strictly regulated and deviations from the norm reduced to a bare minimum. In questions of this nature the potential influence of the individual peasant on the commune was insignificant, whereas the power of the commune over the individual was virtually unlimited.[49]

Peasant Economy

To a significant degree peasant conformism became possible as a consequence of another characteristic of the commune: the commonality of interests among the majority of peasants, their homogeneous social status, their strong internal unity, and the cohesiveness of the commune. In terms of property ownership, of course, the peasantry did not form a single homogeneous whole, notwithstanding the leveling effects of land distribution and collective tax responsibilities. The peasant economy formed a continuum from dispossessed households (families without land, sometimes without livestock and farm tools, subsisting as hired laborers and beggars) to prosperous ones (households with several thousand rubles income per annum, with commercial and nonagricultural enterprises using hired labor)—in other words, stretching from the proletarian to the semiproletarian to the capitalist economic form. This heterogeneity in households may be classified in several categories depending on the particular commune studied and one's research objectives. Yet it is important to keep in mind that qualitative social differences appeared only between the extremes, which constituted an insignificant minority of the entire group.[50] Differentiation among the majority of peasant households (and thus among the peasants themselves) bore not a qualitative but only a quantitative character, given that the socioeconomic essence of all intermediate types of economy was identical: households were units of labor and consumption based mainly on the labor of family members and oriented not to make a profit but to achieve a balance between income and needs.[51] Because of their small size, the rural bourgeoisie and the proletariat were not capable of controlling and directing life in the commune.

That peasant households of the working/consuming type should dominate despite the extensive development of commercial-monetary relations in the village can be explained by the leveling mechanism operating in the commune. It embraced the following subjective and objective factors:

(1)   Systematic, equitable redistribution of communal land among the peasants prevented its concentration in the hands of a rich minority.[52]

(2)   The low level of mechanization and the low productivity of agriculture (in European Russia the average yield of grain on peasant land was 4.64 centners per hectare in 1861–70 and 4.99 centners per hectare in 1871–80) limited both income and the accumulation of capital.[53]

(3)   Increases in agricultural productivity lagged behind demographic growth (for the decades 1861–70 and 1871–80, the per capita harvest of grains and potatoes in European Russia declined from 4.06 to 3.86 centners),[54] and this in turn meant a declining per capita income for the rural population.

(4)   The peasants' tax burdens and obligations exceeded their economic returns. This was especially evident in the provinces that were not part of the black soil region;[55] under the terms of the reforms in the 1860s, the peasants paid more quitrent per desiatina than they had before the reforms.[56] Moreover, by 1882 peasant arrears amounted to 24.2 million rubles, which represented 47.2 percent of the amount owed.[57] For the majority of peasants this severely limited the possibilities of accumulating capital.

(5)   The unfavorable number of working days (nonworking days constituted up to one third of the year)[58] had a negative impact on peasant income.

(6)   The peasants' economic behavior was oriented not toward making a profit but toward satisfying the subsistence needs of their families.

(7)   Mutual responsibility obliged the rich peasants not only to pay the arrears of the poor but also to support them or, in any event, not to contribute to their final ruin.[59]

(8)   The commune also developed measures to retard differentiation in the peasantry.

The final factor merits closer examination. Above all it is important to note that the commune did not—indeed, could not—attempt to achieve complete economic equality among its members. It did, however, seek to establish certain limits to differences in their economic status. The measures that were adopted were diverse and depended on the circumstances of the individual commune; they included public service, welfare and assistance, the system used to choose recruits, and progressive taxation.

The commune had numerous elective offices. The most important ones entailed the greatest loss of work time, the most frequent material losses, and the most frequent distraction from the individual's own economic affairs. These losses were not compensated by the salaries or insignificant privileges accorded the upper official ranks. According to some calculations (which are probably exaggerated, however), public business occupied up to a third of the time of those holding offices.[60] These losses in work time were not evenly distributed among all strata in the commune; to a large extent they fell upon the upper stratum.[61]

The peasantry also preserved a custom of charity which imposed on prosperous peasants the moral obligation to donate resources to widows, orphans, the church, and the school.[62] It was deemed a great sin to refuse assistance to those who begged for handouts in "Christ's name,"[63] and this sustained the custom of "seeking crusts" (*khodit v kusochki*)—that is, asking in the name of Christ for food in one's own village and, if this did not suffice, in neighboring villages as well.[64] As Vladimir G. Korolenko wrote, "begging in Russia [was] a great popular strength, mutable and elastic, either embracing huge masses [in famine years], or once again singling out a few from its depths."[65] Even though charity did not reduce inequities, it did in part assist the poorest peasants to hold out for short periods, to keep their household intact. The custom of "mutual assistance" (*pomoch*) served the same function. When a peasant fell victim to illness, fire, or cattle plague, neighbors and sometimes the entire commune came to help with time-consuming or especially urgent tasks. They worked without pay the entire day, receiving only food and drink on completion of the work.[66]

Another leveling mechanism was the system for recruitment into the army, which, until the introduction of universal military conscription in 1874, fell in the provenance of the commune. The government demanded a specific number and quality of recruits from the commune but did not influence the selection process.[67] Making use of this freedom the commune, following custom, sent in the first instance peasants guilty of deviant behavior, in the second instance the poorest peasants, and finally those whose turn had come in accordance with the ordinary rules of recruit selection. Prosperous peasants could buy their way out of the recruit obligation. Given that prior to the reforms of 1874 recruits practically never returned home, the commune could by this mechanism rid itself of nonconformist elements and the poor, and from the rich it levied a redemption payment. With the establishment of universal military conscription in 1874, the leveling effect of this institution became much less pronounced.

These measures could not, of course, eliminate differentiation altogether, but to a certain degree they served to retard the process. It is no accident that the entire rural bourgeoisie was based not on agriculture but on trade and industry.[68]

The similarity in the socioeconomic profile of most peasant households meant that the main strata of the peasantry generally favored the commune.

Only relatively small groups of peasants began to regard the commune as a burden: the bourgeois elements that could not fully exploit their fellow commune members, and the proletarian elements that could not free themselves from the commune and settle in the city.[69] This also explains why, during the Stolypin agrarian reforms in the early twentieth century, it was chiefly peasants from the extremes of the social order that left the commune.[70]

In assessing the consensus that underlay the commune, it is also important to consider the peasants' own thinking. The peasant economy was exceedingly unstable and insecure—a rich household could become impoverished overnight, a poor one could become rich. A significant majority of the peasants experienced a change in status in the course of their lives.[71] As a consequence the interests of the majority—which kept in mind the instability of their position, equality in rights and duties, and their equal dependence on the state—in principle coalesced to form a cohesive whole. Hence an absolute majority of the peasants in the 1860s and 1870s still supported the commune and indeed could not even conceive of an existence outside its confines. "The commune is something great, greater than man." "Who is greater than the commune? You don't fight the commune."[72]

The impact of communal property on the cohesiveness—both external and internal—of its members is beyond question.[73] Evidence can be found in a comparison of the Russian peasantry with peasants in the Ukraine and Belorussia, where private rather than communal property prevailed and individual household inheritance was the dominant system. As replies to the questionnaire of the Free Economic Society from Belorussian peasants demonstrate, here—to a significantly greater degree than among the Russian peasantry—the abolition of serfdom was followed by competition, by the striving of the rich peasant to prosper at the expense of the poor peasant, and by strong economic differentiation. Correspondents from Vilnius province wrote: "Communal law is very weakly developed here, and hence the other peasants look indifferently upon the decline of a particular household—indeed, they do not forego the opportunity to profit at the expense of the impoverished, for example, by seizing his land, imposing excessive obligations in kind, and so forth."[74]

Social Mobility

To understand the commune, it is important to determine the rates of social mobility that had developed among the peasantry. Horizontal mobility in the 1860s and 1870s took various forms: migration for nonagricultural labor (both in the immediate surroundings and to more distant locations to work in factories, crafts and artisanal enterprises, and commercial firms); brief trips to the city, bazaars, markets; and transfers to neighboring communes (within the same district). For the period 1870 to 1896 the number of migrants—an index for the level of population movement—totaled 3.9 million individuals in the empire as a whole.[75] These migrants, of whom the great majority were peasants, absorbed less than 6 percent of the natural demographic growth in the country.[76] In the 1880s all forms of crafts and industry in the provinces in which communes were located employed about 16 percent of the male peasant population (7 percent working away from home, but generally without severing their ties to the land of the commune).[77] Almost all adult males, moreover, made short trips to the city, market, and bazaar. Transfers to another commune were virtually unknown, as peasants lost their right to land allotments if they left their communes of origin.

Particular provinces sharply differed from one another in the degree of horizontal mobility. Only in a few provinces (Iaroslavl, Moscow, Vladimir, and Tver', for instance) did contemporaries discern a significant impact of horizontal mobility on the peasantry and the rural commune. Even there the influence was apparent chiefly in terms of the standard of living, of external material culture; at the time, at least, it had little effect on *mentalité*, mores, customs, and production.[78] It had an impact only on those peasants who repeatedly went to the two capitals or to other large cities for extended stays.[79] In the city the peasants did not become part of the general urban populace but remained with their artisanal collective (*artel*) and with people from their own geographic area; it was only with difficulty that they yielded to the processes of cultural assimilation.[80] The influence of the city worked through a kind of cultural sieve that determined how urban culture was acquired and what elements were rejected.[81]

Vertical mobility in the peasantry included mobility into other social strata and within the commune itself. As a rule movement from one social category to another resulted from relocation to a city and inscription in official tax rolls as an "urban resident." Hence the dynamics of urban population growth are an important index to the development of intergroup mobility. Between 1863 and 1885 the urban population of European Russia increased from 6.1 to 10.0 million (from 10 to 12 percent of the population).[82] Even if the entire growth in urban population for these years is explained by peasant migration, only 3.9 million (6.2 percent of the rural population) left the countryside over a period of twenty-three years. In sum, intergroup mobility drained off fewer than

177,000 individuals a year—less than 0.28 percent of the rural population.

An important mechanism for vertical mobility, however, was the army. Prior to the establishment of universal military conscription, recruitment exerted a stabilizing influence: the commune sent into the army the poor and the deviant, conducting as it were a purge and social selection of unwanted elements.

The low intergroup mobility of the peasantry is explained by the closed system of social estates (*sosloviia*) in Russian society, by the serious juridical barriers to transfer into other estates, and by the restrictive impact of the commune's tendency to level and retard differentiation among the peasantry.[83]

By contrast, the intracommunal mobility of the peasantry was very high. If one uses the simplified categories of poor, intermediate, and prosperous, then approximately 80 percent of the peasants changed their status in the two or three decades after the mid-nineteenth century and about 60 percent by the turn of the century. As a result, only an insignificant proportion of the children inherited the status of their fathers. Intracommunal mobility followed a cyclical pattern, unifying and consolidating the peasantry within a single commune. Despite the high degree of intracommunal mobility, the commune gradually developed groups of hereditary poor and rich, a process that became increasingly marked as time passed. As a rule, however, these extreme groups abandoned the commune and departed for the city, industry, trade, and the army because they found it difficult to get along inside the commune. By expelling "social rejects" and making access difficult for outsiders, for a long time the commune was able to preserve its socioeconomic homogeneity.[84]

Thus the level and character of social mobility in the peasantry in the 1860s and 1870s allow one to describe the commune as a half-closed social organization, a microcosm dominated by local interests.[85] As a result of the juridical, social, and cultural isolation of the peasantry, it represented not simply a social estate but "a completely separate world, in the very foundations of its civic order profoundly distinct from all other social groups in the Russian population."[86]

"A Separate World"

The following principles governed the functioning of the commune.[87]

(1) Democratic centralism: primacy of the interests of the entire commune over those of individual peasants or families.

(2) Collective responsibility: the commune was responsible for the individual before the government; the family bore that responsibility before the commune.
(3) Members were allowed a measure of individualism and initiative in the practical realization of the principles of communal life, but within the framework of traditions and customs.
(4) Complete equality of rights and obligations of peasants (or families), and regulation of any differentiation among them.
(5) The equal use of communal resources gave all peasants the right to property and labor and assured the means of subsistence for each member of the commune, as well as each family's capacity to pay taxes.
(6) The right to participation in public matters (at the assembly through peasant courts and elective offices).
(7) The right of families to communal assistance in crisis situations.
(8) Nonintervention of the commune in internal family and personal matters so long as these were handled within the limits of custom and tradition and did not violate the interests of the whole community.
(9) Traditionalism, marked by an orientation toward the past as the ideal.

These principles of communal life institutionalized the social, economic, and familial relations of peasants within the commune. They represented the norms, the unwritten laws of communal life, and so bore an ideal character. In the peasants' daily struggle these principles could be an advantage to some and an impediment for others.[88] For example, an assembly's decision on land redistribution might be made after a stubborn struggle that lasted several years, and it was made only when it had become advantageous for the majority of commune members.[89] When peasants who opposed the principles of communal life were dominant, the norms were violated, distorted, and transformed. In addition to temporary conflict, the commune generated a stable minority of members who, as a matter of principle, were opposed to the norms of communal life and made a systematic effort to undermine its traditional foundations.[90] As a consequence the commune witnessed perpetual struggles: among those with different principles—that is, between the bourgeois elements and the traditional majority—and among those who agreed on the norms but differed on how to apply them.[91]

Insofar as these principles in general corresponded to the needs and interests of the middle-level peasants, who constituted the majority in the village, it was that group—and its principles—which most frequently prevailed. This general pattern continued to assert itself amid recurring deviations from the norm. Despite its collective spirit the Russian commune was by no means a charitable institution; the Russian peasant, for all his willingness to sacrifice personal interest for the sake of general interest, was no philanthropist.[92] "Individualism, egoism, and striving to exploit others are extremely well developed among the peasantry," observed A. N. Engel'gardt, a writer of populist convictions. The triumph of communal principles was aided by the propensity of the peasant to become a kulak and exploiter at the first opportunity:

> As long as he is a peasant, as long as he works, toils, and cultivates the land himself, he is not a real kulak—he does not think of seizing everything, does not think how nice it would be if everyone else was poor and needy, and does not work toward this end. Of course, he takes advantage of the needs of others, forces them to work for him, but he does not base his well-being upon the needs of others but upon his own labor.[93]

When the basic principles were observed in their entirety, the result was an ideal commune with a well-developed communal spirit. The ideal was rarely attained, however. Communes formed a continuum from those with a weak communal spirit to those with a strongly developed one. Therefore it is possible to argue that particular communes adapted to diverse and variable conditions within the framework of the general principles but deviated from them in one or another direction, applying specific means for their realization. The following example illustrates this point.

Various methods were used to determine each household's share of the tax payments that had to be sent "up" to the government each year. The tax dues might be based on the size of the land allotment, the number of livestock, income from nonagricultural labor, or the income level of the household. In general the payments corresponded to those features of the economy which characterized the economic strength of households in a given area. Moreover, the commune was guided above all by the principle of proportionality in correlating tax dues with the income of each household. When a family suffered severe reverses from accidents or appeared in a general state of decline, the commune freed it from all or part of the payments, deferred payment, provided interest-free loans, and granted it other temporary privileges. This assistance was given primarily at the expense of the prosperous households and represented an embrionic form of progressive taxation;[94] some communes actually practiced a kind of progressive taxation.[95] The methods used by the communes for the assessment and distribution of taxes thus ranged from "less just" to "more just" ones.

Change in the Post-Reform Era

In order to determine how the commune changed in the postreform era, it is important to compare the commune of the 1860s and 1870s with that of earlier years. As a first step it is essential to examine the conditions under which the commune and the peasantry had to operate.

The reforms of the 1860s intensified bourgeois tendencies of development, especially in large-scale industry, finance, the socioeconomic infrastructure, and urban culture. The village was not left untouched by this progress; it too experienced the strong growth of commodity-monetary relations and a degree of involvement of the peasantry in the countrywide market. Among the peasantry a series of new phenomena appeared, both positive and negative. The positive developments, as yet only weakly expressed, consisted of efforts to intensify agricultural production, the cooperative movement, increased availability of credit, a rise in mobility, and commercial entrepreneurship.[96] The rise in literacy and urban culture encouraged the peasants to develop a feeling of personal individualism, which was especially apparent when peasants worked in the city and established close bonds between the city and their commune. In the opinion of contemporaries, it was individualism which caused the increasing frequency of divisions in family property[97] and the growing fondness for fashionable dress (that is, urban clothing)[98] among the peasants after 1861.

More apparent were the negative phenomena—the heavy yoke of redemption and tax payments, the rise in arrears, agrarian overpopulation, the ever more acute shortage of land, the dwindling pool of livestock, and the resulting pauperization[99] and increase in social inequality.[100] A decline in the purchasing power of the peasants and, consequently, their well-being was graphically apparent in the declining consumption of spirits—especially when one takes into account that the peasants regarded vodka as a necessity, not a luxury. In the fifty provinces of European Russia the annual consumption of purchased spirits per capita declined from 0.36 *vedro* in 1870–74 to 0.32 *vedro* in 1875–79, a reduction of 11.1 percent.[101]

A further indication of the deteriorating condition of the peasantry is found in data from universal military conscription: the number of those found unacceptable for military service (because of illness, physical shortcomings, height, immaturity) increased even though the physical requirements for induction into the army were lowered.[102] It is well known that a poor diet produces especially negative effects in children, retarding their growth, their physical and psychological development.[103] The cohort born between 1853 and 1857 (before the Great Reforms) and called up for service from 1874 to 1878 yielded 335,600 physically unfit recruits (representing 26 percent of all those called up);[104] the cohort born between 1867 and 1872 and conscripted from 1888 to 1893 had 625,500 rejects (33 percent of all those called up); and the cohort born between 1876 and 1880 and drafted from 1897 to 1901 produced 885,500 rejects (38 percent of the pool).[105] It is fair to suggest that the significant increase in the number of rejects reflects the declining health of the peasants (who made up the lion's share of those drafted), which was the product of malnutrition caused by the deterioration in its economic circumstances.[106]

Amid the changing and largely adverse conditions of the 1860s and 1870s the commune exhibited an astonishing vitality. The dualism of the commune and the characteristic struggle of its two fundamental principles—individualism and collectivism—has already been noted. The conflict between these principles grew more intense in these two decades.[107] On one hand, there was a rise in social differentiation and mobility, an improvement in literacy rates and a broadening in perspective, a strengthening of the peasant's sense of self and the development of the nuclear family, a decline in the role of the elders, and an atrophy of certain patriarchal traditions in the life of the commune.[108] On the other hand, one does not find any significant changes in the structure and functions of the agrarian commune. Not only is there no abandonment of basic principles that had been developed in the prereform era,[109] but, on the contrary, their observance became at once more strict and systematic and in some sense more flexible.[110] One obtains the impression that both principles continued to develop and grow stronger but that for the time being the collective one remained dominant. Several factors account for this impression.

After prolonged delays and hesitation,[111] a movement for land distribution began to sweep Russia in the late 1870s which resulted in an affirmation of the established land use practices of the peasantry. This movement was accompanied by a transition to a principle of greater equality in land distribution and the extension of this principle to house plots and woodlands. The norms of communal life established themselves freely, without any pressure from outside, among the former serfs who were used to corvee (*barshchina*). In the overwhelming majority of cases, the peasants supported the commune; only a small number exercised their right to purchase their allotments and separate themselves from the commune. Similarly, the transition from communal to household landholding occurred only in isolated villages, and even there only under the pressure of local authorities. These results emerge not only from an analysis of the questionnaire of the Free Economic Society[112] but also from a comprehensive statistical analysis of 133 districts in twenty-four provinces of European Russia (conducted in the 1880s and early 1890s by *zemstvo* statisticians).[113] As a result, the commune became strengthened in thirty-seven Russian provinces that constituted the main bastion of the communal order. As a proportion of peasant landholding, the communal order encompassed 89.0 percent of all peasant households (92.2 percent of the land) in 1877–78; by 1905 this proportion had increased to 89.5 percent of all peasants (and 93.3 percent of all land).[114]

By the onset of the Stolypin Reform in 1906, the Russian repartitional commune was still alive and active.[115] This fact supports the conclusion that in the effort to survive, the majority of peasants depended primarily on traditional modes. Only an insignificant number of peasants found an alternative to the commune in trade, industry, and the sale of their labor. As in the past, the majority placed their hopes for a better life in the commune and a new agrarian reform, which would transfer all the lands of the nobility to the commune.[116] These divisions within the peasantry persisted until 1917—on one side a significant (if gradually declining) majority that clung to the traditional methods of solving their problems of survival, and on the other side a minority (gradually gaining in strength) which, disillusioned with old approaches, searched for new ways to improve its material condition.[117] The government's decree on land realized the aspirations of the majority, and hence its implementation contributed to a rebirth of the commune.[118]

Among the factors that contributed to the preservation of the commune (and, in a series of instances, its revival), the peasant reform was the most important. By abolishing the authority of the squire, weakening government guardianship, conferring the right of self-government on the peasants, and increasing the administrative authority of the commune over the peasants, it made it difficult for them to leave the commune.[119] At first the peasants were burdened by redemption payments, which in the majority of cases exceeded their revenues from the land and from rents. Having no legal right to renounce the land, they faced the problem not of equitable distribution of profits but of losses from their land allotments.

The peasants became extremely vigilant and persistent in upholding the principles of equitable distribution of land and payments for the simple reason that their very survival depended on it. This accounts for the peasants' unremitting interest in the commune and their strong support for its mechanism for land redistribution.[120] With time, as the allotments were "cleared" of redemption payments, the land rose in value, and by the late 1870s its value surpassed the amount of the redemption payments. Now the peasants' interest in the land was no longer a matter of necessity; cultivation became profitable, and the peasants no longer tried to free themselves of the land and abandon the village. But the available land did not correspond to the existing needs because the reforms had deprived the former serfs of approximately 4.1 percent of their prereform allotment (in the black soil areas this even amounted to 16.0 percent) and left 28.0 percent of all peasants with an insufficient allotment.[121] The rapid growth of the population after 1861 further reduced the per capita allotment. Finally, in the late 1870s, as a consequence of the abundant supply of peasant labor, the possibilities of earning an income outside the commune were diminished. All of these factors worked in favor of the commune and its principles of collective life.[122]

Thus the reforms of the 1860s did not lead to gradual or direct changes in the commune. The commune neither set new social goals for itself nor developed new means of achieving them; rather, it adapted to the new conditions of existence—however painful that may have been—by more strictly observing its traditional principles. Nevertheless, the reform generated a new minority, which aspired to a bourgeois path and gradually won more and more peasants to its banner. These two tendencies, the traditional and the bourgeois, persisted in the development of the Russian peasantry (with the traditional one predominant) until 1917.

The Durability of the Commune

What accounts for the durability of the commune as an institution? Several key elements contributed to its high degree of social stability:

(1) The social and teleological dualism of the commune. This was a source of great vitality, flexibility, and adaptability, first because it enabled the commune to satisfy the interests of both the state and the peasantry and second because communal property (and the social relations to which it gave rise) imparted resilience to the communal foundations, whereas private households, separate cultivation of arable land, and private acquisition of its fruits permitted the development of the individual personality.[123]

(2) The commune was almost impervious to internal dissolution: it provided the peasant with the means for existence, restrained social differentiation, systematically expelled anyone deviating from the norms, regulated the economic activity of its members, responded to the interests of the majority, and enjoyed its support.

(3) The commune received reinforcement from the outside in the form of legal and administrative support by the state and moral support by the church.[124]

(4) Rigid separateness of social estates, limited mobility, socialization by means of direct transmission of experience, a low literacy rate, and

scant knowledge of the external world deprived the peasants of new models for behavior and conserved the norms and values of the commune.[125]

(5) The population density,[126] which retarded development of the social division of labor and nonagricultural employment, for a long time made it possible to practice extensive agriculture through the three-field system and allowed a harmonious agrarian order to develop and to persist.[127]

(6) The weakly developed personal individualism of the peasant and an outlook oriented toward tradition as the fundamental, definitive principle of life.

This combination of factors shows clearly that the commune was not compatible with an intensive market economy,[128] with significant differentiation in property, culture, and social status; with formal rationality; with a clearly expressed individualism; with a constitutional state—in short, with the characteristics of an industrial society. Postreform Russia as a whole was developing along bourgeois lines and acquired precisely those characteristics of an industrial society which were irreconcilable with the values and principles of the commune as an institution of a traditional society. Despite the phenomenal vitality of the commune, its days were numbered because it did not exist in a social, economic, and cultural vacuum. Certain phenomena in the commune itself contributed to this development: insufficient resources, the growth of individualism, differentiation, literacy, mobility, development of the nuclear family. As yet no more than tendencies, these phenomena nevertheless undermined the commune and threatened to destroy it. There were, however, several directions the commune could take as it emerged from this transitional crisis period. As a consequence of its dualism, the Russian rural commune could be transformed into a multifamily collective economy, into a large capitalist agroindustrial enterprise, into a cooperative, or into a commercial operation based on the family. The direction depended on the path of development taken by society at large.[129]

Hence the immediate consequences of the reforms of the 1860s were not those expected by either the state or the ruling class. In lieu of social peace and prosperity based on slow, tranquil modernization, the Russian village experienced a serious social, political, and economic crisis by the late 1870s.[130] For the overwhelming majority of peasants, the conditions created by the reforms precluded the development of a rational economy. Although a certain segment of the peasantry showed affinities for the urban bourgeois culture, an overwhelming majority resisted modernization and strove to preserve the traditional order: the centuries-old, fundamental peasant culture showed its strength.[131] But as the city, in contrast to the village, quickly began to modernize under the impact of the reforms, the social, economic, and cultural differences between city and country turned into total antitheses, the gap between them becoming unbridgeable. All of these developments prepared the way for a general conflagration—a peasant war against the noble landowners, the rural bourgeoisie (whom the peasants perceived as violators of popular justice), and the government. The "Great" Reforms became a prelude to the Russian Revolution. That was the logical outcome of the inconsistent, contradictory reformism of the 1860s, which pursued narrow class goals and left untouched the fundamental institution of Russian society—the commune.

Notes

This article was translated by Gregory L. Freeze; a preliminary version was drafted by Carol S. Leonard.

1. A negative assessment of the reforms is found in N. M. Druzhinin, *Russkaia derevnia na perelome 1861–1880 gg.* (Moscow, 1978), 266–75; and Alexander Gerschenkron, "Agrarian Policies and Industrialization: Russia, 1861–1917," *Cambridge Economic History of Europe*, vol. 6, pt. 2 (Cambridge, 1965), 727, 743, 765, 798–99. More positive evaluations are found in P. G. Ryndziunskii, *Utverzhdenie kapitalizma v Rossii* (Moscow, 1978), 284–94; and R. Portal, "The Industrialization of Russia," *Cambridge Economic History of Europe*, vol. 6, pt. 2, 810–11.

2. Sociologists and anthropologists who have conducted research on the commune hold one of three theoretical positions: (1) typological, (2) ecological, or (3) structural-functionalist. See D. E. Poplin, *Communities: A Survey of Theories and Methods of Research* (New York, 1972); and Jerzy Szacki, *History of Sociological Thought* (London, 1980), 439–43. For the historiography on anthropological and sociological works on the commune, see Alan Macfarlane, "History, Anthropology and the Study of Community," *Social History* 5 (1977): 631–52; Robert Redfield, *Human Nature and the Study of Society*, vol. 1 (Chicago, 1962), 302–10, 375–91; Sydel Silverman, "The Peasant Concept in Anthropology," *Journal of Peasant Studies* 7 (1979): 49–69; R. L. Simpson, "Sociology of the Community: Current Status and Prospects," *Rural Sociology* 30 (1965): 127–49.

3. A model of the commune denotes an approximate analogue that, in a general way, reflects the fundamental features, regularities, and peculiar characteristics of the functioning of thousands of individual communes.

4. The literature on the repartitional commune is enormous: about three thousand books and articles (excluding works about the peasantry that treat the commune only in passing). As a rule, however, scholars have limited their research to particular aspects of communal life, primarily economic and juridical dimensions, and have not examined the commune in all its important aspects as a total, internally coherent system. For the historiography on the commune, see V. A. Aleksandrov, *Selskaia obshchina v Rossii (XVII-nachalo XIX v.)* (Moscow, 1976), pp. 3–24; S. M. Dubrovskii, "Rossiiskaia obshchina v

literature XIX i nachale XX v. (bibliograficheskii obzor)," in *Voprosy istorii selskogo khoziaistva, krestianstva i revoliutsionnogo dvizheniia v Rossii* (Moscow, 1961), 348–61; K. R. Kacharovsky, "The Russian Land Commune in History and Today," *Slavonic Review* 7 (1929): 565–76; M. B. Petrovich, "The Peasant in Nineteenth-Century Historiography," in W. S. Vucinich, ed., *The Peasant in Nineteenth-Century Russia* (Stanford, 1968), 191–320. For a bibliography of literature about the commune, see S. G. Pushkarev, *Krestianskaia pozemelnaia peredelnaia obshchina* (Newtonville, MA, 1976), vi-x.

5.   Thirty-three descriptions of communes have been published in *Sbornik materialov dlia izucheniia selskoi pozemelnoi obshchiny*, vol. 1 (St. Petersburg, 1890) [hereafter *Sbornik materialov*] (the questionnaire format is published in ibid., 1-36). A detailed source analysis is to be found in L. I. Kuchumova, "Iz istorii obsledovaniia selskoi pozemelnoi obshchiny v 1877–1880 godakh," *Istoriia SSSR*, no. 2 (1978): 115–26.

6.   TsGIA, *fond* 91, *opis* 2, *delo* 777, l. 194; d. 779, l. 491; *Sbornik materialov*, pp. 43, 175, 205, 238, 333–34 and passim.

7.   K. Golovin, *Selskaia obshchina v literature i deistvitelnosti* (St. Petersburg, 1887), 7–33.

8.   For an example of a large commune, see TsGIA, f. 91, op. 2, d. 775, ll. 36–87.

9.   Jerome Blum, *Lord and Peasant in Russia from the Ninth to the Nineteenth Century* (Princeton, NJ, 1961), 504–6; Iu. E. Ianson, *Sravnitelnaia statistika Rossii i zapadno-evropeiskikh gosudarstv*, vol. 1: *Territoriia i naselenie* (St. Petersburg, 1876), 38; *Sbornik statisticheskikh svedenii po Moskovskoi gubernii: Otdel khoziaistvennoi statistiki*, 4, no. 1 (Moscow, 1879), 250; L. I. Kuchumova, "Selskaia pozemel'naia obshchina Evropeiskoi Rossii v 60–70-e gody XIX v.," *Istoricheskie zapiski* 106 (1981): 325–35.

10.   Calculated according to data in *Statisticheskii vremennik Rossiiskoi imperii*, ser. 3, no. 10 (St. Petersburg, 1886), 42–43, 113, 121, 129; Blum, *Lord and Peasant*, 504–6; N. A. Blagoveshchenskii, *Svodnyi statisticheskii sbornik khoziaistvennykh svedenii po zemskim podvornym perepisiam.* I: *Krestianskoe khoziaistvo* (Moscow, 1893), 130.

11.   For the various types of communes, see Golovin, *Selskaia obshchina*, 13–22; A. A. Karelin, *Obshchinnoe vladenie v Rossii* (St. Petersburg, 1893), 219–29; K. R. Kachorovskii, *Russkaia obshchina* (Moscow, 1906).

12.   In some cases the communes controlled the quality of fertilization and cultivation of the fields and took measures against "indolent peasants," who were at first "reproved and exhorted at a communal assembly" and then were temporarily stripped of their land allotment. See TsGIA, f. 91, op. 2, d. 769, l. 62; d. 774, l. 61; d. 776, l. 24ob.; *Sbornik materialov*, 366.

13.   The law was enforced only by the *volost* peasant court (the *volost* was the lowest administrative unit, embracing 600 to 4,000 persons). By custom, however, the commune itself had its own court, which took several forms: (a) the family, (b) court of arbitration, (c) elders, (d) neighbors, (e) village elder, and (f) village communal meeting. See TsGIA, f. 91, op. 2, d. 769, l. 66; *Sbornik materialov*, 381; M. I. Zarudnyi, *Zakony i zhizn. Itogi issledovaniia krestianskikh sudov* (St. Petersburg, 1874), 172–73; N. V. Kalachov, "O volostnykh i selskikh sudakh v drevnei i nyneshnei Rossii," in *Sbornik gosudarstvennykh znanii* (St. Petersburg, 1880), 8: 128–48; V. V. Tenishev, *Pravosudie v russkom krestianskom bytu* (St. Petersburg, 1907), 33–69; *Trudy Komissii po preobrazovaniiu volostnykh sudov*, 6 vols. (St. Petersburg, 1873–74). According to field research conducted in ten provinces, communal courts of elders and *stariki* existed everywhere and alongside the *volost* court (ibid, 1: 252).

14.   This characterization of communal activity is based on responses to the Imperial Free Economic Society questionnaire and the general statute on serf emancipation in 1861

(see *Polozhenie 19 fevralia 1861 g. o krestianakh, vyshedshikh iz krepostnoi zavisimosti* [Moscow, 1916]).

15. Zarudnyi, *Zakony i zhizn*, 167–85; P. N. Zyrianov, "Obychnoe grazhdanskoe pravo v poreformennoi Rossii," in *Ezhegodnik po agrarnoi istorii*, vol. 6: *Problemy istorii russkoi obshchiny* (Vologda, 1976), 91–101; S. V. Pakhman, *Obychnoe grazhdanskoe pravo v Rossii*, vols. 1–2 (St. Petersburg, 1877–79); E. I. Iakushkin, *Obychnoe pravo: Materialy dlia bibliografii obychnogo prava*, vol. 1 (Moscow, 1910), i-xxx; vol. 2 (Iaroslavl', 1896), i-xxxvii.

16. S. T. Semenov, *Dvadtsat piat let v derevne* (Petrograd, 1925), 35–40; O. P. Semenova-Tian-Shanskaia, *Zhizn Ivana* (St. Petersburg, 1914), 106; Skaldin, *V zakholuste i v stolitse* (St. Petersburg, 1870), 45.

17. Skaldin, *V zakholuste*, 34–41; K. I. Tur, *Golos zhizni o krestianskom neustroistve* (St. Petersburg, 1898), 9–18; S. I. Shidlovskii, *Zemelnye zakhvaty i mezhevoe delo* (St. Petersburg, 1906), 16; idem, *Obshchii obzor trudov mestnykh komitetov (Vysochaishe uchrezhdennoe osoboe soveshchanie o nuzhdakh selsko-khoziaistvennoi promyshlennosti)* (St. Petersburg, 1905), 119–20, 133.

18. N. N. Zlatovratskii, *Ustoi*, in his *Sobranie sochinenii* (St. Petersburg, 1912), 3: 119; P. Kushner, ed., *Selo Viriatino v proshlom i nastoiashchem* (Moscow, 1958), 96.

19. TsGIA, f. 91, op. 2, d. 770, l. 32; E. P. Busygin et al., *Obshchestvennyi i semeinyi byt russkogo selskogo naseleniia Srednego Povolzhia. Istoriko-etnograficheskoe issledovanie (seredina XIX-nachalo XX v.)* (Kazan, 1973), 59; N. N. Zlatovratskii, "Ocherki krestianskoi obshchiny," *Sobranie sochinenii* (St. Petersburg, 1913), 8: 14, 44; Semenova-Tian-Shanskaia, *Zhizn Ivana*, 111; Skaldin, *V zakholuste*, 223; E. Solovev, "Samosudy u krestian," in Russkoe Geograficheskoe Obshchestvo, *Zapiski Russkogo geograficheskogo obshchestva po otdeleniiu etnografii* (St. Petersburg, 1878), vol. 8, section 3: 15–17.

20. *Shornik materialov*, 201.

21. *Obshchee polozhenie o krestianakh*, arts. 60, 64, 67, 68, 122, 125.

22. According to data compiled by the Ministry of Internal Affairs on thirty-four provinces in European Russia in 1880 (concerning 85,279 village elders), 37.5 percent were currently in their first year of service, 26.9 percent in their second, 25.9 percent in their third, 3.1 percent in their fourth, and only 6.6 percent were in office for more than four years. Given that the single term of an elder was set at three years, it follows that 90.3 percent of the elders were still in their first term and only 9.7 percent had served for two or more terms. Calculated from data in *Statisticheskie materialy po volostnomu i sel'skomu upravleniiu 34 gubernii, v koikh vvedeny zemskie ustanovleniia. Svod dannykh, dostavlennykh po tsirkuliariu MVD 18 ianvaria 1880 g. za no. 4 (Sostavlen v kantseliarii vysochaishe uchrezhdennoi Osoboi komissii dlia sostavleniia proektov mestnogo upravleniia)* (n.p., n.d.), table 4.

23. V. G. Korolenko, "Golodnyi god," in Korolenko, *Sobranie sochinenii* (Moscow, 1955), 9: 297–303; *Krest'ianskoe dvizhenie v Rossii, 1861–69 gg.* (Moscow, 1964), 22–23.

24. *Obshchee polozhenie o krestianakh*, art. 119.

25. V. I. Dal, *Poslovitsy russkogo naroda* (Moscow, 1957), 405.

26. Kuchumova, "Selskaia pozemelnaia obshchina," 341–42.

27. Calculated from data in *Statisticheskie materialy po volostnomu i selskomu upravleniiu*, table 1; see also TsGIA, f. 91, op. 2, d. 776, l. 7.

28. TsGIA, f. 91, op. 2, d. 770, l. 21ob; d. 774, l. 7.

29. Ibid., d. 774, l. 22ob; *Shornik materialov*, 185; Kuchumova, "Selskaia pozemelnaia obshchina," 342.

30. TsGIA, f. 91. op. 2, d. 772, l. 29; d. 774, l. 22ob; *Shornik materialov*, 162–63, 173, 213, 308, 340, 344, 381 and passim; Zlatovratskii, "Avraam," in *Sobranie sochinenii* (St.

Petersburg, 1912), 2: 271; idem, *Ustoi*, 74. See also A. M. Anfimov and P. N. Zyrianov, "Nekotorye cherty evoliutsii russkoi krestianskoi obshchiny v poreformennyi period (1861–1914)," *Istoriia SSSR*, no. 4 (1980): 34–35; Kuchumova, "Selskaia pozemelnaia obshchina," 340.

31. *Sbornik materialov*, 259; P. A. Zaionchkovskii, *Otmena krepostnogo prava v Rossii* (Moscow, 1968), 99–101, 166–77; *Krestianskoe dvizhenie v Rossii v 1861–69 gg.*, 17–26; *Krestianskoe dvizhenie v Rossii 1870–80 gg.* (Moscow, 1968), 39–48; P. P. Maslov, *Agrarnyi vopros v Rossii* (St. Petersburg, 1908), 2: 43–70; V. G. Chernukha, *Krestianskii vopros v pravitelstvennoi politike Rossii (60–70-e gody XIX v.)* (Leningrad, 1972), 79–82.

In 1861–63 4 percent of the conflicts between peasants and the government ended in confrontation with military forces. P. A. Zaionchkovskii, *Provedenie v zhizn krestianskoi reformy 1861 g.* (Moscow, 1958), 131.

32. K. D. Kavelin, *Krestianskii vopros* (St. Petersburg, 1882), 151; see also *Vestnik Evropy*, no. 10 (1886): 745–46.

33. A. A. Kornilov, "Krestianskoe samoupravlenie po Polozheniiu 19 fevralia," *Velikaia reforma*, 6 vols. (Moscow, 1911), 6: 137–57; *Materialy dlia izucheniia sovremennogo polozheniia zemlevladeniia i selsko-khoziaistvennoi promyshlennosti v Rossii, sobrannye po rasporiazheniiu ministra gosudarstvennykh imushchestv*, vol. 1 (St. Petersburg, 1880), 38–43; S., "O krestianskom samoupravlenii," *Ustoi*, no. 2, 72–99; nos. 3–4, 42–182; V. V. Tenishev, *Administrativnoe polozhenie russkogo krestianina* (St. Petersburg, 1908), 1–129.

34. Dal, *Poslovitsy*, 405.

35. Tenishev, *Administrativnoe polozhenie*, 92–94; A. N. Engelgardt, *Iz derevni: 12 pisem, 1872–87* (Moscow, 1937), 407–8; Anfimov and Zyrianov, "Nekotorye cherty," 33–34; P. N. Zyrianov, "Nekotorye cherty evoliutsii krestianskogo 'mira' v poreformennuiu epokhu," in *Ezhegodnik po agrarnoi istorii Vostochnoi Evropy 1971 g.* (Vilnius, 1974), 383–85; Kuchumova, "Selskaia pozemelnaia obshchina," 341, 343.

36. V. Dobrovolskii, "Prozvishcha krestian," *Zhivaia starina* 8, no. 2 (1898): 421–24; A. A. Shustikov, "Prozvishcha krestian," ibid., 9, sec. 2: (1899): 526–28; A. A. Iarkov, "Narodnye slova i prozvishcha," ibid., 12, no. 1 (1902): 127–28; P. S. Efimenko, *Materialy po etnografii russkogo naseleniia Arkhangelskoi gubernii. Chast 1: Opisanie vneshnego i vnutrennego byta* (Moscow, 1877), 161.

37. F. Shcherbina, "Russkaia zemelnaia obshchina," *Russkaia mysl*, nos. 5–8, (1881): 10, 12.

38. For example, see TsGIA, f. 91, op. 2, d. 776, ll. 11–12; and *Sbornik materialov*, 375. See also A. Nikolskii, "Lichnost v obshchinnomu bytu," *Russkoe ekonomicheskoe obozrenie* 1 (1898): 54–95; A. A. Rittikh, *Zavisimost krestian ot obshchiny i mira* (St. Petersburg, 1903).

39. A. F. Mozharovskii, *Iz zhizni krestianskikh detei Kazanskoi gubernii* (Kazan, 1882).

40. Blagoveshchenskii, *Svodnyi statisticheskii sbornik*, 1: 128; N. Bychkov, "Gramotnost selskogo naseleniia (po dannym zemskoi statistiki)," *Iuridicheskii vestnik* (July-August 1890): 310–12.

41. R. Ia. Vnukov, *Protivorechiia staroi krestianskoi semi* (Orel, 1929).

42. Zlatovratskii, *Ustoi*, 119.

43. TsGIA, f. 91, op. 2, d. 773, l. 15; *Sbornik materialov*, 371.

44. V. A. Novakovskii, *Opyt podvedeniia itogov ugolovnoi statistiki s 1861 po 1871 g.* (St. Petersburg, 1891), 18. E. N. Tarnovskii, "Itogi russkoi ugolovnoi statistiki za 20 let (1874–1894 gg.)," *Zhurnal ministerstva iustitsii*, no. 7 (1889), prilozhenie: 187; and idem, "Raspredelenie prestupnosti po professiiam," ibid., no. 8 (1907): 67–68.

45. N. P. Shveikin, "Umershie nasilstvenno i vnezapno v Evropeiskoi Rossii v 1875–1887 gg.," *Vremennik TsSK MVD* 35 (1894): ii, v.

46. P. Bechasnov, "Statisticheskie dannye o razvodakh i nedeistvitelnykh brakakh za 1867–1886 gg.," ibid., no. 26 (1893): 30–31. Data for divorce applied to entire provinces (including the urban areas) and is not broken down by estates. But evidence that divorce rates were higher in cities is suggested by the close correlation between the number of divorces and the percentage of urban population in a given province.

47. V. A. Aleksandrov et al., eds., *Russkie. Istoriko-etnograficheskii atlas. Zemledele. Krestianskoe zhilishche. Krestianskaia odezhda* (Moscow, 1967); Aleksandrov et al., *Russkie. Istoriko-etnograficheskii atlas. Iz istorii russkogo narodnogo zhilishcha i kostiuma* (Moscow, 1970).

48. Georg Simmel, *Philosophische Kultur: Gesammelte Essays*, 2d ed. (Postdam, 1923), 26.

49. For a good description of the status of the individual personality in the commune, see Semenov, *Dvadtsat piat let*, pp. 60–62, 72–76, 120 and passim.

50. Evidence is found in all the responses to the questionnaire. See, for example, TsGIA, f. 91, op. 2, d. 772, ll. 6–7; *Sbornik materialov*, 70–72. See also Blagoveshchenskii, 132–33; V. P. Vorontsov, "Razdelenie truda zemledelcheskogo i promyshlennogo v Rossii," *Vestnik Evropy*, bk. 7 (1884): 330, 332; P. Lokhtin, *Bezzemelnyi proletariat v Rossii* (Moscow, 1905), 156; *Materialy dlia izuchenia sovremennogo polozheniia zemlevladeniia*, 1: 17–18, 62–67; A. Fortunatov, "K statistike raspredeleniia khoziaistvennogo dostatka sredi krestian," *Russkaia mysl*, no. 9 (1894): 156; N. N. Chernenkov, *K kharakteristike krestianskogo khoziaistva* (Moscow, 1918), 68–113; Anfimov and Zyrianov, "Nekotorye cherty," 31.

51. A comprehensive characterization of peasant consumption is given in A. V. Chaianov, *Organizatsiia krestianskogo khoziaistva* (Moscow, 1925).

52. See for instance, *Sbornik materialov*, 366; V. Orlov, "Formy krestianskogo zemlevladeniia v Moskovskoi gubernii," in *Sbornik statisticheskikh svedenii po Moskovskoi gubernii. Otdel khoziaistvennoi statistiki* 4, no. 1 (Moscow, 1879).

53. *Materialy vysochaishe uchrezhdennoi 16 noiabria 1901 g. Komissii po issledovaniiu voprosa o dvizhenii s 1861 g. po 1900 g. blagosostoianiia selskogo naseleniia srednezemledelcheskikh gubernii sravnitelno s drugimi mestnostiami Evropeiskoi Rossii* [hereafter *Materialy komissii 1901 g.*], vol. 1 (St. Petersburg, 1903), 117.

54. Ibid. According to A. S. Nifontov's calculations, based on the governors' annual reports, the per capita harvest of grain and potatoes rose from 2.75 to 3.0 *chetverts* (3.36 to 3.66 centners) in the 1860s and 1870s; see his book, *Zernovoe proizvodstvo Rossii vo vtoroi polovine XIX veka* (Moscow, 1974), 201. Nifontov's calculations, however, occasion some doubt. His data show that for 1861–70 and 1871–80 the absolute measure of grain harvested rose by 13 percent (p. 183) but the rural population grew by 15 percent (*Materialy komissii 1901 g.*, 6). It would follow, then, that the per capita harvest of grain represented a 2 percent decrease, not a 7 percent increase as estimated by Nifontov. In view of this, the data of the commission of 1901 seem preferable.

55. Druzhinin, *Russkaia derevnia*, pp. 132–33; P. Kovan'ko, *Reforma 19 fevralia i ee posledstviia s finansovoi tochki zreniia (vykupnaia operatsiia 1861–1907 gg.)* (Kiev, 1914), 431–33; Iu. E. Ianson, *Opty statisticheskogo issledovaniia o krestianskikh nadelakh i platezhakh* (St. Petersburg, 1877), 25, 39, 45–46, 67, 81.

56. B. G. Litvak, *Russkaia derevnia v reforme 1861 goda. Chernozemnyi tsentr 1861–1895 gg.* (Moscow, 1972), 320.

57. *Ezhegodnik Ministerstva Finansov*, no. xiii (St. Petersburg, 1883).

58. N. M. Astyrev, "Prazdniki v krestianskom bytu Moskovskoi gubernii," in *Ezhegodnik Moskovskogo gubernskogo zemstva za 1887 g.* (Moscow, 1887); Vasilchikov, *Zemlevladenie i zemledelie*, 2: 582–84; *Doklad vysochaishe uchrezhdennoi Komissii dlia issledovaniia*

nyneshnego polozheniia selskogo khoziaistva i selskoi proizvoditelnosti v Rossii [hereafter *Doklad Komisii 1872 g.*], prilozhenie 1 (St. Petersburg, 1873), 201–24; Semenov, *Dvadsat piatlet*, 43, 83.

59. TsGIA, f. 91, op. 2, d. 774, l. 72ob; d. 775, ll. 22, 24.

60. Ibid., d. 774, ll. 14–15.

61. *Materialy dlia izucheniia sovremennogo polozheniia zemlevladeniia*, 1: 40; A. A. Syrnev, "Svedeniia o chisle sotskikh i desiatskikh v 1888 g.," *Vremennik TsSK MVD*, no. 9 (1889): 1–4.

62. For example, see TsGIA, f. 91, op. 2, d. 770, ll. 7ob, 25; *Sbornik materialov*, 173.

63. For an analysis of the attitude of the peasantry toward beggars, and the causes and dissemination of mendicity, see S. V. Maksimov, "Brodiachaia Rus Khrista-radi," *Sobranie sochinenii* (St. Petersburg, 1912), vols. 5–6.

64. Engelgardt, *Iz derevni*, 14–18; Semenova-Tian-Shanskaia, *Zhizn Ivana*, 100; Skaldin, *V zakholust'e*, 195.

65. Korolenko, *Golodnyi god*, 281.

66. *Pomoch'* was so widespread that it is noted on all the responses to the FES questionnaires save one (see *Sbornik materialov*, 189). See also G. I. Kulikovskii, "Olonetskie pomochi," *Olonetskii sbornik*, no. 3 (Petrozavodsk, 1894): 396–97; I. Kh., "Pomoch (iz obychno-obshchinnykh otnoshenii)," *Russkoe bogatstvo*, no. 1 (1879): 66–74.

67. A. Rediger, *Komplektovanie i ustroistvo vooruzhennoi sily* (St. Petersburg, 1900), 85–91.

68. TsGIA, f. 91, op. 2, d. 774, l. 22ob.

69. Besides the responses to the questionnaire, see also Vorontsov, *Krestianskaia obshchina*, 134–44; Orlov, *Formy*, 274–94.

70. S. M. Dubrovskii, *Stolypinskaia zemelnaia reforma* (Moscow, 1963), 222–30.

71. See note 84.

72. Dal, *Poslovitsy*, 404–5.

73. A. M. Anfimov, *Krestianskoe khoziaistvo Evropeiskoi Rossii, 1881–1904* (Moscow, 1980), 92.

74. TsGIA, f. 91, op. 2, d. 771, l. 98ob. See also Vasilchikov, *Zemlevladenie i zemledelie*, 2: 715–18, 734–36, 748–51; I. V. Veretennikov, *Obshchestvennoe i chastnoe zemlevladenie v Zemlianskom i Zadonskom uezdakh Voronezhskoi gubernii* (Voronezh, 1893); N. A. Karyshev, "Podvornoe i obshchinnoe khoziaistvo; statisticheskie paralleli," *Russkoe bogatstvo*, no. 1, (1894): 49–54; no. 6, 106–13; I. Krasnoperov, "Sovremennaia krestianskaia obshchina," *Severenyi vestnik*, no. 10 (1893): 17–29.

75. L. G. Beskrovnyi, I. E. Vodarskii, and V. M. Kabuzan, "Migratsii naseleniia Rossii v XVII—nachale XX vv.," in *Problemy istoricheskoi demografii SSSR* (Tomsk, 1980), 32.

76. *Materialy komissii 1901 g.*, pt. 1, 2–3, 22–23.

77. Blagoveshchenskii, *Svodnyi statisticheskii sbornik*, 1: 133. See also B. Lenskii, "Otkhozhie zemledelskie promysli v Rossii," *Otechestvennye zapiski*, no. 12 (1877): 210; *Materialy dlia izucheniia sovremennogo polozheniia zemlevladeniia*, 1: 26–29; N. F. Rudnev, "Promysli krestian v Evropeiskoi Rossii," *Sbornik Saratovskogo zemstva* (Saratov, 1894), 6: 190–91; P. G. Ryndziunskii, "Krestianskii otkhod i chislennost' selskogo naseleniia v 80-kh godakh XIX v.," *Problemy genezisa kapitalizma* (Moscow, 1970), 423–26.

78. Vesin, "Znachenie otkhozhikh promyslov v zhizni russkogo krestianstva," *Delo*, no. 2 (1887): 119, 123–214; Dobrotvorskii, *Pozemelnaia obshchina*, 26–27; D. N. Zhbankov, *Vliianie otkhozhikh promyslov na dvizhenie narodonaseleniia Kostromskoi gubernii po dannym 1866–83 gg.* (Kostroma, 1887), 33, 108, 113–14; idem, *Otkhozhie promysli v*

Smolenskoi gubernii v 1892–95 gg. (Smolensk, 1896), 3; N. N. Kharuzin, "Iz materialov, sobrannykh sredi krestian Pudozhskogo uezda Olonetskoi gubernii," *Olonetskii sbornik*, no. 3 (Petrozavodsk, 1894), 302–3, 340–41.

79. A correspondent from Moscow province observed that life in the city "develops urban interests in the peasant" and that peasants "appear more defined in their individuality, basically behave in a more original manner, and in a word become more individualistic." TsGIA, f. 91, op. 2, d. 776, ll. 47–48.

80. Vorontsov, *Krestianskaia obshchina*, 90, 99, 102, 110–15, 117; Zlatovratskii, *Ustoi*, 224; Vorontsov, "Krestiane-prisiazhnye," in Zlatovratskii *Sobranie sochinenii*, 2: 162, 175; F. S. Prugavin, *Russkaia zemelnaia obshchina v trudakh ee mestnykh issledovatelei* (St. Petersburg, 1888), 25–30; Robert E. Johnson, *Peasant and Proletarian: The Working Class of Moscow in the Late Nineteenth Century* (New Brunswick, NJ, 1979), 51–98.

81. For this mechanism of "screening," see Stephen Dunn and Ethel Dunn, *The Peasants of Central Russia* (New York, 1967), 129.

82. A. G. Rashin, *Naselenie Rossii za 100 let (1811–1913 gg.)* (Moscow, 1956), 98.

83. A. Vasilchikov, *Sel'skii byt i selskoe khoziaistvo v Rossii* (St. Petersburg, 1881), 74–84; P. A. Vikhliaev, *Ocherki iz russkoi selsko-khoziaistvennoi deistvitelnosti* (St. Petersburg, 1901), 107; N. A. Kablukov, *Ob usloviiakh razvitiia krestianskogo khoziaistva v Rossii* (Moscow, 1899), 294, 300.

84. Boris Mironov, "Sotsialnaia mobilnost i sotsialnoe rassloenie v russkoi derevne XIX-nachale XX v.," *Problemy razvitiia feodalizma i kapitalizma v stranakh Baltiki* (Tartu, 1972), 156–83; Mironov, "Soziale Struktur und soziale Mobilität der russischen Bauernschaft vom 16. bis 19. Jahrhundert," *Jahrbuch für Wirtschaftgeschichte*, no. 4 (1976): 193–208. See also Dunn and Dunn, *Peasant*, 22; Teodor Shanin, "Socio-Economic Mobility and the Rural History of Russia, 1905–1930," *Soviet Studies* 23 (1971): 222–35; idem, *The Awkward Class: The Political Sociology of the Peasantry in a Developing Society: Russia, 1910–25* (New York, 1972). The difference between my view and Shanin's is that I acknowledge the gradual formation of social "sediment" (hereditary strata of poor and rich peasants in the commune), whereas Shanin denies this process.

85. Karl Marx and Friedrich Engels, *Sochineniia* (Moscow, 1961), 19: 405.

86. A. Nikolskii, *Zemlia, obshchina i trud: Osobennosti krestianskogo pravoporiadka, ikh proiskhozhdenie i znachenie* (St. Petersburg, 1902), 109.

87. These principles are postulated on the basis of an analysis of all responses to the FES questionnaire. Particular principles in communal life are noted in the following: Zlatovratskii, *Ustoi*, 14, 24–25; idem, "Ocherki krestianskoi obshchiny," 96–97, 304; Korolenko, *Golodnyi god*, 308; *Selo Viriatino*, 96–97.

88. *Sbornik materialov*, 163, 175, 212 and passim; Zlatovratskii, *Ustoi*, 342; Korolenko, *Golodnyi god*, 46–55; P. Nebolsin, "Okolo muzhikov," *Otechestvennye zapiski* 141 (1861): 432.

89. TsGIA, f. 91, op. 2, d. 769, l. 58.

90. *Sbornik materialov*, 175, 316, 334 passim.

91. TsGIA, f. 91, op. 2, d. 779, l. 318; d. 780, l. 4. See also Kachorovskii, *Russkaia obshchina*, 315; Prugavin, *Russkaia zemelnaia obshchina*, 268; G. I. Uspenskii, "Ravnenie 'pod odno,'" *Russkaia mysl*, no. 1 (1882): 210–39.

92. Efimenko, *Materialy po etnografii*, p. 161; M. Ia. Fenomenov, *Sovremennaia derevnia*, pt. 2 (Moscow-Leningrad, 1925), 91–94; Semenov, *Dvadtsat piat let*, 74.

93. Engelgardt, *Iz derevni*, 395–96.

94. TsGIA, f. 91, op. 2, d. 768, l. 3; d. 769, l. 63; d. 772, l. 4ob; d. 777, ll. 86ob-87ob; d. 779, l. 202ob; d. 782, l. 46; *Sbornik materialov*, 169, 372–73 and passim; N. Karyshev, *Trud,*

ego rol i usloviia prilozheniia v proizvodstve (St. Petersburg, 1897), 554–59; *Sushchestvuiushchii poriadok vzimaniia okladnykh sborov s krestian. Po svedeniiam, dostavlennym podatnymi inspektorami za 1887–1893 gg.*, nos. 1–2 (St. Petersburg, 1894–95).

95. TsGIA, f. 91, op. 2, d. 769, l. 63; d. 772, ll. 13, 5, 36; d. 774, l. 2.

96. For example, see ibid., d. 772, ll. 22, 43; d. 774, l. 42. See also Druzhinin, *Russkaia derevnia*, 147–48; *Materialy dlia izucheniia sovremennogo polozheniia zemlevladeniia*, 1:13–18, 26–29, 43–45, 83–87; Ryndziunskii, *Utverzhdenie kapitalizma*, 152–84.

97. *Doklad Komissii 1872 g.*, appendix, sec. 1, 253; Minkh, *Narodnye obychai*, 7; *Selo Viriatino*, 97; Tur, *Golos zhizni*, 101.

98. *Doklad Komissii 1872 g.*, appendix 1, sec. 1, 225–52.

99. The discussion here refers to the dominant tendency in the great majority of communes. See Druzhinin, *Russkaia derevnia*, 272; A. V. Peshekhonov, "Ekonomicheskoe polozhenie krestianstva v poreformennoe vremia," *Velikaia reforma*, 6: 200–48; A. D. Polenov, *Issledovanie ekonomicheskogo polozheniia tsentralno-chernozemnykh gubernii. Trudy osobogo soveshchaniia, 1899–1901* (St. Petersburg, 1901), 31, 66–67; Chernukha, *Krestianskii vopros*, 99. To be sure, some communes enjoyed unusually favorable circumstances and did not suffer degradation. For an example, see *Sbornik materialov*, 87–88.

100. I. Anisimov, "Razlozhenie nashei zemelnoi obshchiny," *Vestnik Evropy*, no. 1 (1855): 111; Golovin, *Selskaia obshchina*, 255–59; P. N. Zyrianov, "Rol krestianskoi obshchiny v ispolzovanii i vostanovlenii estestvennykh resursov," in *Obshchestvo i priroda: istoricheskie etapy i formy vzaimodeistvii* (Moscow, 1981), 211–12; Karelin, *Obshchinnoe vladenie*, 96, 103–4; Lokhtin, *Bezzemelnyi proletariat*, 55–62.

101. *Materialy Komissii 1901 g.*, pt. 1, 43; pt. 3, 135. Data here refer to the entire populace, not just the countryside; given the predominance of the rural population, however, the data can be taken to represent patterns in the village.

102. Rediger, *Komplektovanie i ustroistvo*, 167–75.

103. *Gigiena pitaniia*, 1 (Moscow, 1971): 223–24.

104. After the introduction of universal military conscription, draftees consisted almost exclusively of youths twenty-one years of age.

105. Data about the physically unfit among recruits are found in the following: *Materialy Komissii 1901 g.*, 1: 32–33; *Stoletie voennogo ministerstva, 1802–1902*, vol. 4, pt. 3, no. 1, sec. 2: *Glavnyi shtab; istoricheskii ocherk. Komplektovanie voisk s 1855 po 1902 god*, comp. V. V. Shchepetilnikov (St. Petersburg, 1914), 178, 298, 317–19. The total number of recruits examined is the sum of those rejected and those actually inducted into military service. The numbers inducted were as follows: 9,439,000 in 1874–78; 12,821,000 in 1889–93; and 14,664,000 in 1897–1901.

106. P. Griaznov, *Opyt sravnitelnogo izucheniia gigienicheskikh uslovii krestianskogo byta i mediko-topografiia Cherepovetskogo uezda* (St. Petersburg, 1880), 142–57, 183; S. A. Dediulin, *K voprosu o prichinakh fizicheskogo vyrozhdeniia russkogo naroda. Doklad vysochaishe utverzhdennomu obshchestvu dlia sodeistviia russkoi promyshlennosti i torgovle, 25 marta 1899 goda* (St. Petersburg, 1900), 1–48; *Doklad Komissii 1872 g.*, appendix 1, sec. 1, 225–52; M. M. Pokrovskii, "Zdorove russkogo naroda v sviazi s usloviiami ego byta," *Russkaia mysl*, no. 2 (1882): 132–33, 149; *Materialy dlia izucheniia sovremennogo polozheniia zemlevladeniia*, 1: 49–51.

107. This has led to contradictory views about the commune in the period under examination. Those contemporaries and researchers who stressed new phenomena in communal life spoke of the decline of the commune; by contrast, those interested in the foundations of the commune regarded the institution as still essentially solid and stable. In my view the commune preserved its collective basis intact in the 1860s and 1870s. It was later

that individualistic, private property tendencies sharply intensified, evoking the acrimonious debate of the 1880s and 1890s among populists, "Westerners," and Marxists about the fate of the commune. An analysis of this later controversy, however, lies beyond the scope of the present paper.

108.   These new phenomena emerged most forcefully in the non-black earth provinces. See A. A. Golovachev, "Kapitalizm i krestianskoe khoziaistvo," *Russkaia mysl*, no. 10 (1882): 71–72; Golovin, *Selskaia obshchina*, 255–59; Efimenko, *Narodnye iuridicheskie obychai Arkhangelskoi gubernii* (Arkhangelsk, 1869), 200; Karelin, *Obshchinnoe vladenie*, 95–104; Nikolskii, *Zemlia, obshchina i trud*, 22–23. See also Anfimov and Zyrianov, "Nekotorye cherty," 31, 35; Zyrianov, "Rol krestianskoi obshchiny," 211–12; idem, "Nekotory cherty," 383–86; Kuchumova, "Selskaia pozemelnaia obshchina," 340–47; Ryndziunskii, *Utverzhdenie kapitalizma*, 168–73; and idem, *Krestianskii otkhod*, 423–26.

109.   Aleksandrov, *Selskaia obshchina v Rossii*; S. G. Alekseev, *Mestnoe samoupravlenie russkikh krestian XVIII–XIX vv.* (St. Petersburg, 1902), 117–59, 193–263; M. M. Gromyko, "Territorialnaia krestianskaia obshchina Sibiri (30-e gg. XVIII v.—60-e gg. XIX v.)," in *Krestianskaia obshchina v Sibiri XVII–nachala XX v.* (Novosibirsk, 1977), 33–103; idem, *Trudovye traditsii russkikh krestian Sibiri (XVIII-pervaia polovina XIX v.)* (Novosibirsk, 1975), 294–342; idem, "Obshchina v obychnom prave sibirskikh krestian XVIII—70-kh godov XIX v.," *Ezhegodnik po agarnoi istorii Vostochnoi Evropy 1971 g.* (Vilnius, 1974), 388–94; N. M. Druzhinin "Krestianskaia obshchina v otsenke A. Gakstgauzena i ego russkikh sovremennikov," *Ezhegodnik germanskoi istorii* (Moscow, 1968), 28–50; A. P. Zablotskii-Desiatovskii, "O nedostatkakh obshchestvennogo vladeniia zemlei," TsGIA, f. 940 (Zablotskii-Desiatovskii), op. 1, d. 16; Zablotskii-Desiatovskii, "Istoricheskii ocherk russkikh obshchin," ibid., dd. 296–97, 313–14; K. I. Zaitsev, *Ocherk istorii samoupravleniia gosudarstvennykh krestian* (St. Petersburg, 1912); I. I. Igantivoich, *Pomeshchichi krestiane nakanune osvobozhdeniia* (Leningrad, 1925), p. 71; V. A. Panaev, *Obshchinnoe zemlavladenie i krestianskii vopros* (St. Petersburg, 1881), 1–69; L. S. Prokof'eva, *Krestianskaia obshchina v Rossii vo vtoroi polovine XVIII-pervoi polovine XIX veka* (Leningrad, 1981); P. A. Sokolovskii, *Ocherk selskoi obshchiny na Severe Rossii* (St. Petersburg, 1877), 158–83; F. M. Umanets, "Selskaia obshchina v Rossii," *Otechestvennye zapiski* 150 (1863): 131–70, 463–500; August von Haxthausen, *The Russian Empire, Its People, Institutions and Resources*, 2 vols. (London, 1956); F. Le-Play, *Les ouvrières européens. Etudes sur travaux, la vie domestique et la condition morale des populations ouvrières de l'Europe* (Paris, 1855); Pushkarev, *Krestianskaia pozemelnaia obshchina*.

110.   N. Dobrotvorskii, *Pozemelnaia obshchina*, 26–27; L. I. Ivaniukov, "Obshchinnoe zemlevladenie," *Russkaia mysl*, no. 1 (1885): 47–48; S. Ia. Kapustin, "Nashe krestianstvo i obshchinnoe zemlevladenie," *Russkaia mysl*, no. 6 (1881): 1–35; no. 2, 25–78; Kapustin, *Formy zemlevladeniia u russkogo naroda* (St. Petersburg, 1877), 70–73; Krasnoperov, *Pozemelnaia obshchina*, 267–68, Polovtsev, *Pervye shagi*, 19; Prugavin, "K voprosu o razrushenii krestianskoi obshchiny," *Russkaia mysl*, no. 7 (1884): 11–22, 28.

111.   Delay in land redistribution resulted from a number of circumstances, of which the following were more significant: (1) waiting for a new population census (*reviziia*): redistribution after a census had already become a tradition, though there had been no such census since 1858; (2) the peasants' belief that if they redistributed the land from one census to the next, at the new census the commune would receive additional land from the state for those landless peasants born after the last census; and (3) the presumption that the delivery of redemption payments would convert the land into its possessor's private property. See *Sbornik materialov*, 360; K. Ermolinskii, "Vykupnye platezhi i kazennye peredely mirskoi zemli," *Slovo*, no. 4 (1881): 49–50; Kachorovskii, *Russkaia obshchina*, 314–15; Prugavin, "K voprosu o razrushenii krestianskoi obshchiny," 8–9, 22.

112. Only two responses to the questionnaire testify to complete atrophy of the communal spirit, a cessation of land redistribution, and the like. See TsGIA, f. 91, op. 2, d. 783, ll. 1–18; *Sbornik materialov*, 37–138.

113. Vorontsov, *Krestianskaia obshchina*, 56–66, 133–53, 193–97, 480, 492–93; Karelin, *Obshchina vladenie*, 23–54, 160–65; Karyshev, *Trud*, 493–521; Kacharovskii, *Russkaia obshchina*, 290-300, 315, 329, 360–61; Prugavin, *Russkaia zemelnaia obshchina*, 267–69, 280.

114. Calculated according to data in A. E. Loistskii, *Raspadenie obshchiny* (St. Petersburg, 1912), 57–65; see also D. A. Tarasiuk, *Pozemelnaia sobstvennost poreformennoi Rossii* (Moscow, 1931), 117.

115. Dubrovskii, *Stolypinskaia zemelnaia reforma*, 189–99.

116. G. A. Kavtaradze, "K istorii krestianskogo samosoznaniia perioda reformy 1861 g.," *Vestnik Leningradskogo gosudarstvennogo universiteta*, Seriia istoriia, no. 14 (1969): 54–64; V. A. Fedorov, "Lozungi krestianskoi borby v 1861–1863 gg.," *Revoliutsionnaia situatsiia v Rossii v 1859–1861 gg.* (Moscow, 1963), 247.

117. V. P. Danilov, "Ob istoricheskikh sudbakh krestianskoi obshchiny v Rossii," *Ezhegodnik po agrarnoi istorii*, no. 6 (Vologda, 1976): 106; Dubrovskii, *Stolypinskaia zemelnaia reforma*, 222–30; I. V. Chernyshev, *Obshchina posle 9 noiabria 1900 g.* (Po ankete Volnogo Ekonomicheskogo Obshchestva), pt. 1 (Petrograd, 1917), i-xxv.

118. V. P. Danilov, *Sovetskaia dokolkhoznaia derevnia: naselenie, zemlepolzovanie, khoziaistvo* (Moscow, 1977), 106; V. Ia. Osokina, *Sotsialisticheskoe stroitelstvo v derevne i obshchina 1920–1935* (Moscow, 1978), 8–9.

119. The commission established early in the twentieth century to review legislation on the peasantry confirmed that prior to 1889, "peasant life was left almost entirely to go its own way, remained outside all supervision by the government, which did not even comprehend what was transpiring in the commune." See *Trudy redaktsionnoi komissii po peresmotru zakonopolozhenni o krestianakh*, vol. 1 (St. Petersburg, 1903), 5.

120. *Sbornik materialov*, pp. 238–56; Anfimov and Zyrianov, "Nekotorye cherty," 31.

121. Anisimov, "Nadely," *Velikaia reforma*, 6: 98, 102; Zaionchkovskii, *Otmena krepostnogo prava*, 196; Tarasiuk, *Pozemelnaia sobstvennost*, 92, 128.

122. Vorontsov, *Krestianskaia obshchina*, 415; Druzhinin, *Russkaia derevnia*, 122–23; Kachorovskii, *Russkaia obshchina*, 290–300.

123. Marx and Engels, *Sochineniia*, 19: 404. See also Zlatovratskii, *Ocherk krestianskoi obshchiny*, 294, 302–4.

124. Chernukha, *Krestianskii vopros*, 123–304; I. V. Chernyshev, *Agrarno-krestianskaia politika Rossii za 150 let* (Petrograd, 1918), 121–53.

125. *Selo Viriatino*, 96.

126. In 1861 the average population density of European Russia was thirteen persons per square kilometer, and the average distance between settled points was 4.3 kilometers: *Voenno-statisticheskii sbornik*, no. 4: *Rossiia* (St. Petersburg, 1871), 46, 178.

127. The predominant system of land utilization (three-field, open-field, and strip farming) was integrally related to the entire way of life in the Russian countryside at the time—its agricultural technology and practice, its social structure, and the mentality of the peasantry. See A. V. Sovetov, *Izbrannye sochineniia* (Moscow, 1950), 317–59; M. Confino, *Systèmes agraires et progrès agricole. L'assolement triennal en Russie aux XVIIIe–XIXe siècles.* (Paris, 1969).

128. Vasilchikov, *Selskii byt i sel'skoe khoziaistvo*, 118; A. I. Skvortsov, *Ekonomicheskie etiudy. Ekonomicheskie prichiny golodovok v Rossii i mery k ikh ustraneniiu* (St. Petersburg, 1894), 73–92; G. Shults-Gevernitz, *Ocherki obshchestvennogo khoziaistva i ekonomicheskoi politiki Rossii* (St. Petersburg, 1901), 274–84.

129. V. P. Danilov, "K voprosu o kharaktere i znachenii krestianskoi pozemelnoi obshchiny v Rossii," *Problemy sotsialno-ekonomicheskoi istorii Rossii* (St. Petersburg, 1901), 274–84.

130. P. A. Zaionchkovskii, *Krizis samoderzhaviia na rubezhe 1870–1880-kh godov XIX v.* (Moscow, 1964); M. I, Kheifets, *Vtoraia revoliutsionnaia situatsiia v Rossii (konets 70-kh—nachalo 80-kh gg. XIX v.)* (Moscow, 1963).

131. As the noted Russian historian N. P. Pavlov-Silvanskii perceptively observed, "beneath the upper stratum of the squire's authority ... there always lay the ancient and fundamental bedrock of communal self-government: the peasant commune." Thus it was, he added, that "this foundation protruded into the open when the government removed the squire's authority over the peasantry, as was done for all of Russia under Alexander II." N. P. Pavlov-Silvanskii, *Feodalizm v udelnoi Rusi* (St. Petersburg, 1910), 210.

2

Peasant Women and Their Work

Rose Glickman

The core of peasant life from which all relationships radiated and which determined values, obligations, rewards, and behavior was land. And land was a male attribute. Although the land was not the private property of any individual male, the right to the land devolved from father to son or, in the absence of sons, to other male relatives. Similarly, the homestead, kitchen garden, farm implements, and domestic artifacts were the collective property of the household and passed indivisibly from one generation of males to the next. Women had rights only over their dowries, which consisted primarily of clothing and kitchen utensils, occasionally a sheep or a cow. As a student of Russian peasant society put it, "Peasant law did not consider women, strictly speaking, members of a household. . . . Therefore, a woman did not hold property rights over a household if male members of a family lived."[1]

Marriage was virtually universal and patrilocal. The peculiarities of patrilocalism in Russian contributed to the woman's instability and contingency within the household:

As a girl the essence of her existence is to leave her own family for a strange one, that is, to marry. When she is married—taken, that is—from [her own] family, she is bound to the [new] family only by her husband; should he die, she can return to her kin. She may, of course, remain in her husband's family, but in both cases only to work according to her strength in return for sustenance. In other words, there is no solidity to

45

the woman's position, no organic knots to bind her to the family. This is one of the reasons why the woman is at the bottom of the family. Her entire significance ... consists of undertaking every task assigned to her in the household economy and providing it with new members—most important, sons, who are its real representatives. Girls are accepted only as a necessary evil.[2]

The multiple-family household controlled by the male parent was the most prevalent form of family organization until the Revolution. The patriarch's authority over the household's life from the smallest detail to the largest included the right to sexual intercourse with daughters-in-law, a practice sufficiently common to merit a special word in the Russian language: *snokhachestvo*. Adult sons had a consultative voice in common family affairs and dominance over their wives. As for the woman, "she may not participate in the governance of common [household] affairs. Every male has the right to participation once he is of age: she, in the final analysis, is considered lower than any adult male."[3]

The rigid patriarchy of peasant society was hardly unique to Russia. In Russia, however, the peasant woman was subordinate not only to one father or one husband but to the entire male community. Peasant households were organized into communes and governed by elders, male heads of households who acted in the name of the entire commune. The peasant courts, which were the courts of original and final jurisdiction over all civil and some criminal disputes between peasants, consisted of judges chosen from among male peasants. Women were represented neither in the commune nor in the courts.[4]

Thus the peasant woman had neither direct access to land, the most vital component of subsistence, nor a role in the conduct of domestic or communal life. She was mute and powerless, a condition expressed in a pithy peasant proverb: "A hen is not a bird, a woman is not a person." Her contribution to family survival was nonetheless great.

The multiple-family household often included as many as four sons and their families and could be as large as twenty-five or thirty people.[5] Domestic obligations were allocated among the unmarried daughters and the daughters-in-law by the wife of the male head of household. The mother-in-law, however, commanded only the activities of the women, for like all other women, she had no power in the male establishment and was herself under the thumb of the patriarch. The mother-in-law's power and abuse of power over the women in the household was notorious, and for good reason. As the popular peasant saying described the daughter-in-law's lot: "And who carries the water? The daughter-in-law. And who is beaten? The daughter-in-law. And why is she beaten? Because she is the daughter-in-law."[6]

According to the mother-in-law's dictates, the women took turns doing all the domestic tasks, first and foremost those that served the needs of the entire household: cleaning and maintaining the hut, grinding the grain, baking the bread, preparing the daily food, and preserving food for the future. They looked after the livestock and prepared butter and cheese. Sometimes the patriarch assigned the dairy work to the daughter-in-law lowest in his favor as a punishment, for it was heavy and demanding work. The kitchen garden, which produced the larger part of the household's food, was also the women's responsibility.

After attending to the common needs of the household, each woman worked for her own family. She cared for her children and dressed herself, her husband, and her children from head to foot. In some families she was also obliged to provide clothing for the mother-in-law and her husband's unmarried sisters and brothers. No mean task, it often involved the initial preparation of material from the sheep or communal hemp field. Each woman took complete care of her allotment in the household's hemp field from sowing to harvesting, and then prepared garments from the cloth, which she spun and wove.

The peasant woman's responsibilities were not limited to the hut and its environs, for the survival of the household depended on her labor in the fields as well. By tradition fieldwork was strictly divided between men and women. Generally men kept the bees and sheep and ploughed and sowed the land. Women were responsible for fertilizing and weeding before the harvest. During the harvest they mowed the hay (sometimes jointly with the men), stacked it, turned and bound the sheaves. In some regions of the empire even joint obligations such as mowing were traditionally divided by sex; women mowed the hay with a sickle; men, with the scythe.[7] But the sexual division of field labor was not designed to allocate less work to women, nor were these sexual divisions invulnerable to the influence of changing economic forces.

In this period Russian agriculture was suffering from serious underproduction. The land, exhausted by centuries of primitive cultivation, was unable to support a rapidly growing population. Thus by the 1880s the peasant household was rarely self-sufficient. The land provided neither the surplus necessary for payment of taxes nor food for the peasants, and they were forced to buy goods that they had once produced themselves. Wage labor became a necessity and directly influenced the position and role of the peasant woman in the household and in the larger economy.[8]

As agricultural production declined and the market intruded into the rural economy, the raison d'être of the multiple-family household was undermined. Although the multifamily household remained the dominant form of family organization to the end of the period under study, gradually it became more common for married sons and their wives to disengage from the larger household. The smaller family was probably a welcome relief for both men and women. The literature abounds with attestation to the tyranny of the parental generation. The control and independence that the peasant woman acquired may well have been adequate compensation for the increase in her workload. One of the few nineteenth-century sources that investigated the peasant woman noted that in the multiple-family household "she is simply a machine for the execution of predetermined and preallocated family tasks," whereas "in the smaller family the woman does not work less—perhaps even more, as peasant women themselves acknowledge, especially if they have small children . . . but she controls and manages her own work."[9] Moreover, in the multifamily household the individual wife's importance was diluted by the other available work hands. In the small family the husband depended mainly on her labor, and her stature must have been enhanced accordingly. She was no longer only one daughter-in-law among many. To abuse the wife unduly, to kick her out of the family (not uncommon in the multiple-family household), or to lose her labor for other reasons could be a catastrophe for the small family.

But we can only speculate about the nature of these changes. The evidence is rare and impressionistic and our own judgment is clouded by the uncomfortable tensions between present-day romanticization of larger extended families and the acceptance of the nuclear family as the norm. Moreover, traditional attitudes and relationships are fiercely tenacious and capable of withstanding serious alterations in the material and economic bases from which they derive. In important ways the woman's position in both the family and the peasant community remained as it had been. The small family gave her neither greater rights to land inheritance—or even to land use in her own right—nor the right to the slightest participation in village affairs. Patriarchy may have been of a gentler variety with only one male superior to contend with, but patriarchy it remained, down to the husband's prerogative to beat his wife, fully sanctioned by tradition and customary law. His liberal utilization of this prerogative appears to have been preserved intact: "Beating [the peasant woman] is not [considered] an abuse of power, but completely legal and natural to such an extent that the absence of beating is considered abnormal."[10] That observation, made in 1884, could have easily been made in 1914 as well.

The changing economy led to more obvious and tangible changes in the peasant woman's work obligations. Paradoxically, industrialization and the concomitant decline in peasant agriculture increased her share of field labor. The peasant was enormously reluctant to forsake the land entirely, clinging to it as long as it yielded something, however minimal, to family survival. A 1912 *zemstvo* report stated:

> To cast off agriculture completely, to reduce it to nothing, is a decision very few [peasants] can make. But to leave it in the hands of women to carry on some way or other is a decision the majority come to.... Therefore, women not only plough, plant, rake, and gather the hay and grain, but often execute the social obligations of men as well.[11]

From all parts of the empire, transcending the kaleidoscope of regional variations, came reports of women's growing responsibility for the land as men left to seek outside earnings: "Children and old men who remain at home cannot cope with the field work by themselves. Women must take the most active role even in such purely male work as ploughing and haymaking."[12] In 1891 a colorful example was provided in a report from Kostroma province, a province with relatively poor agriculture and many factories: "The stronger representatives of the local peasantry [men] have been driven from here by need, and we find ourselves in a mythical kingdom of amazons."[13] Here, the report continues, women were fulfilling all the duties reserved for men in earlier times, such as the heavy fieldwork, road repairs, and tax collection: "Even in the inns and taverns these days the shrill, drunken voices of women drown out the hoarse bass notes of men."[14]

The erosion of traditional divisions of agricultural labor was linked to less flexible sexual divisions in the world of wage labor. Men were more likely than women to seek wage labor that took them from the land—not merely because women were responsible for child-rearing and therefore less mobile, and certainly not because peasants considered work to be inappropriate for women. Men left the land first, quite simply, because they could earn more than women. Nonetheless, peasant women were forced to earn money as well. Predictably, they looked first to occupations that could be reconciled with their domestic and agricultural obligations.

The picture of women's remunerative work in the countryside must be pieced together from a jumble of inchoate information. The main sources of information are the voluminous *zemstvo* studies and the works of individuals who were devoted to the preservation of peasant crafts. The data range from sophisticated statistical compilations to communiqués from "volunteer correspondents"—village priests, rural intelligentsia, barely literate peasants.

The varieties of women's work were not distributed uniformly throughout the empire and depended on the geographical and economic characteristics of each region. For our purposes the country is best divided into three major areas: the Central Industrial Region, the province of St. Petersburg, and the black earth provinces. Although this threefold division does not exhaust the country's geographical, climatic, and socioeconomic regions, it encompasses the kinds of wage-earning alternatives available to peasant women throughout the Russian Empire.

Wage-Earning Alternatives

The Central Industrial Region was densely populated, and all arable land had been under the plow for more than a century. Long before the spurt of population growth in the mid-nineteenth century,[15] the land had ceased to support the local population, and by 1900 only 6 percent of peasant families survived by the cultivation of their plots alone.[16] In the Central Industrial Region, one of Russia's most heavily industrialized regions, factories were dispersed throughout the countryside as well as concentrated in the city of Moscow. It also had a long and vigorous tradition of *kustar* production—that is, independent domestic production of handmade finished products for an undefined market that, since the growth of industry, included putting-out work from the factories.

Women's *kustar* production fell into three groups. In Group I the woman worker was completely independent; she bought or made her own materials, owned her tools, and sold to merchants either directly or through an intermediary. In Group II a merchant provided the materials and tools and bought back the finished product. Group III was work given out by factories to peasant women "because they [peasant women] could be paid less than women working in large factories where the identical work is done on machines."[17]

In the 1880s the knitting of woolen gloves and stockings occupied the greatest number of women:

> Come autumn or summer early in the morning on a market day. On the roads that lead from the countryside to Moscow you will see a strange spectacle. You will see row upon row of wagons loaded down with grass, hay, wood, potatoes, and other vegetables, and driving or walking beside them women talking loudly among themselves as their hands move and their fingers flash. They are knitting stockings. You will see women carrying sacks with jugs full of milk and cream, knitting as they walk.[18]

Under the best of circumstances women took the wool from their own sheep. But as sheep raising declined, the wool had to be purchased. In both cases the women were independent of middlemen for materials, tools of production, or access to the market. The knitter was poorly paid for her efforts, and the work was performed "in addition to her customary family contributions: field work, housework, satisfying the demands of custom, dressing herself, her husband and her children. She is an essential member of the family. . . . In times of need [her earnings] even pay for bread or a cow or sheep."[19] Knitting was completely subject to the vagaries of urban demand and therefore mainly occupied women who lived within a 30-verst radius from Moscow city. As urban tastes changed and factory-produced stockings and gloves triumphed over the handcrafted articles, the latter slowly dropped from the woman's repertoire. In 1889 knitting was still singled out as a major woman's craft, but by 1898–1900 it was not even mentioned in the *zemstvo* reports.[20]

The second largest occupation, unwinding cotton, was a job put out by the factory; "Despite the existence of machines for this work, most of the cotton used in cotton-weaving factories is unwound by hand by peasant women in the countryside."[21] The work of unwinding cotton thread had several convenient features for the peasant woman. The factories that put out the work were widely distributed throughout the province and easily accessible. This was important because it eliminated the middleman, who could otherwise eat into the woman's earnings. Simple enough for a six-year-old child, unwinding required nothing more than a bobbin and a roller, which could be purchased for a pittance or made at home. The work could be done in the peasant hut without encroaching on living space; it required neither the cleanliness, good vision, nor concentration of the more skilled crafts.[22] Yet unwinding cotton was not considered a desirable occupation, for the work was dirty and poorly paid. Women were driven to it either by the decline of better-paying crafts or by their lack of skill—two factors that increased over the years. It was always the choice of last resort. By 1900 more than twice as many peasant women in Moscow province were unwinding cotton as in 1882.[23] But from then on the craft declined steadily, so that by 1912 it had become a "victim of machinery."[24] Similar victims of mechanization were flax and wool spinning, also putting-out processes. Employing 12,000 women in 1882, flax and wool spinning had been swallowed up by the factory by the turn of the century.[25]

Some crafts followed an interesting trajectory from the factory to the village and back again to the factory. The craft of sewing kid gloves is one example. In the 1780s small glove factories using serf labor had begun to appear around Moscow (and St. Petersburg) in response to urban demand. After the emancipation of the serfs, the preparation of leather was so perfected that it became cheaper to put out the prepared leather to peasant women to sew the gloves together. This craft, though not highly skilled, was more demanding than many others. It required a degree of cleanliness not easy to come by in the peasant hut, agile fingers (in wet weather it was not possible to sew the gloves because the fingers tended to swell), and good vision. Still, it was a desirable occupation because it paid well—until the factories began to reclaim it. In 1882, 3,000 women in Moscow province sewed kid gloves at home.[26] By 1900 only 575 women were thus employed, and in 1904 *zemstvo* statisticians noted that even that vestige of a formerly important village craft had totally vanished.[27]

A host of luxury crafts catering to urban taste were brought from the city of Moscow to a small number of women in the village. The crafts of lace-making with gilded threads, embroidering crosses and stars for vestments, and knitting fringes to be sewn onto fashionable garments all had a transient life in Moscow province in the 1880s. Subsequently other minor crafts appeared and disappeared in rapid succession in response to the ephemeral dictates of fashion.[28] But by 1911 the demand for domestic handwork of every kind had diminished radically as "the machine continues to bear down relentlessly on home industry, primarily for women and child workers."[29]

Male peasant wage earners were rather evenly distributed throughout the provinces of the Central Industrial Region. By contrast, the distribution of women workers was irregular and contingent on a greater variety of local conditions. To illustrate, let us compare three districts (*uezdy*) in Vladimir province which, like Moscow province, had a rich *kustar* tradition and a heavy concentration of industry.

Shuiskii district was one of the most highly industrialized areas of Russia. It contained within its borders Ivanovo-Voznesensk, known as the "Russian Manchester," as well as the city of Shuia and the industrial villages of Teikovo and Kokhma. Altogether the factories in Shuiskii district employed at least 100,000 workers.[30] Outside earnings, mostly from factory work, predominated heavily over agricultural earnings in the peasant budget, and 26 percent of the peasant women were wage earners. Half of the women who worked for wages were employed in the factories and came mostly from households whose land did not produce crops. The other half, nine-tenths of whom had heavy fieldwork obligations, engaged in domestic hand weaving (only three-fourths of male domestic *kustar* workers simultaneously worked the land).[31] Domestic production was strictly divided between men's and women's work in Shuiskii district. Most men made goods from sheepskin, work that paid very well in comparison with women's primary work, domestic hand weaving on a putting-out basis.

Vladimir district was less industrialized and agriculturally more prosperous than Shuiskii district. Nevertheless male emigration for outside work was extremely high even in households with relatively large parcels of land, mainly because of the shortage of livestock. But only 7 percent of the district's peasant women were wage earners. Women could not be spared for wage-earning work because the burden of working the land fell on their shoulders. Half of the women wage earners worked in factories. The other half were divided between agricultural day labor and domestic service because Moscow was too far from Shuiskii district to stimulate *kustar* production.[32]

Pokrovskii district exhibited yet another configuration. Like Shuiskii and Vladimir districts, it was highly industrialized, and less than 7 percent of the men were engaged exclusively in farming. Of the remainder, two-thirds emigrated to the factories "so that all the field work is the women's obligation when the men go out for summer earnings."[33] In spite of the remarkably heavy burden of fieldwork, 47 percent of the district's women were domestic wage earners. Putting-out work from local cotton factories remained available as late as 1908, and domestic silk weaving occupied many women because "machine weaving cannot yet be applied to silk and . . . the factory is still in competition with *kustar* production."[34] However, half the silk weavers were men because silk weaving was a skilled craft requiring two years of apprenticeship. Wages were high, 70–90 rubles per year compared with 20 rubles per year for cotton weaving, a woman's craft. Another option for women, found only in this district, was tearing the nap from woven velveteen, a fulling process that could not yet be done by machine. In the 1880s it had been men's work. But remuneration was very small, and it passed into women's hands when factory work became available to men.[35]

Throughout the Central Industrial Region, then, uniform and growing economic distress forced most men into wage labor. Women stayed on the land as long as something could be scratched from it. Nonetheless, in addition to playing a large and often major role on the land, women worked for money. Whether they did and what they did depended on the local economic landscape—in other words, on whether urban markets or local factories made work available to them.

In the province of St. Petersburg peasant women had a substantially different array of wage-earning alternatives. Here the climate was harsher, the land stingier, and the population sparse compared with the Central Industrial Region. Although the province was highly industrialized, industry did not go out to meet the peasant in the countryside as it did in the Central Industrial Region. Factories were almost entirely concentrated in and near St. Petersburg city, and only peasants who lived close to the city worked in factories. Proximity to the city was, however, instrumental in determining women's contribution to family survival, but *kustar* production, so prominent in the Central Industrial Region, played a negligible role, a few women here and there making gloves and weaving fishing accouterments.[36] The great majority of women engaged in and dominated the sale of agricultural and dairy products, mainly to the city of St. Petersburg. Of the 4,110 families in St. Petersburg district who owned cows, 3,507 sold milk products.[37] The sale of produce from kitchen gardens to the city or, in the summer, to the resort population was exclusively women's work, as was the collection and sale of wild berries, mushrooms, and flowers. Women had complete responsibility not only for growing and gathering but for carrying the produce to the St. Petersburg markets as well.[38] Calculating their earnings is not possible because in this type of wage-earning activity the contribution was lost in the household total.

The outlying areas of the province were popular holiday places for the inhabitants of St. Petersburg city and also drew a large number of peasant immigrants from other parts of Russia who were looking for factory work in the city.[39] Thus second in importance among the local peasant women's earnings was the renting of summer accommodations to vacationers and to immigrants, as well as the provision of a number of related services such as cleaning and laundering.[40]

These occupations were created by St. Petersburg's rapid growth in the decades after the emancipation of the serfs. The city's growing appetite for food and services was never satisfied by the meager resources and sparse population of St. Petersburg province, but it provided a stable seasonal market for those peasant women with the resources to accommodate it. Like women's work in'the Central Industrial Region, it allowed women to remain close to the household. The important difference between the two areas was the absence in St. Petersburg of factory putting-out work and domestic *kustar* production.

The more prosperous agricultural areas of Russia, the so-called black earth provinces, in some cases had no industry and relatively little in others.[41] In these provinces fewer peasants sought outside earnings because the land yielded, if not abundance, at least reasonable subsistence. Urban markets for *kustar* products were few and not easily accessible. Consequently, women's work was largely on the land. In 1884 the *zemstvo* report of Saratov province indicated that the "outstanding characteristic of peasant women is the great variety of their occupations. Divisions of agricultural work into men's and women's hardly exist, unless we count mowing and ploughing as men's work and care of the kitchen gardens as women's. But this is not a systematic division, and one can find many places where men and women exchange jobs."[42] Even more remunerative work was related to the land, mainly the selling of various edibles.[43] The major nonagricultural option of women was the knitting of woolen socks and gloves, which in some parts of the province occupied women the year round, interrupted only by the most necessary fieldwork. Women took the wool from their own sheep and were responsible for selling the finished product in the city of Saratov or to itinerant merchants. The average income for knitters was fifteen to twenty rubles per year.[44]

As the demand for hand-knit articles declined in competition with cheaper factory-made goods, women found new occupations. In the famine year of 1892, for example, the weaving of goat down for handkerchiefs, a great luxury item, was brought to two of the most agriculturally productive districts of Saratov province and took a firm hold. "The female population of the countryside has joyfully seized on this new auxiliary occupation. Almost all the women and girls spin on hand wheels, while adolescents and children clean and comb the down."[45] But local opportunities for outside earnings were so few in this agricultural province that peasants were forced to emigrate when the land did not provide adequate subsistence. Men and women left the countryside in equal numbers. In 1904 a survey of *kustar* production in the city of Kuznetsk, the most important *kustar* center of the province, indicated that the city's working population was equally divided between men and women.[46]

In the black earth province of Kharkov there was yet another configuration of opportunities to earn money. As in Saratov, very few of the inhabitants (only 10 percent) sought outside earnings. But here industry was growing, and the city of Kharkov offered nonindustrial urban work opportunities as well.

By 1912 peasants in the factory far exceeded those who stayed behind to work locally in *kustar* production: 130,000 in the former and 34,389 in the latter; the opportunities for female *kustar* work had suffered most. Obviously, many women were going to the factory—or at least to the city—as the steady increase in passports given to women indicates.[47] But for those who remained behind there was a significant shift in available work. In 1891 *zemstvo* statisticians noted that in this basically agricultural province, weaving had always been a very important woman's job:

> Women have guarded this craft as a necessary way to cover their needs by the labor of their own hands, since by custom all clothing which is not made at home must be acquired somehow by the woman alone. Neither husband nor father give a kopek. Therefore, the year round, women have no rest. In every home there are one or two weaving looms. Each woman works for herself; the mother, the bride, the daughter. All winter they prepare wool and hemp.

Spring, summer, and autumn they weave woolens, linen, belts, foot-cloths. . . .
With this they dress themselves, their husbands, and their children and sell the
surplus at an average of twenty-five rubles per year per household.[48]

In 1891, then, all women wove; by 1912 only 76.7 percent did. But
as weaving declined, a variety of small *kustar* occupations emerged to
take up the slack. The most important was the production of spinning
cards and looms, a craft that had not existed at all in 1891. By 1912 it
was entirely in women's hands. The second was a significant increase of
women tailors, from 4.0 percent in 1891 to 15.7 percent in 1912, catering
to urban demand. Further, women had moved into some traditionally male
occupations such as basket making, coal working, and shoemaking, albeit in
small numbers.[49] Thus even in the provinces with more sustaining agriculture
where outside earning was a small part of family survival, women had a
growing wage-earning role determined in these provinces, as elsewhere, by
land conditions and urban demand.

Despite the diversity of regional conditions that influenced the proportions of peasant women wage earners and the kinds of work they did,
we can make some generalizations about the nature of women's work
in the countryside. The most ubiquitous consequence of the changing
economy between the 1880s and 1914 was that women took increasing
responsibility for working the land to free men for outside wage work.
When male earnings could not assuage growing peasant need, women
too sought remunerative work. But unlike men, they engaged first in a
variety of occupations that could be combined with household and field
obligations. The traditional division between men's and women's work on
the land, collapsing under the impact of altered economic forces, was
transmitted intact to the world of remunerative labor. Women's work
invariably required relatively little training and skill. Although it enabled
women to move easily from one occupation to another, it also invariably
commanded less money than men's work—and less respect. Indeed, the
more skilled *kustar* production that men did exclusively, such as blacksmithy,
metal working, carpentry, and stonecutting, was called by another name,
remeslo.

Women earned less even in those rare occupations they shared with
men. Agricultural day labor, which employed both sexes throughout European Russia, is a good example. According to a 1907 survey of agricultural
wages, women earned from one-fifth to two-thirds of men's wages, depending
on the region.[50] As a *zemstvo* report observed in 1908:

Women's remunerative labor is not only technically simpler [than men's]
and closer to the domestic hearth, but is also very low on the social

ladder. As a result, the social position of the woman worker is lower and more difficult than men's. For this reason women's work is considered less valuable and is paid less than male labor. Women do not have equal rights with men in labor as they do not have equal rights in social life.[51]

For some decades expanding urban markets and putting-out work from factories enhanced peasant women's opportunities to combine household and fieldwork with wage work. But by the turn of the century the factory's tentacles began to choke off the demand for handmade crafts and, concomitantly, encroached on the work that it had itself created—the various putting-out processes. Many factories that closed during the slump of the first years of the twentieth century abolished their putting-out departments when they reopened, and the manual work previously done by peasant women in their homes was absorbed within the factory walls to be performed on mechanized apparatuses.[52] A limited amount of putting-out work remained available, however, for the absolute number of peasant women thus employed, province by province, remained stable between 1902 and 1910.[53] Many peasant women—perhaps most—continued to seek work that was compatible with remaining on the land and eagerly accepted whatever came their way. The salient point is that such work no longer accommodated peasant need. Over the years as more peasant women had to, or wished to, earn money, domestic *kustar* production simply occupied relatively fewer women, and they went to the factory in ever-increasing numbers.

The Subjective Dimension

Unfortunately, the subjective dimension of the peasant woman's life and work cannot be deduced from quantitative information on agriculture and labor. Nor has she left memoirs or other tangible sources from which we can make direct judgments. We must therefore rely on the perceptions of the observers of rural life, who only infrequently recorded the voices of women themselves but whose observations, sometimes direct and at other times oblique, evoke an impressionistic picture of how the peasant woman experienced her life.

For the most part, those who observed and reported on rural work were biased in favor of preserving village life. It would have violated tradition to suggest that the peasant woman do nothing but care for children and hut, considering that fieldwork had been an indivisible component of her existence from time immemorial. Nor was the transformation of production for home consumption to market production regarded as a threat to rural stability and the stability of sex roles. New crafts introduced to the village were hailed as a good thing, for they replaced dying crafts and permitted women to continue working in the village. Therefore, the conditions under which peasant women worked, the extra burden they bore, and the physical effects of various kinds of work were irrelevant. In fairness to the observers, they seldom put forth the kind of saccharine and sentimental stereotypes of the jolly, healthy farm woman which appeared so often in Western European literature. The distortions are rather in the absence of analysis.

Most observers assumed that women's wage work could easily be slotted into the crevices of her daily activities. It is more likely that women worked many hours a day in addition to their normal obligations. Often women themselves were at a loss to calculate how much time they spent on a craft: "We have no hours, we just do not know," they would say and then explain that because candles were expensive, they simply arranged their working hours to fit the available light.[54] Even the paltriest of earnings could cost the woman ten to fourteen hours a day.[55] Some kinds of *kustar* work, such as sewing kid gloves, were harmful to the eyesight and could be done for only a limited number of years. Women's *kustar* work was rarely skilled, creative, or innovative. Most of it was, as one *zemstvo* observer noted, a "daily, monotonous grind, requiring long, exhausting hours. Such work not only exhausts the body, but dulls the mind as well."[56] Once a process had been assimilated, it was simply repeated mindlessly as long as demand remained—and sometimes, however futile, longer.[57]

Given the constraints of their lives, their poverty, illiteracy, and lack of skill, it is not surprising that as eagerly as peasant women seized new opportunities, they were rarely capable of creating them or ferreting them out. For the most part, peasant women were the passive beneficiaries of benevolent chance. It was not uncommon for an entire village to ply a craft that had been introduced fortuitously by a woman from another village who married a local peasant.[58] The following report from the Ministry of Education illustrates the obstacles faced by even the most energetic of peasant women:

> The peasant women of Iashchery [a tiny village in St. Petersburg district] appealed to the Zemstvo for help in learning how to make lace. As their households live in extreme poverty, they wish to make some contribution. They invited a teacher, Mrs. Pushkareva ..., rented a space in the village and began to make lace. In the first year the women were able to sell part of their work. In view of the current winter unemployment this kind of work would

be a great advantage to them, but they do not have the means to pay a teacher [for further training] or to rent a space.[59]

Cooperation was rare among peasant women engaged in *kustar* production. Occasionally they would render one another certain kinds of services. For example, factories issued only one packet of cotton at a time to women who unwound cotton thread, thereby limiting the amount of money they could earn. Sometimes when a women decided to stop unwinding temporarily she would pass her workbook on to a friend so the latter could have more work.[60] Many crafts would have lent themselves to cooperative marketing, especially those that depended on a middleman to fetch materials and return the finished product to the factory. The middleman, who absorbed some of the producer's already meager earnings, could have been circumvented if the women took turns going to the Moscow markets or the factories. But apparently it never occurred to them.[61] Their isolation and illiteracy also left them prey to the calculated errors of merchants and factories; because the women were unable to read what was written in their workbooks, how much material had been given them, and what the prices were, they were easily cheated.[62]

A thin stratum of peasant women became *khoziaiki*—that is, they abandoned production and worked as middlemen between merchant and producer. From all reports *khoziaiki*, or any kind of intermediaries, were exploitative in many ways. Women workers often had to accept whatever form of payment the middleman chose to hand out. Payment in kind could be in the form of useful goods such as bread or tea, but frequently it was in useless goods that had to be sold back to the shops at half the market price. The only way to mitigate the exploitation was to work through several middlemen so as not to be dependent on one.[63]

Women were indeed aware of their exploited position, but this was balanced by "their gratitude, even when [the middleman] cheated them all the time. . . . Some women sincerely looked upon the *khoziaiki* as their benefactresses, for they did not know how they would feed themselves without the work."[64] But it is clear that when there was a choice, jobs that paid women directly were more appealing than those in which earnings accrued to the family unit, at least among unmarried women. In Moscow province, for example, women lace-makers would help the family make brushes when lace-making was slow. "But they do this reluctantly because they do not get their earnings 'in hand' . . . and have to wait until the father doles out the money."[65]

A few *zemstvo* observers, less intent on preserving the village intact at any price, perceived that the sharp distinction between men's and women's work made women "the victims of extreme exploitation."[66] To be sure, these divisions were sometimes based on relative physical strength, but by no means invariably. More often the divisions were based on patriarchal definitions of what was appropriate to women. After the turn of the century, then, the more sensitive *zemstvo* observers approved women's increasing choice of factory work over domestic production. For to the peasant women, long accustomed to contributing to their own and their family's survival, "it is a misfortune not to work. . . . It is painful and distressing to sit without occupation; bread is dear."[67]

Among Russian peasants, qualities attributed to women and prized by other classes such as beauty and grace, were at most of secondary importance. The most desirable wife was one who even as a girl had demonstrated her capacity for work. Work, paid and unpaid, was the focal point of existence for peasant women as well as men. The specific economic niche occupied by peasant women assigned them by tradition and modified by the exigencies of an industrializing economy thus provided them with a legacy of expectations quite favorable to the move from farm to factory. To work hard, to contribute to their own survival and that of their families, was in no way a transformation of their destiny.

Peasant women also brought to the factory a legacy of subordination: in the family hierarchy, in community governance, in occupational divisions, in remuneration and rewards, and in status. A romantic view of precapitalist and early capitalist society postulates that when the family was the basic unit of production, the woman "had a respected role within the family, since the domestic labor of the household was so clearly integral to the family as a whole."[68] The logic in this assumption is belied by historical reality. True, in my discussion of the peasant woman's world I have not speculated on the informal arrangements that may have been negotiated in subtle and unarticulated ways but not reflected in the codifications of law or inheritance relationships. The bonds of love and affection, of loyalty and other emotional commitments, may have palliated the humiliating effects of patriarchal dominance. I have alluded to but not explored the possible enhancement of the woman's position as multiple-family households fragmented into smaller family units, as peasant women took on greater agriculture and wage-earning burdens. These subtleties of her life remain to be investigated, if indeed there is evidence of them in unexplored sources. It is unlikely, however, that either informal familial accord or the influence of the changing economy seriously dented the double legacy of work expectations and subordination that characterized the woman's life as a peasant.

Notes

1. Teodor Shanin, *The Awkward Class* (Oxford, 1972), 222.
2. Aleksandra Efimenko, *Izsledovaniia narodnoi zhizni* (Moscow, 1884), 68–69. A married woman's return to her own kin was not welcomed. Her labor was rarely valued, and her sons were superfluous because they were not entitled to be counted in land redistribution. See also Peter Czap, Jr., "Marriage and the Peasant Joint Family in the Era of Serfdom," in David Ransel, ed., *The Family in Imperial Russia* (Urbana, IL, 1978).
3. Efimenko, *Izsledovaniia*, 76.
4. Peter Czap, Jr., "Peasant Class Courts and Peasant Customary Justice in Russia, 1861–1912," *Journal of Social History* 1 (Winter 1967).
5. Ibid., 92.
6. Efimenko, *Izsledovaniia*, 79.
7. V. A. Aleksandrov et al., eds., *Narody evropeiskoi chasti SSSR* (Moscow, 1964), 1: 174–89; Sula Benet, ed. and trans., *The Village of Viriatino* (New York, 1970), 14, 17, 95; Efimenko, *Izsledovaniia*, 80. The interplay of tradition and relative physical strength in determining men's and women's agricultural tasks in England is discussed in Eve Hostettler, "Gourlay Steell and the Sexual Division of Labour," *History Workshop*, no. 4 (1977); and Michael Roberts, "Sickles and Scythes: Women's Work and Men's Work at Harvest Time," *History Workshop*, no. 7 (1979).
8. See Lazar Volin, *A Century of Russian Agriculture* (Cambridge, MA, 1970), 57–76.
9. Efimenko, *Izsledovaniia*, 91, 94.
10. Ibid., 81.
11. *Statisticheskii ezhegodnik kostromskoi gubernii za 1911*, chast 1 (Kostroma, 1913), 78. The *zemstva* were district and provincial councils in thirty-four of Russia's fifty provinces. Governed by elected boards of peasant and gentry landowners, they were designed to look after local needs, such as education, roads, medical care, and agriculture. The *zemstva* hired appropriate professional personnel and published reports (7,000 between 1864 and 1914) on a great variety of local conditions.
12. *Materialy dlia otsenki zemel vladimirskoi gubernii*, t. 2, *Vladimirskii uezd*, vyp. 3 (Vladimir na Kliazme, 1912), 4.
13. D. N. Zhbankov, *Babia storona (Statistiko-etnograficheskii ocherk)* (Kostroma, 1891), 1.
14. Ibid., 3.
15. The Central Industrial Region consisted of the provinces of Moscow, Vladimir, Kostroma, Tver, Nizhnii Novgorod, and Kaluga.
16. *Moskovskaia guberniia po mestnomu obsledovaniiu 1898–1900*, t. 4, vyp. 2 (Moscow, 1908), 1–3; Jerome Blum, *Lord and Peasant in Russia* (New York, 1964), 330: "Data for 1783–1784 for the province of Tver', directly northwest of Moscow, showed that cash income from agriculture of the peasants covered only 40–50 percent of the money they needed to meet expenses."
17. Ibid., iii.
18. Ibid., 143.
19. Ibid., 146.
20. *Statisticheskii ezhegodnik moskovskoi gubernii za 1889* (Moscow, 1889), 4; *Moskovskaia guberniia po mestnomu obsledovaniiu 1898–1900*, 92–94.
21. M. K. Gorbunova, comp., *Sbornik statisticheskikh svedenii po moskovskoi gubernii*, vol. 7. *Zhenskie promysly*, facs. 4 (Moscow, 1882), 279.

22. Ibid., 279–84.

23. A. S. Orlov, *Kustarnaia promyshlennost moskovskoi gubernii* (Moscow, 1913), 7.

24. Ibid., 8.

25. Ibid., 7.

26. Gorbunova, 174–84.

27. Orlov, 7. *Statisticheskii ezhegodnik moskovskoi gubernii za 1904* (Moscow, 1905), 15.

28. Gorbunova, 8–9, 45–56, 89–91.

29. *Statisticheskii ezhegodnik moskovskoi gubernii za 1911*, chast 2 (Moscow, 1912), 17.

30. The information for Shuiskii district comes from *Materialy dlia otsenki zemel vladimirskoi gubernii*, t. 10, vyp. 3, *Shuiskii uezd* (Vladimir, 1908), 1–25.

31. Ibid.

32. Ibid., t. 2, *Vladimirskii uezd*, 160–65.

33. Ibid., t. 12, *Pokrovskii uezd*, 1, 12.

34. Ibid., 17.

35. Ibid., 42–46.

36. *Materialy po statistike narodnogo khoziaistva v s-peterburgskoi gubernii* (St. Petersburg, 1887), 270.

37. Ibid., 238.

38. Ibid., 244.

39. The immigrant (*prishlye*) peasant population had no land and rarely came to St. Petersburg province with children or elderly family members. Therefore, a larger proportion of immigrant women than indigenous women were wage earners and factory workers. Of immigrant wage-earning women, 22 percent were in the factory, as were 14 percent of the indigenous wage-earning women. Ibid., 270.

40. Ibid.

41. The black earth provinces in the southern steppe region of Russia stretched from west to east almost the entire width of the European part of the country. They contained Russia's most fertile land and included the following provinces: Kursk, Orel, Riazan', Tula, Tambov, Voronezeh, Penza, Kharkov, Ekaterinoslav, Kiev, Podol, Saratov, Simbirsk, Kazan, Viatka, and Perm.

42. *Sbornik statisticheskikh svedenii po saratovskoi gubernii*, t. 3, chast l, *Promysly krestianskogo naseleniia saratovskogo i tsaritsynskogo uezdov* (Saratov, 1884), 129.

43. Ibid.

44. Ibid.

45. *Issledovanie kustarnykh promyslov saratovskoi gubernii*, vyp. 5, *Balashovskii i serdovskii uezdy* (Saratov, 1913), 1.

46. *Issledovanie kustarnykh promyslov saratovskoi gubernii*, vyp. 1, *Gorod Kuznetska* (Saratov, 1904), 2.

47. In 1897, 28,149 passports were issued to women. By 1905 that figure had grown at a very steady rate to 37,600. This was a 25 percent increase, whereas passports issued to men had increased by only 19 percent. *Kratkii ocherk mestnykh i otkhozhikh promyslov naseleniia kharkovskoi gubernii* (Kharkov, 1905), 100.

48. *Doklad v kharkovskuiu zemskuiu upravu o kustarnykh promyslakh po kharkovskomu uezdu* (Kharkov, 1891), 27–28.

49. *Kustarnye promysly v kharkovskoi gubernii po dannym issledovaniia 1912 g.* (Kharkov, 1905), 6.

50. "Otsenka zhenskogo i muzhskogo truda na selskikh rabotakh," *Zhenskii Vestnik*, no. 2 (1907): 48–49.

51. *Materialy dlia otsenki zemel vladimirskoi gubernii*, t. 10, *Shuiskii uezd*, vyp. 3 (Vladimir, 1908), 33.

52. *Svod otchetov fabrichnykh inspektorov za 1906* (St. Petersburg, 1908), iv.

53. *Svod 1902*, 34–35; 1906, 41–42; 1907, 44–45; 1908, 44–45; 1909, 44–45.

54. Gorbunova (see note 19), 42.

55. Ibid., 89–91, 180–84, 209.

56. *Statisticheskii sbornik po iaroslavskoi gubernii*, vyp. 14, *Kustarnye promysly* (Iaroslavl, 1904), 46.

57. *Statisticheskii ezhegodnik kostromskoi gubernii 1909 g.*, vyp. 1 (Kostroma, 1912), 55.

58. Gorbunova, passim.

59. TsGIA, f. 741, op. 8, d. 11, l. 2.

60. Gorbunova, 280. The author noted that although this kind of service was rare, even rarer was the fact that it was rendered free.

61. Ibid., 175.

62. Ibid.

63. Ibid., ix, 97.

64. Ibid., 17.

65. Ibid., 5.

66. *Materialy dlia otsenki zemel vladimirskoi gubernii*, t. 10, 33.

67. Gorbunova, 5.

68. Eli Zaretsky, *Capitalism, The Family and Personal Life* (New York, 1976), 29.

3

The Woman's Side: Male Outmigration and the Family Economy in Kostroma Province

Barbara Engel

In the last decades of imperial Russia, peasant migrants from all over Russia swelled the ranks of urban dwellers. Impelled by the increasing impoverishment of their villages and the hope of a steady wage, they poured into the cities, some to remain for months or years, others to stay for life. The number of male migrants always exceeded the number of female, though the proportion of women was growing steadily. Even so, the majority of men either remained single or left wives and children in the village.

Thus far the attention of most social historians has focused on the migrant: his relation to the means of production; the extent to which his experiences in city and factory contributed to the transformation of his consciousness from peasant to proletarian. This approach has yielded rich scholarly results. But that scholarship has addressed the peasant migrant almost exclusively as male and regarded his relation to his village primarily as an obstacle on the path to proletarianization.[1]

This paper will shift the focus away from the migrant and onto the village, the family, and the woman he left behind. There is much to be learned from such an approach, both as a complement to the customary one and on its own terms. Emphasizing the rural component of the urban-rural nexus sheds light on such neglected topics as the effect of outmigration on peasant women, village demography, and the rural way of life; and, far more than the customary approach, it serves to highlight the significance of the family economy and family relations as a factor in the development of the Russian working class.

It is easy to forget that in many cases a young man departed for the city as a member of a family economy and that, if his father remained alive, the decision to leave was rarely the migrant's alone. Often marriage forged the crucial link in his attachment to the village. As one historian has observed: "It is hard to say whether the obligation to marry and leave a worker (*rabotnitsa*) in the household was always a painful one, but it was a rather typical occurrence." He quotes a worker from Tver, subsequently a Bolshevik, who remembered: "After lengthy efforts and a struggle with my family, in 1896 I succeeded in . . . going to Petersburg; but to do this I had first to marry, so as to leave a worker in the household."[2] Drawing on data from the census of 1897, Shuster points out that among adult male workers in St. Petersburg—among whom married men constituted 43.7 percent (compared with 53.0 percent in European Russia as a whole)—only 8.1 percent of married men were heads of households residing with their families; 5.2 percent were members of families living with their families; and 86.2 percent lived apart from their wives and children.[3]

In Russia the traditional peasant household was also a family economy in the sense that every able-bodied member, including children, worked to ensure that the household survived. Or as Teodor Shanin puts it: "A peasant household is characterized by a nearly total integration of the peasant family's life and its farming enterprise."[4] The members of the multigenerational family were arranged hierarchically according to age and gender and subordinated to the *bolshak* (its head), whose decisions concerning the disposition of their labor were absolute according to law and custom. This tradition meant that males as well as females remained subject to the father's will so long as the father lived and they remained members of his household, and he had final say as to whom they married, whether and where they migrated, and what sort of work they did. As Shanin has observed, until 1906 the head of the household could have one of its members "arrested, sent back to his village under escort, or flogged by simple application to the peasant court."[5]

Patriarchy in so pure a form, however, was not to be found everywhere in rural Russia despite the attempt by the government to reinforce it during the emancipation of the serfs. The proliferation of capitalist relations and the expansion of nonagricultural employment that followed the emancipation undermined the authority of the *bolshak* and the economic allegiance of the family's absent members. The rapid industrialization of the late nineteenth century, by shifting production of many manufactured goods from household to factory, undermined these attitudes still further. Nevertheless, economic development did not do away entirely with patriarchal authority, and though it may have made absent members' responsibility to the family economy seem more burdensome, economic development rarely freed them from that responsibility altogether. "If the family that lives in the city is only part of the extended agricultural family, then that family, as well as a man living on his own . . . must send part of the wages to the village."[6] Instead, industrialization modified patriarchal authority and adapted it to new economic circumstances at the same time that it altered the character of the family economy and the manner by which men and women contributed to it and received benefits from it.[7]

Migration and the Peasant Household

This modification and adaptation varied enormously according to the history and patterns of development of a particular locale, even of a particular village. The degree of variation means that case studies are the best way to analyze continuity and change. I have chosen to examine two districts of Kostroma province, Soligalich and Chukhloma. The two districts, though comparable to some areas in the Central Industrial Region that had long-standing, extensive, and far-ranging male outmigration, are for these very reasons atypical of others. Nevertheless, they set into particularly sharp relief patterns that distinguished the Central Industrial Region from more sedentary agricultural areas. The data relating to Soligalich and Chukhloma are unusually abundant. In the first decades following its establishment, the Kostroma *zemstvo* provided an assiduous collector and publisher of demographic information concerning the peasant population, and D. N. Zhbankov, who spent six years (1883–89) serving as a *zemstvo* physician for the two districts, wrote remarkably detailed accounts of the lives of the people.[8] Born a serf, the illegitimate son of a peasant and her landlord, and a "liberal-populist" in his sympathies, Zhbankov was a sensitive and sympathetic observer of village life.[9] These materials will be verified and supplemented by ethnographic and other information relating to the neighboring district of Galich, which had similar, if less extreme, patterns of outmigration, and to other comparable areas of the Central Industrial Region.

In contrast to the agricultural regions of Russia, the peasant households of Soligalich and Chukhloma districts had long supplemented agricultural production with income in cash. The districts were located in the northwestern section of Kostroma province, far from major cities or centers of trade. Generally poor soil, inadequate pastureland, and cool summers and long winters made supplementary income essential, and the lack of local industry and indigenous raw materials (with the exception of some forestlands) and the distance from trading centers made it almost imperative that income be sought elsewhere.[10] As a result, outmigration in Soligalich and Chukhloma districts had a long history. Under serfdom the two districts had the highest level of feudal dues in the entire province—30, 40, even 50 rubles for each tax unit—and peasants sought work in the cities to pay them.[11] These peasant migrants were almost exclusively male and constituted more than 20 percent of the adult male population at the end of the eighteenth century; the percentage continued to grow. Owners with an eye to gaining the maximum return from their serfs sent them to be trained early, around the age of twelve. As a result, migratory laborers usually engaged in skilled trades, working as coppersmiths, metalworkers, joiners, carpenters, or blacksmiths, or became petty tradesmen—butchers and tanners, for example.[12] The income from such occupations created an unusually high level of material well-being. According to a survey of Kostroma province on the eve of the emancipation, the families of migrants lived "a step above the rather dirty and not particularly fastidious life of the ordinary peasantry, and their life-style resembled that of petty merchants."[13]

The emancipation of the serfs intensified these patterns and left the peasant households of Soligalich and Chukhloma still more economically dependent on male outmigration. Peasant land allotments were reduced, and redemption payments were set high—close to two and a half times the productivity of the land, according to one source; more than one and a half times its productivity, according to another. The land yielded only enough grain to last about seven and a half months of the year. After that, grain, the staple of the peasant diet, had to be purchased. The loss of meadow and pastureland caused the number of cattle and horses steadily to decline.[14]

In response to declining opportunities at home, even the more well-to-do peasant families resorted to the customary practice of sending their sons elsewhere for training when they reached the age of twelve, and as a result, some sort of training was the norm for young men from the districts. Of the 21,210 candidates reviewed by the Chukhloma military recruitment center between 1874 and 1916, only 525 had learned no trade (498 more were engaged in intellectual professions).[15] Their skills enabled the painters, carpenters, joiners, and other craftsmen from Soligalich and Chukhloma to earn a decent wage, but only if they migrated elsewhere, usually to St. Petersburg. As measured by the number of passports issued, male outmigration showed a substantial overall increase in the fifty years following the emancipation.

This, however, does not tell the entire story. The number of departing migrants fluctuated considerably from year to year. Moreover, in any given year some men left for the first time while others, seasoned migrants, returned to the village and remained there until they regained their health, recovered from an accident or from alcoholism, or otherwise recuperated. It is therefore likely that the proportion of men with outmigratory experience was more substantial than the numbers suggest.

The vast majority of these migrant workers were married. Although the Kostroma *zemstvo* data do not tell us whether they married earlier than city-born workers or peasants from sedentary agricultural areas, as Robert Johnson has argued they did,[16] they do tell us that men in Chukhloma district, the area of highest outmigration, married much more frequently than the norm for Kostroma province as a whole. The data also indicate that men from Soligalich married on the average slightly more frequently.

These comparatively high rates of nuptiality served a number of practical purposes. Most important, marriage to a village girl provided the vital link in the urban-rural nexus and ensured the maintenance of the family economy. A wife in the village tied a young man more firmly to it, made his "heart more inclined toward home."[17] It was important that the bride be a peasant because a wife was first and foremost a worker who lived with her in-laws, laboring in place of her migratory husband. A city-bred wife was unlikely to have either the experience or the inclination to do agricultural labor; in addition, peasants believed that city people had a different morality from countryfolk and were subject to greater temptation. As a result, even a short stint of service in a city often disqualified a peasant girl as a suitable match.[18] Parents not only preferred that their sons marry peasant girls; they also preferred that they marry early.[19] Men who went off to work in St. Petersburg, however, usually enjoyed the freedom to choose their own brides, in contrast to the sedentary peasants of Kostroma province or those of the agricultural regions, whose parents arranged marriages for them.[20] Around the end of October, young migrants returned to the village bearing trinkets, yards of silk, and other presents, prepared to court the local maidens.

Even the relative freedom to choose his bride, however, served in the end to consolidate a migrant's commitment to the family economy. Marriage was "an economic and physiological agreement," in the words of one observer.[21] Whatever the attachment between husband and wife, the struggle for survival came first. Having married in January, the migrant was off to St. Petersburg again by March. He had lived with his bride for about two months, and he left her "neither a maiden nor a widow, a real orphan," as they sang in one local folksong.[22] Only young wives without children could visit their husbands, and then only rarely because of distance and cost (twenty-five to thirty-five rubles per round-trip, according to Zhbankov). Once children arrived, mothers stayed home. Thereafter, the migrant might see his wife during the slow winter months, but in some cases he visited as rarely as every three to five years.[23]

When men did return to the village, they often lived there "like guests," doing no work around the house or yard.[24] This treatment underscores the distinguishing characteristic of the migrant's contribution to the family economy: cash and goods that could be purchased with cash. The majority of women, by contrast, contributed exclusively in kind. Indeed, the very extent of male outmigration helped to keep the level of female outmigration low and to restrict it almost entirely to nonmarriageable women (those over age twenty-three) and to childless widows. So long as there was land to be worked in the household of parents or in-laws, female hands were needed to work it. This need led families to place far greater constraints on women's migration than on men's.

The number of female migrants was very small during the days of serfdom, and it increased slowly, if steadily, after 1861 (see table 3.1). Those women who did leave were the most marginal members of the peasant household, and they tended to remain in the city. Other women left as members of families. Between 1874 and 1883, approximately the same number of passports were issued to families as were issued to individual women. Because family members were not listed separately, however, it is impossible to be sure about the precise number of sisters, mothers, or, most commonly, wives who left the countryside with their menfolk. Rarely did these women earn independent wages. Their role was to contribute to the family economy by reducing men's expenses, acting as cooks and housekeepers in the apartments or workshops where the husbands, sons, or brothers plied their trades.[25] If it is assumed that the number of women departing on a family passport was approximately the same as the number

Table 3.1
Number of Yearly and Half-Yearly Passports and Tickets Issued to Women (for each 100 women)

Locality	1869	1875	1880
Chukhloma	1.3	1.3	2.1
Soligalich	1.3	1.6	2.3

Source: *Materialy dlia statistiki Kostromskoi gubernii*, vyp. 3, 159; vyp. 4, 284; vyp. 6, 79.

leaving alone, it means that about 95 percent of adult women remained in the countryside.

For these women the evidence indicates that marriage to men who migrated was not only the expected but the preferred order of things. From among the candidates who presented themselves, it was the woman—not her parents—who usually made the selection.[26] Even in the days of serfdom, women's sewing circles would grow more lively when migrants returned from St. Petersburg, signaling the start of the courting season. Then and later, women favored the migrant, who sent money home, displayed sophisticated urban ways, and dressed modishly in a short jacket and overcoat. Men who remained in the village, even those who were financially better off, were clearly not *"Petersburgers."*[27] In the words of two local folk songs, "peasant lads are nitwits."[28]

Marrying a man who worked elsewhere tied a woman still more closely to the soil and increased her burden of physical labor. In the districts that Zhbankov called "the woman's place" and another writer entitled "the woman's kingdom" (*Babe tsarstvo*), heavy agricultural labor—men's work in sedentary areas—was conducted primarily, sometimes exclusively, by women, either by themselves or with the aid of a hired hand.[29] So demanding was this labor that it sometimes interrupted women's biological cycles: during the thirty to sixty days when work in the fields was most intensive, "a significant minority" of women, in the words of one physician, "the great majority" according to another, who were neither pregnant nor nursing ceased to menstruate altogether.[30]

Even as men's absence increased women's burdens, it made their lives easier in other respects. First, they endured less frequently the pains and risks of childbearing. Perhaps the cessation of menstruation, certainly outmigration itself, served as an inadvertent form of birth control. Whereas the rate of marriage in Soligalich and Chukhloma was higher than the average for rural Kostroma, the birthrate per thousand inhabitants was considerably lower.

Moreover, during these same years the peasant mothers of Soligalich and Chukhloma buried fewer of their nursing infants than did mothers in all other districts of rural Kostroma except Galich. Physicians writing at the time provide no explanation for these comparatively low rates of infant mortality, because to a man they believed that outmigration *raised* the rates by intensifying women's physical labor and leaving them no time to care for infants.[31] Whatever the negative effect of outmigration, in Soligalich and Chukhloma (and Galich) it was apparently offset by the positive effect: better nutrition of pregnant and nursing mothers, the result of a comparatively high standard of living.

The relative well-being that Krzhivoblotskii observed in Soligalich and Chukhloma before the emancipation continued into the decades that followed. By October 1873, for example, arrears in redemption and tax payments had reached 7.0 percent of the total in Kostroma province as a whole but only 0.9 percent in Soligalich and 0.8 percent in Chukhloma.[32] In 1880 a correspondent for *Kostromskie gubernskie vedomosti* wrote glowingly from Soligalich: "In the past twenty years, the level of well-being of the local population has risen to such an extent that people of former times simply wouldn't recognize peasant life." As evidence of this he pointed to houses that looked better and were kept more neatly, the widespread use of tea, and the number of women who wore wool and silk dresses.[33] Later reports confirm this positive tone, and for a more extensive area. Peasant houses were becoming more spacious and noticeably cleaner and neater: "Each peasant woman washes her hut once and sometimes twice a week without fail. Peasants no longer sleep on the stove or on planking between the stove and the ceiling, as the agricultural population does, but in separate beds with cotton curtains."[34]

Although it is necessary to treat such favorable accounts with caution, they are indirectly confirmed by the survival rate of infants as compared with children over the age of one. Children in Soligalich, Chukhloma, and Galich ate the food of peasants, were subject to the scourges of rural childhood, and perished at about the same rate as children did in other districts of Kostroma. Infants, on the other hand, were sustained by the milk of their mothers; and if infants in Soligalich, Chukhloma, and Galich died less often, it is very likely because their mothers ate better and were in better health on the average than peasant women elsewhere in Kostroma.

Migration and Women's Lives

In addition to stimulating a taste for manufactured goods and providing a means to purchase them, outmigration fostered peasant women's connection to a larger world by increasing their literacy. During the years that followed the emancipation, literacy among women of Soligalich and Chukhloma rose noticeably. Even when parents refused to spend money to educate daughters, literate brothers and fathers would sometimes teach them.[35]

In less measurable ways, too, marriage to a migrant offered women greater control over their own lives, as well as a measure of dignity that distinguished them sharply from women in more sedentary areas. The wife's contribution in kind was essential to the family economy, and the fact that often she alone sustained the rural household served to make the marital union more of a partnership. Moreover, during most of the year migrant husbands and fathers were not on hand to discipline women, and the high mortality rates of migrants reduced the number of men present still further. Like other workers in St. Petersburg, migrants from Soligalich and Chukhloma labored long hours, lived crowded together in damp and dingy rooms, and ate very poorly. As a result, many died prematurely; this was especially true of painters, whose susceptibility to tuberculosis was usually high because they inhaled paint fumes during apprenticeship.[36]

In his account of village life Zhbankov included a description of the composition of sixty-one peasant households in four villages, where there lived twenty-six widows, ranging in age from twenty-two to one hundred, and only two widowers.[37] Other sources suggest that these households were not idiosyncratic. In 1884 from a parish in neighboring Galich district, where, as in Soligalich and Chukhloma, a large proportion of men worked as painters, a correspondent wrote that every year two or three men died on the job and that in one year seven had perished (the male population totaled 302 at the time). He counted sixty-five widows but only six widowers among his parish population; thirty-five women over sixty, but only fifteen men.[38] In 1906 a participant at the ninth annual congress of Kostroma physicians reported that whereas one would expect about 120 old women for every 100 old men, in Soligalich and Chukhloma for every 100 old men "there were 212 and even 286 old women."[39] Of the fifty-three households with land in Zhbankov's sample, only twenty-two contained an adult (over age sixteen) male year round; and sixteen of them (close to one-third) were headed by widows over the age of forty-five.[40]

The result was that physical violence against women was relatively rare in the peasant marriages of Soligalich and Chukhloma. The folk songs Zhbankov recorded serve as one example: although the picture they portray of the relations between the sexes is rarely happy, it is almost never brutal. In Zhbankov's words: "In the songs, there are no complaints about cruel treatment or beatings, while songs from the more remote 'uncultured' locales are filled with such complaints."[41] In neighboring Galich, too, all "industrious Petersburgers spoil[ed] their wives a lot," mistreating them only when drunk and regretting it afterward.[42]

This treatment led women to conduct themselves more independently. By contrast with the "oppressed pariahs of the black earth regions, who are frightened of saying a word in the presence of their master[s]," "the women of Soligalich and Chukhloma were independent, self-reliant and self-assured," and they knew "the value of their labor and themselves."[43] Women's desire to become mistresses of their own households could prompt household divisions in the two districts, as elsewhere.[44] Women even participated in village self-government. In Kostroma, as in other areas of substantial male outmigration, women assumed their husbands' places at the village assembly and fulfilled the offices of representative and elder.[45]

Yet another index of the extent to which traditional constraints on women had eroded is the fact that some were unfaithful to absent husbands, either in casual encounters or in relationships serious enough to prompt the woman to move in with her lover. Although not precisely common, wifely infidelity seems to have been widespread and connected directly to outmigration. It was most likely to occur in places where men were absent over extended periods of time, depriving their wives of regular sexual congress.[46] Zhbankov himself claimed personally to have observed twenty-two cases of illegal cohabitation, and two such illegally cohabiting couples can be found among the sixty-one households he describes. One case of wifely infidelity wound up in court. The accused, Sidorova, resided in Chukhloma district and had rarely seen her husband since their wedding twelve years before. When she bore a child by another man, terror of what her husband might do led her to murder it. The husband proved understanding in this particular instance and treated his wife "with great compassion."[47] Nevertheless, Sidorova's murderous terror reflected the commonly held belief that a betrayed husband had the right to punish his wife as he chose. Reinforced by lack of opportunity, women's physical exhaustion, and perhaps a greater degree of loyalty and more romantic attitude toward marriage, this belief very likely served to restrain other women from sexual infidelity altogether.

Whatever the reasons, all commentators agree that although outmigration increased wifely infidelity, women strayed less frequently than did their absent husbands. In the realm of sexual activity, as in other areas, women's actions remained more circumscribed than men's and more subject to the constraints of family and community. The peasant women of Soligalich and Chukhloma were more closely linked than men to a natural economy and a traditional way of life and were far less exposed than were men to modern sectors of society; nevertheless these women lived differently from women in more sedentary areas of the province. Their standard of living was higher, and their consumption patterns demonstrated the influence of urban ways; they were more likely to be literate, and they exercised a greater degree of control over their own lives, both at home and in village self-government.

Change and Stability

These elements of "modernity," however, occurred within a culture that in fundamental respects varied little from one generation to the next. In contrast to their migrant husbands, fathers, and brothers, the women of Soligalich and Chukhloma lived like peasants. A growing proportion of spinsters and childless widows might leave, but female migrants remained a minority. Most followed in the footsteps of their mothers, marrying migrants, remaining in the village, and maintaining the family economy.

In the early twentieth century, as conditions on the land worsened and opportunities in the cities multiplied, the number of outmigrants from Soligalich and Chukhloma increased substantially, and so did the proportion of women among them. Nevertheless, the migratory patterns described in this paper apparently remained essentially unchanged even after the Revolution of 1917. As an early Soviet historian of Kostroma province put it: "Generally speaking, outwork is closely intertwined with all other aspects of life in the villages of Kostroma, and to describe it is essentially to describe that life in all its variety."[48]

There were many reasons for the stability of outmigratory patterns. Some, such as tradition and a feeling for the land, are hard to measure. Others—for example, the economic advantages of continuing outmigration—are much easier to determine. The age levels of men and the seasonal nature of their employment meant that a wife and children in the village were the only family most men could afford. In the 1880s the maximum a migrant could hope to earn, unless he worked as a petty tradesman, was 100–300 rubles a year, and this figure was possible only if he became a highly qualified metalworker or blacksmith. A painter working from March to November earned between 70 and 150 rubles a year; a carpenter working from April to November earned between 60 and 120. In Zhbankov's time the average wage of a migrant from Soligalich and Chukhloma was around 100 rubles.[49] By the eve of World War I, these wages had more than doubled, reaching 240.9 rubles for a painter and 221.6 for a carpenter.[50] This income was enough to rent a cot in a damp basement, buy a few presents for the folks at home, contribute to the peasant economy, visit the village occasionally, and have a few drinks and a good time once in a while, but it was insufficient to raise a family in St. Petersburg.

According to a study conducted by S. N. Prokopovich in 1909, in order for a worker in St. Petersburg to marry and keep his wife with him, he had to earn between 400 and 600 rubles a year; only when his wage exceeded 600 rubles could he afford to educate his children. Men who earned less could marry only because they had an allotment in the village and a wife who would stay there, cultivate it, and raise the children. Prokopovich's calculations assume that only male heads of households contributed to the family income. In fact, only a minority of working-class families conformed to such a picture. Wives, accustomed to contributing to the family economy however they could, worked in factories, did day labor, took in boarders, and earned money in other similar ways, and even children did what they could to pay their way. Yet even if the contribution of other family members is included, overall family income at the wage level of workers from Soligalich and Chukhloma would still fall below the levels calculated by Prokopovich. This situation kept many fully urbanized workers from marrying at all. Men, such as the artisans of Soligalich and Chukhloma, who maintained their village ties, were in a far better position to have a family and to provide decently for their children than either fully proletarianized workers who earned a comparable wage or their sedentary peasant brothers.[51] Until economic circumstances changed dramatically, outmigration of the sort described in this paper remained the most effective way for families of the majority of the peasant-workers from Soligalich and Chukhloma districts to allocate their human resources. In fact, not even the Revolution of 1917 altered the rhythm of outmigration. It ended only with the industrialization drive and the collectivization of agriculture, which broke the urban-rural connection and forced men to choose a "side."

As a family strategy, outmigration had a significant effect on others besides the migrant. It removed adult men from some households for months and even years. It left other households, made up of nuclear families and widows, without a *bolshak* altogether. In such cases outmigration altered the patriarchal family patterns usually regarded as typical for the peasantry and provided some women with an unusual opportunity to be their own mistresses, even as it added to their labors. Moreover, the children of such households were likely to spend their early years in a world peopled primarily by women.[52] According to Zhbankov's data, of the forty-one households that included children aged ten or below, twenty-five contained no males older than sixteen for at least part of the year. Did children, like wives, gain greater autonomy because of the absence of a male authority figure? It would be useful to know what such long-distance relations did to people's concepts of marriage, the family, and fatherhood, for popular attitudes concerning these matters provided a significant factor in shaping family life in the postrevolutionary era.

In Soligalich and Chukhloma, and perhaps in other areas with comparable patterns, outmigration offered fundamentally different experiences to men and women. Though men might return in winter months, they took no part in the agricultural labors of their wives; women, in turn, might visit the city, consume manufactured products, and learn to read and write, but in the end women's connection to a cash economy and the wider world depended on men.

We still have much to learn about the consciousness of both these migrants and the women who stayed at home, but their disparate experiences make it likely that there would be differences between them and that women's consciousness would be the more "conservative," more bound up with the familiar, more resistant to change.[53] This, of course, is conventional wisdom. What the analysis in this paper suggests, however, is that in areas such as Soligalich and Chukhloma, married women's conservatism was less the product of women's "backwardness" and more the result of their perfectly understandable effort to hold on to a world that was not only familiar and secure but also, comparatively speaking, substantially under their control.

Although it is not the task of this paper to explore such questions, it seems to me that the line of inquiry I have adopted might shed considerable light on the upheavals in the relations between sexes in the postrevolutionary period, first in the early 1920s, when the complementarity of men's and women's roles in certain parts of the Central Industrial Region was broken by the flow of migrants back to the countryside in the wake of urban devastation, and then in the late 1920s by industrialization, collectivization, and the imposition of centralized control. It is time to attend to the "woman's side."

Notes

1. Rose Glickman, *Russian Factory Women: Workplace and Society, 1880–1914* (Berkeley: University of California Press, 1984).

2. Iu. A. Shuster, *Peterburgskie rabochie v 1905–1907 gg.* (Leningrad, 1976), 31.

3. Ibid., 26.

4. Teodor Shanin, "Peasantry as a Political Factor," in *Peasants and Peasant Societies*, ed. Teodor Shanin (Harmondsworth, England: Penguin, 1971), 30–31. See also Louise Tilly, Joan Scott, and Miriam Cohen, "Women's Work and European Fertility Patterns," *Journal of Interdisciplinary History* 6 (Winter 1976): esp. 452–54.

5. Shanin, "Peasantry as a Political Factor," 35.

6. Shuster, *Peterburgskie rabochie*, 31.

7. See Ann Whitehead, "'I'm Hungry, Mum': The Politics of Domestic Budgeting," in *Of Marriage and the Market*, ed. Kate Young et al. (London: Routledge & Kegan Paul, 1981), 93–116, for a penetrating discussion of the need to attend to the sexual division of labor, as well as to the "changing nature of the production, distribution and consumption relations within the household, especially as they are affected by its position in the overall socioeconomic structure, or the changes in that structure over time" (p. 94).

8. D. N. Zhbankov, *Babia storona* (Kostroma, 1891); idem, "K voprosu o plodovitosti zamuzhnikh zhenshchin. Vliiani otkhozhikh zarabotkov," *Vrach* 7, no. 39 (1886): 700; idem, "O gorodskikh otkhozhikh zarabotkakh v Soligalichskom uezde, Kostromskoi gubernii," *Iuridicheskii vestnik*, no. 7 (September 1890): 130–49; idem, "Vliianie otkhozhikh zarabotkov na dvizhenie narodonaseleniia Kostromskol gubernii po dannym 1866–1883," *Materialy dlia statistiki Kostromskol gubernii*, vyp. 7 (Kostroma, 1887).

9. S. I. Mitskevich, *Revoliutsionnaia Moskva 1888–1905* (Moscow, 1940), 108–10. See also Nancy M. Frieden, *Russian Physicians in an Era of Reform and Revolution, 1856–1905* (Princeton: Princeton University Press, 1981).

10. Zhbankov, "O gorodskikh," 131–32; G. M. Gertsenshtein, "K voprosu ob otkhozhikh promyslakh," *Russkaia mysl* (1887), kn. IX, 151–52; N. N. Vladimirskii, *Otkhozhie promysly krestianskogo naseleniia Kostromskoi gubernii* (Kostroma, 1926), 12–18. In the late 1850s in both districts combined, four distilleries employed ninety-one workers, three brickmaking workshops employed five men, two cheese dairies hired twenty workers, and five shops manufacturing soap employed twelve. Te-ov, "Zametki o Kostromskoi gubernii," *Vestnik promyshlennosti*, no. 2 (1860): 281–82. On wooden handcrafts, see *Materialy dlia izucheniia Kustarnoi promyshlennosti i ruchnogo truda v Rossii* (St. Petersburg, 1872) chap. 1, 133. The towns of Soligalich and Chukhloma were utterly insignificant as trade or manufacturing centers and were considered backwaters in every respect. N. N. Vladimirskii, *Kostromskaia oblast'* (Kostroma, 1959), 131.

11. *Materialy dlia statistiki Kostromskoi gubernii*, vyp. 3 (Kostroma, 1872), 155.

12. Vladimirskii, *Otkhozhie*, 18–20; A. Iatsevich, *Krepostnye v Peterburge* (Leningrad, 1933), 8; *Ocherki ekonomicheskoi istorii Rossii pervoi poloviny XIX veka* (Moscow, 1959), 79.

13. Ia. Krzhivoblotskii, *Materialy dlia geografii i statistiki Rossii, sobrannye ofitserami General'nogo shtaba* (St. Petersburg, 1861), 500.

14. Concerning land allotments, see E. V. Matveeva, "K voprosu o sviazi rabochikh tekstil'shchikov Kostromskoi gubernii s zemlei v 90 e gody XIX veka," in *Promyshlennost i proletariat gubernii Verkhnego Povolzhia v kontse XIX-nachale XX vv.* (Iaroslavl, 1976), 2.

15. Vladimirskii, *Kostromskaia oblast*, 113.

16. Robert E. Johnson, "Family Relations and the Rural-Urban Nexus: Patterns in the Hinterland of Moscow, 1880–1900," in *The Family in Imperial Russia*, ed. David Ransel (Urbana: University of Illinois Press, 1978), 263–79.

17. S. Kanatchikov, *Iz istorii moego bytiia* (Moscow-Leningrad: *Zemlia i fabrika*, 1929) 1: 20, 45. Or as an observer of peasant life in Tver put it, "peasants regard marriage as a way of attaching a person to the household." Tenishev Archive, Gos. Muzei etnografii narodov SSSR [hereafter refered to as Tenishev Archive], fond 7, opis, 1, delo 1724, 19.

18. Tenishev Archive, d. 588, 3 (Galich, Kostroma).

19. Ibid., 9; Zhbankov, *Babia*, 24–25, 27, 63, 80–82.

20. Krzhivoblotskii suggests that even under serfdom, migrants chose their own brides, *Materialy dlia geografi*, 55, 516–17. If he and Zhbankov are right, then Soligalich and Chukhloma provide evidence of how much developmental patterns might influence social mores. The ethnographic correspondent from neighboring Galich, where outmigratory levels were somewhat lower, reported that in Galich, "rarely do men follow their hearts, and how can they, when they visit such a short time. Parents run it all." Tenishev Archive, f. 588, 5–6. On the other hand, weddings in Galich rarely occurred without the consent of the couple.

21. Tenishev Archive, d. 588, 5. Or, as Zhbankov put it: "If marriage in the agricultural zone is strongly subject to economic needs, then here its character is primarily economic." Zhbankov, *Babia*, 82.

22. Tenishev Archive, d. 589 (Galich), 19; Zhbankov, *Babia*, 134.

23. Zhbankov, *Babia*, 72, 83. Lengthy separations are also discussed in P. G. Timofeev, *Chem zhivet zavodskii rabochii* (St. Petersburg, 1906), 13–14.

24. *Materialy dlia statistiki*, vyp. 3, 103–4.

25. Zhbankov, *Babia*, 71–72.

26. Tenishev Archive, d. 588, 11; Zhbankov, *Babia*, 82.

27. Writes the correspondent from Galich: "If some boy is home over the summer, no girl will accept his attentions, because he's not a *Pitershchik*." Tenishev Archive, d. 587 (Galich), 5; Krzhivoblotskii, *Materialy dlia geografil i statistiki*, 516.

28. Zhbankov, *Babia*, 27; 126, n. xxv; 127, n. xxvii.

29. V. P. Semenov, ed., *Rossiia: Polnoe geograficheskoe opisanie nashego otechestva*, 11 vols. (St. Petersburg, 1899) 1: 110; A. Balov, "Ocherki Peshekhoniia," *Etnograficheskoe obozrenie* 35, no. 4 (1897): 57. I. Krasnoperov provides a detailed description of the physical labor that the peasant women of Tver performed in their husbands' absence in "Zhenski promysly v Tverskoi gubernii," *Mir bozhii*, no. 2 (1898): 22–24.

30. Z. G. Frenkel, "Osnovnye pokazateli, kharakterizuiushchie dvizhenie naseleniia v Kostromskoi gubernii v tri poslednie piatiletiia (1891–1905)," in *Trudy IX gubernskogo sezda vrachei Kostromskoi gubernii*, vyp. 3 (Kostroma, 1906), 65. Zhbankov, *Babia*, 91, and "K voprosu," 700. In Riazan province, A. O. Afinogenov observed the same phenomenon. *Zhizn zhenskogo naselniia Riazanskogo uezda v period detorodnoi deiatelnosti zhenshchiny i polozhenie dela akusherskoi pomoshchi etomu naseleniiu* (St. Petersburg, 1903), 44.

31. M. S. Uvarov, "O vlianii otkhozhego promysla na sanitarnoe polozhenie Rossii," *Vestnik obshchestvennoi gigieny i sudebnoi meditsiny* 31, no. 7. (July 1896): 34–39; S. N. Karatenko, "O sanitarnom znachenii otkhozhego promysla v Rossii," *Zhurnal Russkago obshchestva okhraneniia narodnago zdraviia*, no. 2 (1895): 127; Krasnoperov, "Zhenskie promysly," 22.

32. *Materialy dlia statistiki*, vyp. 3, 115.

33. "Iz Kostromskoi volosti Soligalichskogo uezda," *Kostromskie gubernskie vedomosti*, no. 37 (1880): 213.

34. Semenov, *Rossiia*, 103.

35. Zhbankov, *Babia*, 93–98.

36. *Trudy IX gubernskogo sezda vrachei*, vyp. 2, 28. For average life expectancy of a fifteen-year-old male in the years 1874–1910, see V. V. Paevskii, *Voprosy demograficheskoi i meditsinskoi statistiki* (Moscow, 1970), 290.

37. Zhbankov, *Babia*, 103–10.

38. N., "Zametka ob otkhozhikh promyslakh krestian Ignatovskogo prikhoda," in *Materialy dlia statistiki Kostromskoi gubernii*, vyp. 6 (Kostroma, 1884), 143–45.

39. *Trudy IX gubernskogo sezda vrachei*, vyp. 2, 28. For the period 1874–1910, Paevskii has calculated that on the average the life expectancy of women at age fifteen was only marginally higher than that of men. *Voprosy demograficheskoi*, 290.

40. Zhbankov, *Babia*, 103–10.

41. Ibid., 119. For examples of traditional plaints, see A. Borovikovskii, "Zhenskaia dolia po malorossiiskim pesniam," *Chteniia v Imperatorskom Obshchestve Istorii i Drevnei Rossii*, no. 4 (1867): 96–142; N. I. Kostomarov, "Velikorusskaia narodnaia poeziia," *Vestnik Evropy*, no. 6 (1872): 557, 574–77.

42. Tenishev Archive, d. 588, 22. In Iaroslavl district of Iaroslavl province, another area of high male outmigration, women had become "almost completely men's equals," and men's authority had declined so far that "occasionally it was the wife who exercised authority over her husband"; Tenishev Archive, d. 1832, 10, 11.

43. Zhbankov, *Babia*, 68; F. I. Pokrovskii, "O semeinom polozhenii krestianskoi zhenshchiny v Kostromskoi gubernii po dannym volostnogo suda," *Zhivaia starina*, 1896 otd. 1: 459, 462.

44. F. I. Pokrovskii, "Semeinye razdely v Chukhlomskom uezde," *Zhivaia starina*, 1903, vyp. 1–2: 43–44; *Obzor Iaraslavskoi gubernii*, vyp. 2, chap. 1. "Otkhozhie promysly krestian Iaroslavskoi gubernii" (Iaroslavl, 1896), 191; Tenishev Archive, d. 1725 (Tver), 66; Zhbankov, *Babia*, 81–82.

45. Semenov, ed., *Rossiia*, 110; *Obzor Iaroslavskoi gubernii*, 166; Krasnoperov, "Zhenskie promysly," 22; Zhbankov, *Babia*, 68. In Peshekhonov district of Iaroslavl women attended the district assembly as well, and without having to don a man's hat as apparently was the custom elsewhere. Tenishev Archive, d. 1788, 27.

46. Semenov, *Rossiia*, 110; Tenishev Archive, d. 40 (Vladimir), 4; d. 588 (Galich), 16; d. 1462 (Riazan), 41; d. 1767 (Iaroslavl), 31; d. 1832 (Iaroslavl), 11.

47. *Sudebnyi vestnik*, no. 14 (1873): 4.

48. Vladimirskii, *Kostromskaia oblast*, 40–42.

49. Zhbankov, "O gorodskikh," 136–37.

50. Vladimirskii, *Otkhozhie*, 38–40.

51. S. N. Prokopovich, *Biudzhety peterburgskikh rabochikh*, 26–29. Bernshtein-Kogan notes that workers who had families in the villages were financially in far better positions to marry than workers who were fully urbanized, *Chislennost*, 48–61. For a detailed account of the expenses of urban working-class families, see M. Davidovich, *Peterburgskii rabochii vo ego biudzhetakh* (St. Petersburg, 1912).

52. A. P. Zvonkov, writing of an outmigratory area of Tambov, noted that women and children had much in common, "but they are far apart from the head of the family; their interests are different." "Sovremennyi brak i svadba sredi krestian Tambovskoi gubernii," *Sbornik svedenii dlia izucheniia byta selskogo naseleniia Rossii*, vyp. 1 (Moscow, 1889), 70–71.

53. For example, Nancy Frieden describes how the collectivity of women within the household could serve as an obstacle to the modernizing practices of physicians: "Child Care: Medical Reform in a Traditionalist Culture," in Ransel, *The Family*, 236–59.

4

Peasant and Proletariat: Migration, Family Patterns, and Regional Loyalties

Robert E. Johnson

The family patterns of nineteenth-century Russia stood in sharp contrast to those of most of Western Europe. There private landownership and single-share inheritance were predominant throughout the modern era. Bachelorhood and spinsterhood were relatively common; many individuals did not marry until their late twenties, and the average household included not many more than four members.[1] In Russia, where land tenure was often communal and a father's inheritance was divided among his sons, different patterns prevailed: households were larger, marriages were earlier, and bachelorhood and spinsterhood were extremely rare.

Not surprisingly, the growth of cities and the expansion of factories seemed to threaten many of these patterns. Nineteenth-century observers attached great significance to the movement of families into industrial centers. Populists saw in it the disintegration of a traditional way of life and the undermining of inherited values and authority; advocates of capitalist development believed that a hereditary class of skilled workers would be a cornerstone of future industrial development; revolutionary Marxists expected such workers to become the vanguard of future struggle.[2] All agreed, however, that the worker whose family was with him in the city or factory was in a very different position from the one who had left wife and children behind in the village.

How were traditional peasant family patterns affected by industrialization and urbanization? Was a new, factory-based family unit emerging? Did family life become more "European" or did it retain its distinctive qualities? Did traditional family patterns put their own stamp on the future course of industrial and urban growth? Here the most interesting questions are the hardest to answer. Certain aspects of family behavior are easily described: the age at marriage, the proportion of the population that ever married, the size of the average household in city and country. Describing the family environment of workers or peasants, or the transmission of attitudes and habits from generation to generation, is a much more difficult task. From the limited evidence available, however, one can still draw some cautious inferences about the interaction between village and factory life.

Family Life in the City

The conditions of city and factory life, in Moscow as elsewhere in Russia, tended to discourage workers from maintaining families. Low wages and the terms of employment made it virtually impossible for workers to secure separate living quarters of their own. In the more primitive industrial establishments, those who slept in the workshops could keep their families beside them in extremely unhygienic conditions. One example was the bast-matting industry, in which workers customarily slept on the floor under their hand-powered looms, children began working as early as age five, and most workers lived with their families. Elsewhere, however, workers were crowded into factory-owned barracks or rented a fraction of a room in nearby flophouses. Toward the end of the nineteenth century an "enlightened" minority of employers began to build living quarters to accommodate workers' families, but the families were often crowded several to a room, making domestic life quite difficult. Often, too, these facilities were available only if the husband and wife were both working: if either quit or was fired, the family could be evicted.[3]

Employers, moreover, made little if any provision for the exigencies of child rearing. Nurseries or kindergartens were almost nonexistent, and mothers might even be denied permission to nurse their babies during work hours.[4] The employers' motive was mainly financial: building and maintaining nurseries cost money, and so did any interruption of the work schedule, especially when expensive machinery was involved. To avoid this expense, some factory owners hired only childless women, but even where this was not an explicit policy most mothers found it impossible to keep young children with them.

As a result of these conditions, only a minority of city dwellers, and a much smaller minority of factory workers, lived with their families. Only about one-third of the 650,000 people who occupied ordinary living quarters in Moscow city in 1882 were independent householders or members of their immediate families. Altogether there were 84,000 independent households, of which roughly 60 percent included children of the head of household. Of the total population, 12.6 percent were clerks and workers who resided in their employers' households, and an additional 20 percent resided in nonfamily units such as factory barracks.[5]

A comparison of figures from 1882 and 1897 suggests that the number of dependents was increasing over time; but even so, such individuals remained an insignificant minority at the end of the century. In 1902 fully four-fifths of all migrants living in Moscow city were self-supporting; in contrast, just over one-third of city-born residents were self-supporting.[6]

Who were these workers without families? In the early decades of the nineteenth century the population of Moscow's factories had consisted almost entirely of males.[7] With the spread of mechanization, however, many factory tasks (especially in the textile industry) no longer demanded much strength or skill, and greater numbers of women and minors began to be hired. By the end of the century women accounted for almost half of the total work force in textile manufacturing, and in certain divisions such as cotton spinning males had become an insignificant minority.[8] Between 1871 and 1902 the proportion of women in Moscow city's entire population rose from 40 to 45 percent.[9] Some observers, including the eminent Soviet demographer A. G. Rashin, have taken this growth as a sign that the number of permanent city-based households was increasing—evidence, in other words, that capitalism was advancing and old patterns of life were eroding.[10] Although it would be wrong to deny that *any* such households were formed, a close examination of female labor and migration patterns indicates that they were the exception rather than the rule.

Moscow's female population grew through inmigration. The women who moved there, like their male counterparts, were mostly from the peasantry and came to Moscow to find wages. Roughly two-thirds of them were self-supporting, with domestic service accounting for the greatest proportion (33 percent) followed by factory work (13 percent) and small-scale manufacturing (9 percent).[11] The conditions of their work and living arrangements generally prevented them from having children with them (true not only for factories but for domestic service and most other employment), so those who were mothers commonly left their children in the country to be raised by relatives.

Even so, women of childbearing age who moved to Moscow tended to depart within a short time.[12] The peasant women who stayed longest in Moscow were older, mainly widows and spinsters, who faced fewer obstacles if they wished to renounce their land allotment and depart permanently from the village.[13]

Thus although the overall proportion of women in the population of Moscow city was increasing, the ratio of women to men remained least favorable for the ages of marriage and childbearing. It was lower for migrants than for the city-born population, and lower in the industrial suburbs than in the central districts. Among migrants aged fifteen to thirty-nine in the suburbs, there were only thirty-nine women for every one hundred men.[14]

In short, only a small minority of the women who came to Moscow were likely to stay there, marry, and raise children. An increase in the overall proportion of women did not necessarily mean that the proportion of marriageable women increased, nor did an increase in the number married necessarily lead to an increase in the number of families. When migrant women did bear children, they were more likely to raise them in the countryside.

The Bifurcated Household

Many factory workers and city dwellers chose to maintain households in the countryside. The extent of this practice can be gauged from the fact that there were almost twice as many married men as married women living in Moscow city in 1902.[15] The population of factories and urban centers was composed largely of husbands without wives and parents without children. In the countryside thousands of households relied on the monetary contributions of absent members in order to make ends meet.

What effect did this system have on family composition? Did departing wage earners still follow the marital patterns of the village, or were new proletarian patterns beginning to appear? Demographic statistics reveal that there were indeed sharp differences between the marital patterns of native Muscovites and those of the rest of Russia; migrants and factory workers, rather than falling between the two, seem to follow one extreme or the other, with males maintaining the patterns of peasant Russia and females assimilating to the patterns of the city.

The urban and rural extremes seem to represent what J. Hajnal has called "European" and "non-European" patterns of marriage.[16] City-born Muscovites seem to have married much later than the rest of the population, and a greater proportion never married at all. Their rates are comparable to those found in such countries as Sweden in the nineteenth century, whereas the national Russian figures resemble those of Asia or southeastern Europe (e.g., Serbia). Knowing that the Russian national statistics pertain to a population composed predominantly of peasants, one could easily picture the city and countryside as two opposite poles, analogous to the differences between Western Europe and the rest of the world at the end of the nineteenth century. At one extreme, Moscow city could be taken to symbolize modernity and technological progress. The factors that discouraged or prevented marriage in this setting might include increased labor mobility, more years devoted to education and specialized job training, and a work situation in which, in contrast to agrarian society, a spouse and children are more a liability than an asset. At the opposite extreme, peasants who spent their entire lives in the villages could be expected to follow age-old patterns, marrying early and producing large families.

Following this line of reasoning, migrants and factory workers who spent much of their adult lives in cities and towns should have been exposed to most of the same "modernizing" pressures as the rest of the population. They should therefore have occupied a position between the extremes of city and peasant marital patterns. The males, however, do not fit this prediction. Instead of postponing or avoiding marriage, workers and migrants appear to have married at least as early as other peasants. Male factory workers, in fact, married even earlier: 63 percent in the age group twenty to twenty-nine were married compared with 58 percent of males throughout Russia.

These figures cannot readily be explained by reference to a peasantry in transition whose members were progressing step by step from the backward village to the modern city. Employment away from the native village seems, on the contrary, to have reinforced or exaggerated the preexisting marital pattern of peasant men. The apparent paradox can be explained if one looks again at the idea of rural-urban interaction. Given the possibility of maintaining families in the countryside, peasant workers may have encountered fewer obstacles to marriage than did pure peasants or city-born workers. Unlike other workers, they might not have been inhibited by the lack of housing or the high cost of living in the city; unlike other peasants, they were receiving a relatively reliable money income independent of their land allotments. From the available statistics one cannot determine whether wage-earning peasant youths were defying their fathers by contracting early marriages, or whether the migrant's wages, by enhancing the prosperity of the parental household, encouraged the parents to seek a daughter-in-law. In either case, however, the logic of the rural-urban nexus would seem to encourage young men to marry early. . . .

The same factors that encouraged male migrants to marry early may also have led them to produce large families.[17] Preliminary investigations suggest that migrants' households were not smaller than those of nonmigrant peasants and may even have been larger. Workers at the Tsindel cotton mill in Moscow city, for example, reported an average family size of 7.3, whereas the average household in the regions from which they had migrated was just over 6.[18] . . .

If labor migration (otkhodnichestvo) encouraged men to marry early and have large families, it seems to have had the opposite effect on women. Instead of maintaining the "peasant" marital pattern, female migrants and factory workers appear to have quickly assimilated themselves into the "city" pattern. Their rates of marriage for all ages were lower than the rates for Russia as a whole; for all ages over twenty-five, they were virtually indistinguishable from those of city-born women. The reasons for this phenomenon are not hard to find, especially in light of the previous discussion. Male migrants married earlier because they could leave their families in the countryside; to the extent that they did so, however, their wives would be excluded from the population of cities and factories. The proportion of unmarried, childless, and widowed women in cities and factories would thereby be inflated.

Women, it seems, had to choose between raising families and migrating for wages. To the extent that they did assimilate themselves into the urban-industrial order, their rates of marriage went down. The Moscow provincial *zemstvo*'s survey of factories throughout the province in the early 1880s found that the proportion of married women in different populations varied inversely with the degree of urbanization or industrialization. . . . Studies of a somewhat later period found a negative correlation between literacy and the rate of marriage, and this too suggests that assimilation to urban-industrial life inhibited women from marrying.[19]

The city and factory, it seems, were not preventing marriage and may not have reduced fertility. They were, however, attracting (and rejecting) specific segments of the peasant population. Males with families were encouraged to migrate, as were unmarried and childless women; but given the apparent integration of *otkhodnichestvo* with the village economy, traditional family patterns stood a good chance of survival in the country.

This seems likely to have intensified a pattern, still enduring today in much of the Third World, in which able-bodied young adults go off to the city and leave agriculture to the very old and the very young. (It is true that able-bodied young women also stayed behind, but the reason was usually that they were burdened with young children, and this necessarily limited their role as agricultural producers or potential innovators.) An indirect effect of *otkhodnichestvo* may thus have been to perpetuate small-scale production and inefficiency in the countryside.

Fathers and Sons at the Factory

One further way of measuring the influence of cities and factories on family life is to ask whether sons followed their fathers to the factory. If many did so, this could mean that acquired skills and attitudes were being passed from generation to generation, helping to create a hereditary proletariat.[20] Conversely, if each successive generation was recruited anew from the peasantry, there might be more disruption and discontinuity in migrants' lives and less opportunity to come to terms with the conditions or problems of a new environment.

The implications of this issue were recognized as early as the 1880s, with the result that several different studies collected information about workers' origins. The data they compiled suggest a high degree of continuity and generational succession at the factories of Moscow combined with the continuance of strong rural ties. Children followed their parents to the factory, but they still spent their formative years in the village. If their work was hereditary, this did not necessarily make them proletarian. Studies conducted between 1881 and 1899 show that 43 to 55 percent of workers were second- or even third-generation factory workers.

This pattern would seem to follow logically from the pattern of child labor mentioned earlier in this chapter. Young people entered the factory at a tender age, and those whose parents or relatives were working there may have found their way to the factory more readily than other peasants.[21] Is it proper to conclude from this, however, that the younger generation constituted a true proletariat? Were these younger workers really cut off from village life—propertyless and, in E. M. Dementev's words, "living from day to day"[22] In the main, nineteenth-century researchers answered these questions in the affirmative, and later generations of economists and historians, from Lenin and Tugan-Baranovskii to Soviet scholars of the 1960s, have tended to agree. A close scrutiny of the available evidence, however, reveals several flaws in this argument.

First, the factories described in the 1880s did not employ substantial numbers of women or children. The majority of their workers were male, and, like the males discussed earlier, most lived in barracks without their families. Their children were raised in the countryside by their mothers (or, if the mothers were also working at the factory, by grandparents or other relatives). The existence of a second generation at the factory was no proof that its members had severed ties with the "patriarchal" village.

Second, the cited statistics were compiled during the depression of the early 1880s, when many workers had been laid off and few new ones had been taken on at the factories. This may have inflated the proportion of long-term experienced workers and understated the proportion of green new recruits.[23]

Third, most of those who were listed as second-generation factory workers retained land allotments in their native villages. At the Tsindel factory more than 90 percent of all peasant workers had allotments.[24] A more extensive study of workers in Vladimir province in the years 1894–97 found that of a total of some 35,000 hereditary (i.e., second-generation) peasant workers, 40 percent (13.8 thousand) possessed allotments.[25]

An allotment might have been an involuntary tie to the village, yet additional evidence suggests that many workers had more than a nominal tie to agriculture. In Peskov's study occupational groups with the very highest proportion of second-generation workers were also the ones with the highest proportion of summer departures to the countryside: handweavers in silk, cotton, or wool and hand dye-printers.[26] . . .

P. A. Peskov's breakdown of occupational groups suggests that hereditary workers were actually concentrated in several traditional occupational groups in which mechanization had had little impact (hand-weaving) or had been introduced at a very early point (spinning). The data do not suggest that such individuals were likely to acquire new skills or move into trades other than those of their fathers. When factories mechanized and needed new categories of workers, they were more likely to seek them among first-generation recruits; this was so even for better-paying positions that should have been especially attractive to experienced workers.[27]

If hereditary workers were more common in handcrafts than in mechanized labor, and if sons were most likely to remain in the same occupation as their fathers, this casts doubt on the process of proletarianization that Lenin and most Soviet historians have postulated. Far from undermining outmoded customs or opening workers' eyes to the new realities that surrounded them, the hereditary occupations that existed in Moscow seem to have locked workers into a system reminiscent of the era of serfdom, when sons involuntarily inherited their fathers' trades.[28] This impression is reinforced by other evidence from Vladimir province (1899) which suggests that the proportion of hereditary workers was highest among those who lived less than roughly one kilometer from the factory and that it fell in direct relation to the distance traveled from home to the workplace.[29] In this instance the workers' hereditary experience would seem to have bound them to a particular enterprise, thereby limiting their horizons literally as well as figuratively. . . .

The hereditary workers described in these latter studies were not skilled craftsmen and should not be equated with the relatively privileged and better-paid artisans of Western Europe. The Russian textile workers, unlike European artisans, had no guild tradition to look back to or any independence or other status to lose. They were not labor aristocrats but rather semiskilled or even unskilled laborers whose forebears had been performing the same tasks for many decades at subsistence wages. Their hereditary status was associated with an unchanging environment and bound them all the more tightly to the countryside.

In short, the existence of second-generation, or hereditary, workers was sometimes associated with traditionalism and backwardness rather than with progress and change; thus it need not imply the deterioration of patriarchal family structures in the countryside. It was not necessarily associated with geographic or occupational mobility (it may even have inhibited both), nor did it automatically encourage the acquisition of "modern" skills and attitudes.

Endurance of Village Family Patterns

The conditions of city and factory life were not at all conducive to the formation of new family units. As a result townspeople married later than peasants, had fewer children, or avoided marriage altogether. Male peasant migrants, however, showed no tendency to assimilate into this pattern. It appears that their nonagricultural earnings, when combined with their families' traditional agricultural pursuits, gave migrants a certain measure of economic security and enabled them to continue the rural pattern of early marriage and large households. There was more incentive for a migrant to divide his life (and his family) between factory and village than to move away from the countryside and begin a truly proletarian existence.

This discussion tends to reinforce the suggestion that tradition and continuity outweighed disruption and innovation in migrants' lives. A distinctively Russian pattern of family life was perpetuated, in turn helping to perpetuate other traditions. In the countryside migration seems likely to have reinforced conservatism: a household whose adult members were residing elsewhere was less likely to experiment with new crops, techniques of cultivation, or patterns of landholding. At the factory each new generation of workers was recruited from the countryside. True, many were the sons of older workers and thus may have been prepared in some ways for the transition to factory life. Nonetheless, most had spent their childhoods in the countryside, making them likely to retain some psychological or cultural allegiance to the village in later life.

Certainly there were some innovative or disruptive forces at work in the family patterns of the Moscow hinterland. The abandonment of village traditions was most apparent among female migrants. As they grew older, women without families may have found agricultural activities too difficult to continue. The city offered such individuals a meager but possibly less strenuous existence in such fields as domestic service. The important point for this discussion, however, is that these older female migrants were destined for a solitary life in the city. They would have little direct impact on the lives of future migrants or proletarians, and the next generation of workers, like its predecessor, would have to be recruited from the countryside.

In assessing the traditionalism of Moscow's family life, one more point must be reiterated: the factories themselves were part of the region's tradition. Moscow's peasants had been traveling to urban and industrial centers for a century or more, and thus village family patterns were shaped by long interaction with cities and factories. The data in this chapter suggest that the village and factory were not opposites but were joined together in a symbiotic relationship. Each helped to meet the needs of the other, and each in turn was shaped by the other's needs. The bifurcated household described in these pages was not an innovation of the 1880s or 1890s but had been in existence for as many decades as the Moscow region's oldest factories. . . .

Regional Loyalties

Migrants in many historical and cultural settings have shown a tendency to settle together and provide various kinds of assistance to one another. In North America this pattern was widespread among many immigrant groups. Jewish immigrants formed *landsmanshaftn*, mutual aid societies whose members were drawn from a single town or village in Eastern Europe. For Italians, whose regional dialects and traditions were strongly developed, ties among *paesani* from a village or district provided a basis for employment and settlement in the New World. Analogous patterns can be found among internal migrants in other parts of the world, especially in the rapidly growing cities of the Third World, whose inhabitants are drawn mostly from the countryside.[30]

The migrants who flocked to the factories and working-class districts of Moscow had traveled a much shorter distance than immigrants to North America. Their background was essentially homogeneous, without major differences of speech, religion, ethnicity, or life experience. Thus they lacked some of the incentives that have kept migrants together in foreign lands, the multitribal cities of Africa, or the multiracial ones of Latin America.[31] All the same, many of the peasants who streamed to Moscow in the 1880s and 1890s came with no previous training or craft skills, and even those such as cottage weavers who had acquired such skills might be bewildered and distressed by the complexities of city or factory life. It was natural that the newly arrived migrant should seek support and assistance from someone. Evidence suggests that "someone" was most often a *zemliak*.

The Idea of Zemliachestvo

Smirnitskii's dictionary defines *zemliak* as "fellow-countryman, person from the same land." In popular usage today, the term may be applied to people from an area as large as Siberia, yet it connotes a special kind of relationship. The "land" a Russian claims as his own is often a much smaller territory—a province, district, or even village.[32] The Russian government's suspicious attitude toward public organizations, together with employers' regulation of everyday life, made the establishment of formal associations among workers or migrants impossible at least until 1905. Peasant *zemliaki*, however, continued to seek one another out, and their informal contacts became an important bridge between village and city life. Years later workers recalled how they had kept up ties with *zemliaki* across many decades: "They still remember their fellow villagers, migrants from a neighboring village or from the same county."[33]

I. I. Ianzhul, a Moscow factory inspector, noted in 1884 that children often came to work at large factories in the care of a *zemliak* while their parents remained behind or traveled elsewhere to work.[34] F. P. Pavlov, an engineer at an unnamed textile factory in central Russia, asked a woman worker how she and her husband could stand sharing a room with another family and received the reply, "What of it? They're our own people (*my svoi*), from the same village."[35] . . .

Surveys of whole branches of industry reveal that workers from a particular place were concentrated in a particular occupation, not only at one or two factories but throughout an entire industry. In brickmaking, for example, workers from a single county of nearby Kaluga province constituted an overwhelming majority of all workers.[36] A survey of male textile workers in Moscow city (1880–81) showed patterns of regional concentration on an even larger scale. For example, 43 percent of all cotton weavers came from Kaluga; yet that province provided only 3.8 percent of all dye printers and 6.6 percent of all shearers. . . .

Occupational Motives

There are several ways of explaining this clustering of migrants. One factor of considerable importance was the existence of handcraft traditions through which the peasant population of a region specialized in a particular craft or trade. As peasants moved farther from their villages and into factory production, some of the old regional distinctions were preserved. Thus workers from Vladimir were known as carpenters; those from Tver province, as stove makers and stonecutters.[37] An extreme example of such specialization was the production of bast matting. Of 1,040 workers in this industry in three counties of Moscow province in 1884–85, all without exception came from a single county of Kaluga province.[38]

In other cases peasants acquired particular skills in one industrial center, then migrated elsewhere. For example, concentrations of workers from Ardatovskii county (Nizhnii-Novgorod province) and Tambov province at the Kolomna machine-building works (Kolomenskii county) could be explained by the existence of metalworking enterprises in their home provinces.[39]

Craft skills alone, however, cannot account for the phenomenon of regional concentration because many of the clearest examples of clustering involve unskilled or semiskilled workers. Textile industries, requiring in general much less skill and experience than metalworking plants, included such operations as dyeing, pressing, shearing, and scutching, which required only the "simplest manipulations, or mere physical strength."[40] Yet according to Peskov's study of seventy-eight Moscow city factories in 1881, migrants traveled relatively great distances to work in these occupations, and migrants from one or two regions were predominant in each occupational group.[41] The pattern of regional speculation, moreover, was not consistent from one industrial center to another. . . .

Nor can previous work experience in other localities explain the migration patterns of most textile workers. Although particular branches of textile production were sometimes concentrated in individual counties of Moscow province, those regions were not the ones that supplied migrants to Moscow city's factories. In almost every branch of textile production, Moscow city's workers were recruited from regions where requisite skills and experience were least likely to be found.[42]

Another reason for migrants to work or live together was the pattern of hiring. In certain regions recruiters were sent each year to particular districts. Elsewhere work crews (*arteli*) of peasants hired themselves out as a unit.[43] Both practices were common in small-scale or antiquated industries such as brickmaking and bast mat weaving. In the latter case manufacturers sent subcontractors to the aforementioned regions of Kaluga province; there they sometimes dealt directly with local peasant officials, who contracted to supply a stated number of workers and sent mostly *nedoimshchiki* ("people whose taxes were in arrears"). Workers recruited in this fashion were almost exclusively male, and those who had families were obliged to leave them in the countryside.[44]

Although published references are few, the pattern of hiring through such agents seems to have been most common in occupations that were seasonal either by necessity (as in the digging of clay or peat) or by tradition (as in the bast-matting industry, which was carried on only in the winter months). Workers thus spent about half of each year in the countryside, though not necessarily in agricultural pursuits.[45] Hiring agents usually traveled to the country in late winter, the hardest season for peasants, in order to strike the best possible bargain over the terms of the work contract.[46]

Regionally based work groups, formed at the hiring agents' insistence, were certainly the cornerstone of this system.[47] Workers accepted these arrangements only with the greatest reluctance. Those who took part were the most unstable element of the working class and were prone to depart for the countryside without warning, even when this involved forfeiture of pay.[48] This pattern seems inconsistent with the needs of large enterprises, which operated year-round and preferred to have workers stay on for many years. In the newly developing mining-metallurgical areas of the south, employers had to take workers where they could find them, sometimes resorting to the system of recruitment whereby peasants who had worked at an enterprise for a time returned to their native villages to enlist their neighbors.[49] This arrangement was, however, viewed as a temporary expedient, and the southern enterprises did their best to recruit and retain a permanent labor force. In the Moscow region contemporaries make no mention of such groupings at large enterprises.

Village-based *arteli*, which in principle were formed at peasants' own initiative, were parallel to and in some cases indistinguishable from groups recruited by special agents. They operated under the direction or leadership of an elected "elder," who collected the group's wages from the employer and distributed them among the members. *Arteli* of this type were sometimes formed by itinerant craftsmen but were most common among unskilled workers and day laborers.[50] At large factories this type of *artel* was used only for auxiliary tasks, such as construction or repair work, and even then it was a rarity. Such groupings, then, can hardly explain the settlement patterns of *zemliaki*.

The term *artel* was also used to describe a group whose members shared room and board. These groups were sometimes formed at the employer's initiative, in which case the members might not be *zemliaki*, but they also flourished among villagers who traveled together to the factory and rented quarters nearby. Old-time workers at the Sormovo metal works outside Nizhnii-Novgorod described such units as *zemliachestva*. They were most common among newly arrived or short-term workers, who sometimes traveled back and forth to the village on Sundays for provisions.[51]

Migrants seem, then, to have stayed together in the cities and factories for reasons that had little to do with work contracts or previously acquired skills. This is not to suggest, however, that employment was not a paramount concern of migrants or a prime motive for maintaining ties among *zemliaki*. Rather, *zemliaki* assisted one another in ways not directly related to skills or village-based work groups. A common pattern that endured in Russia well past the Revolution of 1917 was for a peasant to follow his *zemliaki* to a particular part of the city and factory. Petr Moiseenko, a worker-radical of the 1880s, describes his efforts to find work in St. Petersburg in 1873:

> [Having heard that the Shaw factory was hiring] I went up to the gates and asked. They were hiring. I looked for *zemliaki*, and it turned out that one of the assistant foremen was a *zemliak*. It turned out that there were a fair number of *zemliaki*. I was hired and put into a [living] *artel* of *zemliaki*.[52]

In such a case the migrant's choice of occupation, workplace, or residence was governed by the presence or absence of *zemliaki* among the foremen or the rank and file. (Although rank-and-file workers had no direct say in hiring, they could provide the mutual guarantees many employers required.) The system of hiring through *zemliak* networks and of subunits in large factories dominated by "families" of *zemliaki* was noted in many parts of Russia.[53]

The persistence of juridical and familial ties to the countryside, and the constant movement back and forth between the village and the urban or industrial centers, enabled migrants to maintain networks of communication between their two worlds.[54] These could bring the city dweller news from his family or village and could also advise villagers of opportunities in the city. In the winter of 1885 the number of passport applications in Moscow province was high, but by June the number was greatly reduced; local officials concluded that the grapevine had warned villagers that jobs were scarce that year, owing to the continuing industrial depression.[55] Similar networks are known to have existed between central Russian peasants and agricultural migrants who settled in Siberia.[56]

Peasant Culture Survives in the City

Beyond the material assistance migrants could provide to one another, *zemliaki* had other, less tangible reasons for preferring one another's company. The population of Moscow's hinterland may have been homogeneous, but it was not an undifferentiated mass. Despite the basic similarities in their backgrounds, peasants from the surrounding provinces still conserved local traditions and customs. In Moscow at the beginning of the twentieth century, the pioneer ethnologist-musicologist M. E. Piatnitskii devoted considerable attention to the distinctive folk song traditions of three central Russian provinces. Each region, he realized, had its own style of choral singing, and these traditions were kept alive in Moscow by peasant migrants. In 1911 Piatnitskii recruited a choral group whose members were mostly factory workers, and in their first concerts they performed only as groups of *zemliaki*.[57] Local folkways, though weakened, have survived in parts of Russia down to the present, and they were undoubtedly much stronger at the turn of the century.[58]

These cultural patterns, together with the closed nature of the factory community, kept *zemliaki* together long after they had left the village. The bonds between them were especially apparent on ceremonial occasions. Moiseenko recalls being asked to serve as godfather to a *zemliak's* child in Orekhovo in 1884. At that time Moiseenko was an experienced weaver who had not lived in his native village for more than ten years. He had spent time in prison and Siberian exile for his role in the revolutionary underground and the strike movement in St. Petersburg and considered himself a revolutionary and an atheist. These experiences had not erased the ties between *zemliaki*, nor did his atheism prevent him from participating in the child's christening.[59]

Other evidence suggests that marriage between *zemliaki* was a common pattern among migrants. Although male and female migrants usually worked at different jobs or even at different factories, their patterns of migration were virtually identical. Men and women came to Moscow in identical proportions from the surrounding eight provinces, and their patterns of settlement in the various precincts of the city were almost exactly the same. Aggregate census data on residential patterns cannot, of course, prove that male and female *zemliaki* were marrying one another, but this suggestion is consistent with other accounts of factory life—for example, the description, cited earlier in this chapter, of married couples who shared quarters with "their own people." Evidence from the peasant villages seems to point in the same direction. D. N. Zhbankov, who studied outmigration from certain regions of Kostroma province in the late 1880s, described courting rituals in which eligible males were introduced to young women from neighboring villages. A wife was sometimes chosen from a village as much as twelve to twenty-four miles away, Zhbankov reported, but more often from a much narrower radius. Girls who had never been to the city themselves were nonetheless determined to marry a migrant and were scornful of the country manners of young men who stayed in the village.[60] . . .

Rural-urban ties . . . exercised a continuing influence on social life in the city. Like migrants in other settings, central Russian *zemliaki* often lived and worked together. Without having any formal organizational structure, networks of *zemliaki* could provide information and material assistance to the newly arrived migrant. They also helped to maintain village traditions and folkways in the new setting, thereby helping to perpetuate the migrant's identification with peasant society.

The role of these networks was partially one of mediating between agrarian traditions and urban-industrial structures. The stability and continuity they provided, however, did more than merely ease the transition to city life; in certain instances it provided a focus for social action and collective protest.

Notes

1. J. Hajnal, "European Marriage Patterns in Perspective" and Peter Laslett, "Mean Household Size in England since the 16th Century," in *Household and Family in Past Time*, ed. Peter Laslett (Cambridge, England, 1972), 126 ff.

2. See for example Gerhart von Schulze-Gaevernitz, *Ocherki obshchestvennogo khoziaistva i ekonomicheskoi politiki Rossii* (trans. from the German, St. Petersburg, 1901), 120 ff.; compare V. I. Lenin, *The Development of Capitalism in Russia* (Moscow, 1960), 552.

3. The Prokhorovskaia Trekhgornaia cotton mill was considered a model employer for supplying family accommodations; its barracks included fifty-one rooms housing four married couples each and 132 family rooms with four to seven persons in each; *Prokhorovskaia Trekhgornaia manufaktura* (Moscow, 1900), 50–51; S. Lapitskaia, *Byt rabochikh Trekhgornoi manufaktury* (Moscow, 1935) 40 ff.

4. Moscow factory inspector I. I. Ianzhul noted in 1883 that only 4 of 174 factories he visited made any provision for the care of children; I. I. Ianzhul, "Zhenshchiny-materi na fabrikakh," *Ocherki i isseledovaniia*, 2 vols. (Moscow, 1884), 391.

5. These facilities had an average of fourteen to fifteen persons per room; the total included certain industries in which workers slept in the same rooms they worked in; *Perepis Moskvy* (PM) 1882, pt. 1, sec. 1, 37.

6. PM 1902, pt. 2, table 2, 8–9 (my calculation).

7. B. N. Kazantsev, *Rabochie Moskvy i Moskovskoi gubernii v seredine XIX veka* (Moscow, 1976), 77–79.

8. A detailed account of female and child labor in Moscow is found in R. Johnson, "The Nature of the Russian Working Class: Social Characteristics of the Moscow Industrial Region, 1800–1900" (Ph.D. diss. Cornell University, 1975), 93–95.

9. Moscow: Stolichnyi i gubernskii statisticheskii komitet, *Statisticheskie svedeniia o zhiteliakh goroda Moskvy: po perepisi 12 dekabria 1871* (Moscow, 1974), iii; PM 1902, pt. 1, sec. 1, table 1, 4.

10. A. G. Rashin, "Dinamika chislennosti i protsessy formirovaniia gorodskogo naseleniia Rossii v XIX-nachala XX vv.," *Istoricheski zapiski* 34 (1950): 83–84.

11. PM 902, pt. 2, table 2, 11.

12. Ibid., pt. 1, sec. 1, table 5, 11. See also P. A. Peskov, *Sanitarnoe issledovanie fabrik po obrabotke voloknistykh veshchestv v g. Moskve*, 2 pts. (Moscow, 1882), pt. 1, 122.

13. Peasant customary law varied from region to region in the rights accorded to widows or spinsters. Presence or absence of minor children was sometimes decisive. See Teodor Shanin, *The Awkward Class: Political Sociology of Peasantry in a Developing Society: Russia 1910–1925* (Oxford, 1972), 222–23.

14. PM 1902, pt. 1, sec. 1, table 1, 2–4; sec. 2, table 1, 54–56.

15. Ibid., pt. 1, sec. 1, table 4, 9–10.

16. J. Hajnal, "European Marriage Patterns in Perspective," in *Population in History*, ed. D. V. Glas and D. E. C. Eversley (London, 1965), 102.

17. Robert E. Johnson, "Family Relations and the Rural-Urban Nexus: Patterns in the Hinterland of Moscow, 1880–1900" in *The Family in Imperial Russia*, ed. David Ransel (Champaign, 1978), 273 ff.

18. P. M. Shestakov, *Rabochie na manufakture tovarishchestvo 'Emil' Tsindel'' v Moskve: Statisticheskoe issledovanie* (Moscow, 1900), 36–37.

19. I. M. Kozminykh-Lanin, *Semeinyi sostav fabrichno-zavodskikh rabochikh Moskovskoi gubernii* (Moscow, 1914), table I, 2–11. Data refer to 69,000 workers and were collected in 1908. A study of female workers in St. Petersburg (1905–14) found that the percentage married was higher in more backward industries and enterprises; E. E. Kruze, *Peterburgskie rabochie v 1912–1914 gg.* (Leningrad, 1961), 84.

20. The most recent and comprehensive treatment of this question is that of L. M. Ivanov, "Preemstvennost fabrichno-zavodskogo truda i formirovanie proletariata v Rossii," in *Rabochii klass i rabochee dvizhenie (1861–1917)*, ed. L. M. Ivanov (Moscow, 1966), 58–140.

21. According to P. M. Shestakov's findings, workers who entered the factory before age sixteen were 80 percent second generation; those who began factory work after age twenty-one were 78 percent first generation; Shestakov, *Rabochie*, 24.

22.   E. M. Dementev, *Fabrika, chto ona daet naseleniiu i chto ona u nego beret* (Moscow, 1893), 46.

23.   On this point, see Reginald Zelnik, "Russian Workers and the Revolutionary Movement," *Journal of Social History* 6 (1973): 217–19.

24.   Shestakov, *Rabochie*, 26.

25.   "Otchet fabrichnoi inspektsii Vladimirskoi gubernii 1894–1897," as cited by Ivanov, "Preemstvennost," 81.

26.   Peskov, *Sanitarnoe issledovanie*, pt. 1, 134.

27.   Peskov, *Sanitarnoe issledovanie*, pt. 1, 137–41.

28.   On the operation of such a system in post-Petrine Russia, see Arcadius Kahan, "The 'Hereditary Workers' Hypothesis and the Development of a Factory Labor Force in 18th and 19th Century Russia," in *Education and Economic Development*, ed. C. A. Anderson and M. J. Bowman (Chicago, 1965), 291–97.

29.   "Materialy dlia otsenki zemli Vladimirskoi gubernii," as quoted in Ivanov, "Preemstvennost," 103.

30.   Arthur A. Goren, *New York Jews and the Quest for Community* (New York, 1970), 20–21; Phyllis H. Williams, *South Italian Folkways in Europe and America* (New York, 1969 [1938]), 9–17; William Mangin, ed, *Peasants in Cities* (Boston, 1970).

31.   See Donald W. Treadgold, *The Great Siberian Migration: Government and Peasant in Resettlement from Emancipation to the First World War* (Princeton, 1957), 241–42, on the apparent lack of territorial loyalties among peasants who migrated to Siberia. .

32.   Vladimir Soloukhin, *A Walk in Rural Russia* (trans. from the Russian, London, 1966), 12.

33.   T. S. Vlasenko et al., "K voprosu o formirovanii proletariata v Rossii v kontse XIX-nachale XX v." in *Iz istorii rabochego klassa i revoliutsionnogo dvizheniia*, ed. M. V. Nechkina (Moscow, 1958), 282.

34.   I. I. Ianzhul, *Fabrichnyi byt Moskovskoi gubernii* (St. Petersburg, 1884), 89. He specifically mentions the Prokhorovskaia Trekhgornaia factory as one at which this pattern was observed.

35.   F. P. Pavlov, *Za desiat let praktiki* (Moscow, 1901), 55.

36.   *Sbornik statisticheskikh svedenii po Moskovskoi gubernii, Otdel sanitarnoi statistiki* (SSSMG), vol. 3, pt. 2 (Moscow, 1885), app., 1–17. In those few cases where workers from other localities were present, a clear division of labor occurred.

37.   M. Balabanov, *Ocherki po istorii rabochego klassa v Rossii* (Moscow, 1925), vol. 2: 62.

38.   Dementev, *Fabrika*, 3.

39.   SSSMG, 3, pt. 13, 123; app., 1–45.

40.   Peskov, *Sanitarnoe issledovanie*, pt. 1, 115.

41.   Ibid., 121. Peskov concludeed that skilled workers were almost exclusively "local," (i.e., had traveled from no farther than Moscow province), whereas unskilled workers had come greater distances from other provinces.

42.   This conclusion comes from a comparison of Peskov's tables on workers' places of origin (*Sanitarnoe issledovanie*, pt. 1, 103–12, 117) with tables presented by F. F. Erisman (SSSMG, vol. 4, pt. 1 [Moscow 1881], 130–31) on the distribution of industry through Moscow province.

43.   On the numerous meanings of the term *artel*, see Robert Johnson, *Peasant and Proletarian: The Working Class of Moscow in the Late Nineteenth Century* (New Brunswick, 1979), chap. 5, 91–92. The meaning here is a group of individuals who joined together before leaving their native village.

44. Ianzhul, *Fabrichnyi byt*, 86–88.

45. Those who went home in the winter were not, of course, working the soil; instead they hauled timber, engaged in such cottage industry as the squeezing of oil from hempseed, or simply stayed at home waiting for the spring (SSSMG, vol. 3, pt. 2, 189). Bast-rug weavers returned home in the spring and hired themselves out almost immediately as agricultural laborers in other provinces (ibid., vol. 4, pt. 2, 292).

46. On this system and its abuses, see Iu. Kharitonova and D. Shcherbakov, *Krestianskoe dvizhenie v Kaluzhskoi gubernii (1861–1917 gg.)* (Kaluga, 1961), 69–72.

47. This system was not unique to Russia. Among Italian immigrants in North America, the *padrone* system operated in almost identical fashion; the *padrone*, like the *podriadchik*, relied on the workers' loyalty to fellow villagers; Lawrence Frank Pisani, *The Italian in America* (New York, 1957), 81–88. On comparable practices in England at the beginning of the nineteenth century, see Reinhard Bendix, *Work and Authority in Industry*, 2d ed. (Berkeley, 1974), 54–56.

48. SSSMG, vol. 3, pt. 2, 187.

49. I. M. Lukomskaia, "Formirovanie promyshlennogo proletariata Donbassa 70–80kh godov XIX v.," in *Iz istorii rabochego klassa*, ed. M. V. Nechkina, 297–300.

50. D. N. Zhbankov, *Babia storona* (Kostroma, 1891), 10, 22–23. According to this author, who studied outmigration from Kostroma province in the 1880s, *arteli* were used in the time of serfdom as a device for collecting the migrant serfs' quitrent (*obrok*). The elder who collected these payments was sometimes able to line his own pockets in the process, and this was the origin of several private fortunes in the region Zhbankov studied.

51. Vlasenko, "K voprosu o formirovanii," 279.

52. P. A. Moiseenko, *Vospominaniia starogo revoliutsionera*, 2d ed., rev. (Moscow, 1966), 17. An almost identical account is given by Ivan Gudov, who first traveled to Moscow in the 1930s looking for work; *Sudba rabochego*, 2d ed., rev. (Moscow, 1974), 5–6.

53. For example, I. V. Babushkin, *Recollections of I. V. Babushkin* (Moscow, 1958), 93. Compare Zhbankov, *Babia storona*, 48-49. After 1905, with the partial legalization of trade union activity, union leaders complained that this practice was an obstacle to worker solidarity because it put the interests of *zemliaki* ahead of those of fellow unionists; see K. Dmitriev, *Professionalnoe dvizhenie i soiuzy v Rossii*, 2d ed. (St. Petersburg, 1909), 69.

54. Zhbankov, *Babia storona*, 84, notes that a certain proportion of villagers made their living by carrying parcels and messages back and forth.

55. *Statisticheskii ezhegodnik Moskovskogo gubernskogo zemstva za 1885 g.*, sec. VI ("Vidy na zhitelstvo"), 13.

56. V. N. Grigorev, *Pereselenie krestian Riazanskoi gubernii* (Moscow, 1886), 76–77, 82–83, 146–92.

57. I. Martynov, *Gosudarstvennyi russkii narodnyi khor imeni Piatnitskogo*, 2d ed., rev. (Moscow, 1953), 9 ff. In time the local traditions were blended into a common repertoire and the Piatnitskii chorus became famous as one of the Soviet Union's outstanding folk music ensembles.

58. I observed impromptu singing and dancing in Moscow's Izmailovskii park on Sunday afternoons in 1969 and was told by native Muscovites that this was a tradition among "country people." Those who took part were not performers or semiprofessionals but picnickers who sang or danced for their own pleasure. Soloukhin, *A Walk*, presents numerous examples of surviving regional traditions, (e.g., pp. 185–86 on the horn blowers of Kobelikha).

59. Moiseenko, *Vospominaniia*, 72.

60. PM 1902, pt. 2, table 5, 28–45, my calculation. For residence patterns, see PM 1882, pt. 3, table 10, 220–32.

5

Peasants in Uniform: The Tsarist Army as a Peasant Society

John Bushnell

A colonel in the Tsarist army by the name of A. Rittikh wrote in 1893 that service in the army turned ignorant peasants into civilized human beings. The peasant conscript's military career began "with a bath and a haircut," then proceeded to "cleanliness and neatness in dress." At the same time, conscripts were "taught to speak, look, turn and move with military precision." They learned new words and concepts. In sum, "the wholly rough-hewn and rude [peasant conscript] receives, in the broad sense of the word, a human finish."[1] This has a familiar ring. What Col. Rittikh thought of as the civilizing process we have lately called modernization, and it has been argued that service in the armed forces is one of the routes through which peasants in underdeveloped countries are modernized.

To take just one example, Lerner and Robinson have observed that the Turkish army performed a modernizing function in the 1950s because for the army to absorb large quantities of sophisticated weaponry, Turkish soldiers had to be educated in its use and maintenance. An important by-product of this military schooling was that Turkish soldiers "acquired new habits of dress, of cleanliness, of teamwork. In the most profound sense, they acquired a new personality." The army became "a major agency of social change precisely because it spread . . . a new sense of identity—and new skills and concepts as well as new machines. Young Turks from isolated villages now suddenly felt themselves to be part of the larger society."[2]

It might be conceived that the Tsarist army played a similar modernizing role in the late nineteenth and early twentieth centuries. Following its defeat in the Crimean War, the Russian army under the leadership of Minister of War Dmitrii Miliutin embarked on an ambitious program of reforms. One of Miliutin's many goals was to upgrade the army's weaponry, but because the change in weapons technology was undramatic by mid-twentieth-century standards, the starting point for a modernization process cannot be located here. However, we might look for a similar ripple effect from the implementation of Miliutin's principal goal, the capstone of his reforms: the conversion of the Tsarist army from long-term (twenty-five years) to short-term service (six years as of 1874, reduced to three by 1906). One immediate consequence of reducing the conscript's term of service was that military training had to be greatly compressed: the leisurely development of military skills possible in the prereform army had to give way to more intensive instruction. To this end Miliutin introduced compulsory schooling in the three "R's" for all conscripts, and for a time the Tsarist army became the single most important source of literacy for Russian peasants (25–30 percent of all males of draft age went into the army in the last quarter of the nineteenth century).[3]

Given that the intended effect of the many military reforms introduced by Miliutin was to make the Tsarist army a more modern and more professionally competent institution, it is reasonable to ask how these reforms affected peasant conscripts. Was the Tsarist army a modernizing institution, did it instill the habits of discipline and regularity, a sense of abstract order, an openness to change, an orientation toward the future, and all those other traits we associate with modernity? Was service in the army at the least a qualitatively new experience for peasants, bringing them—even if against their will—into contact with a world beyond their villages?

It must be noted at the outset that after Miliutin's retirement in 1881 the army high command lost interest in educating soldiers, and many officers shared the feeling of their new chief, Vannovskii, that education was positively harmful. Junior officers who continued to think of themselves as educators were suspect and were occasionally ordered to cease teaching the rudiments of literacy to conscripts. Although some peasants who came into the army with a semblance of literacy—reading newspapers rather than smoking them, as the saying went—did receive further instruction if they were chosen to be NCOs, the mass of peasant soldiers left the army no more literate than when they had entered it.[4]

However, the lack of a program of formal education need not mean that the army failed to impart modern attitudes. The civilizing experience described by Col. Rittikh could proceed whether or not soldiers could read and write, and many officers shared Col. Rittikh's perception that military service in and of itself was an educational experience.[5] At any rate, service in the army, with its formal hierarchy, its abstract rules and complex patterns of behavior, seems at first glance a world away from life in the village and might be presumed to have undermined the traditional mentality of peasant soldiers. Furthermore, in the late nineteenth century Dragomirov's precepts on training were gospel; soldiers were not simply to be drilled but were to be made to internalize military discipline, to think about and understand the rationale behind the military system.[6] We might add that it was precisely in this period—from the 1880s on—that the army became a predominantly urban institution. Whereas before many regiments had been scattered around the countryside and soldiers quartered in peasant huts, units were now concentrated in the cities and housed in proper barracks.[7] Military society thus became more self-contained, and what extramilitary experience soldiers had was now urban rather than rural.

The case for modernization by way of military service can be taken one step further: the conscript's initial experience in the army was utterly unlike anything he had ever known. During the first four months of service the conscript was immersed in an intensive process of military socialization. It was during this period that the soldier was taught, none too gently, to "speak, look, turn and move with military precision," that he memorized the intricate grammar of the military hierarchy, and that he was catechized on the duties of a soldier and the military virtues. It was in this period, too, that soldiers were introduced to the complete spectrum of the Tsarist army's vices—beatings, extortion by noncoms, outright theft, and so on. Naturally enough, for the conscript this was a time of extreme disorientation, depression, and homesickness; he frequently wasted away bodily and occasionally maimed himself for the sake of a discharge.[8] The severity of the psychological stress was proportionate to the abruptness of the transition from village to barracks. The conscript was well on the way to being modernized, or at least uprooted.

The Regimental Estate

At that point, however, the modernizing process—if that is what it was—ended; of his initial military experience only the vices carried over in any major way to the remainder of the soldier's term of service. The case for sociopsychological modernization breaks down as soon at it becomes clear just how unmilitary life in the Tsarist army was. The soldier's duties, his *byt*, were functions of the economic rather than the properly military life of his unit. In fact, the Russian regiment's economic functions left little room for martial matters. Not only did the regiment cook its own food and bake its own bread; where possible it grew its own fruit and vegetables and even kept some cattle. The regiment produced its own uniforms and boots. (As of 1907, 150,000 soldiers—12 percent of all enlisted personnel—spent their duty hours tailoring.) All regiments produced or otherwise provided for themselves—at no cost to the government—blankets, coats, felt boots, utensils, and other military accoutrement. Every regiment maintained a production complex (*masterskaia*) staffed by soldiers permanently detailed to provide for its economic needs. However, soldiers from line companies as well did duty as tailors, cobblers, carpenters, carters, cooks, and gardeners. They also served as stable hands, singers, musicians, church attendants, batmen, and lackeys in the officers' club. (If this incomplete list calls to mind the organization of a large estate before the emancipation, it should.) During the eight or nine months a regiment spent in its barracks, forty or more of the hundred-odd men in a company were performing these unsoldierly duties. Because most other soldiers were on guard duty or serving as duty orderlies, the total number of men free for the training that was called for in the regulations was low. One estimate put it at one or two, rarely as many as ten. This figure is surely too low, but just as surely, after the first four months of intensive training roughly half the strength of the company on any given day were on details that were in no way military, and most of the rest were simply standing guard. What military training a soldier received was episodic, and it is not difficult to believe a report that a Russian soldier's military skills deteriorated the longer he was in the army.[9]

The unsoldierly life of the Tsarist soldier resulted above all from the fact that once provided with some working capital by the commissariat, regiments were expected to be economically self-sufficient. However, the commissariat was stingy, and the regiment's capital was insufficient to provide for its needs. The only resource the regiment had in excess was labor, so in order to make good the deficit in material, soldiers were dispatched to earn money in the civilian economy, a practice known as "*volnye raboty.*" General Dragomirov observed:

> In July enlisted personnel fan out in hay-mowing, in forests, along railway lines, in town for building; they sew clothing; they acquire an external aspect entirely unsuitable [for military service], they become unaccustomed to discipline and lose their military bearing.[10]

The soldiers' migratory labor was so obviously detrimental to the army's military mission that there was frequent discussion of ending the practice. Yet as one officer noted, his men needed blankets, the blankets had to be paid for, and the only recourse was to collect the money soldiers earned at their civilian work.[11] *Volnye raboty* were built into the military economy.

If the money earned through migratory labor balanced the regimental budget, it did not entirely balance the individual soldier's budget. Prior to 1906 soldiers were required to provide their own soap, spoons, boot brushes and polish, oil and rags for cleaning rifles, bed linen, shirts, in many instances blankets, and on and on. Equipment that *was* issued to the soldiers was so inadequate that considerable expense was involved in keeping it up to specifications. Army-issue boots, for instance, were of such poor quality that they lasted no more than three months. Soldiers had either to purchase their own or pay for repairs—and repairs, even if performed by the company cobbler, could easily cost the soldier as much as four rubles a year, yet before 1906 soldiers were paid only 2 rubles, 70 kopeks a year. The soldier's minimum monthly budget ranged anywhere from 90 kopeks to 1 ruble, 74 kopeks a year. However calculated, it far exceeded his monthly pay of 22 1/2 kopeks (raised to 50 kopeks per month as of January 1906).[12] Soldiers were allowed to keep some of the money from their *volnye raboty*, and roughly half the soldiers received money from home; in addition soldiers sold part of their daily bread ration to civilians, this providing up to 30 extra kopeks per month.[13] In any event, in addition to the regiment's involvement in the civilian economy, soldiers as individuals were also peripheral participants in the market.

It should be evident by now that as an economic entity the Tsarist regiment functioned in a way quite familiar to the peasant soldier. Like the peasant household and village, the Tsarist regiment aspired to self-sufficiency but was bound up in a larger market system. Individual soldiers sold what surplus they had in order to cover the expense of maintaining their military household. But because the regiment's marketable surplus was meager, soldiers joined the migratory labor force and sent their earnings "home."

The similarity between the peasant and military economy extended to the seasonality of the military-economic cycle. Units set off for their summer encampments in early May. Field exercises, the most exhausting part of the yearly cycle, were over by the end of July or early August. At that point soldiers who had completed their term were discharged from service, others were given home leave, and most of the rest went in search of civilian work. The regiment withered from 1800 to roughly 300 men, with no more than 20 percent in a company. Military duties were supposed to resume in mid-October, but with soldiers off doing one thing or another no start could be made until mid-November, at which point end-of-the-year holidays intervened. What training there was during the winter was confined to the four months between the new year and the onset of field exercises—but as we have seen, training was hardly regular even then.[14] Not only was military life as cyclical as peasant life, the modulations of the two cycles were virtually identical.

Relations between officers and men were congruent with the peasant experience. It was not merely that officers thought of their men as the rude peasants they had been prior to service, though this was an important element of the overall pattern. Denikin remarked in 1903 that officers could not conceive of their soldiers as fellow men.[15] This attitude came through most clearly in the distinction officers drew between ordinary conscripts and the educated volunteers: striking a simple soldier was a matter of course, but it was unthinkable to strike a volunteer, who came from a social world much like the officer's own and might actually file charges. The simple soldier was quite aware of his inferior standing, which was entirely independent of his subordinate position in the military hierarchy. That he could be beaten was as natural to him as it was to his officer. Soldiers drew the line only at officers from other companies—their own officers could strike them, but the "gentleman" from another company who did so was violating the social proprieties.[16]

These attitudes were reminiscent of the master-serf relationship, but they were rooted more in the socioeconomic reality of the unit than in tradition. The structure of which such attitudes were a part was most exposed to view in the *volnye raboty*. General Dragomirov commented that

> so-called "civilian work" is in essence *forced labor*, with overtones of serfdom. Formerly the *lord* hired out his own peasants, now the military commander does the same. ... Such an application of authority sometimes leads to an individual who does not want to do civilian work being courtmartialed.[17]

Another officer added that not only did *volnye raboty* "accustom the commander to view his men as serfs; from this it is not far to the use of soldiers as free labor."[18] And indeed, officers employed their men not only to sustain the unit but for all personal labor and other services. The attitude of officers toward the regimental shops was frankly proprietary; outfitting an apartment with new table, desk, and curtains was as simple as issuing an order. Setting soldiers to constructing comfortable summer cottages at the regimental camp was just as easy. In Saratov in the early twentieth century, one enterprising regimental commander ran a funeral procession business, employing in this enterprise the men and horses of his unit. Less imaginative officers merely used their men as household labor.[19]

Like peasants, soldiers were at the mercy of the strong of the world, and the world was one in which formal regulations against striking soldiers or exploiting them for economic gain—formal regulations of any kind—were irrelevant. Custom alone counted, and Tsarist military custom was weighted heavily against the soldier. Yet the soldier's peasant *persona* was more deeply rooted in military society than that. Even when regimental custom conformed to military regulations, the ordinary functioning of the unit recalled for the soldier the familiar peasant world. The officer was not merely the soldier's military superior, he was simultaneously master of the unit's economy. If nothing else, this was a situation ripe for abuse. There was ample opportunity—indeed, necessity—for officers to divert money intended for provisioning soldiers to other needs of the unit, or to their own pockets. (To the soldier, of course, it made no difference whether money meant to purchase their food was gambled away by the company commander or was spent repairing barracks.)

Furthermore, whether or not officers were in fact "stealing" from their men, they could be doing so, and it was impossible for soldiers to complain because the officers' economic functions were vested in their authority as military superiors. This may seem a minor point. But if officers had had primarily military functions, if they had not controlled the finances for feeding and clothing their men, if they had not allocated their men to production duties, they would not automatically have been perceived to be living at the expense of the soldiers. (As one contemporary observer put it delicately, the fact that the officer's military and economic functions were indivisible undermined his moral authority.) As things stood, there was nothing more natural than for soldiers to view their officers as economic drones, or at least as competitors for scarce goods.[20] Certainly officers alone were not responsible for this situation—in the military economy was in fact one of scarcity. Yet the socioeconomic pattern that derived from the army's scarcity economy could only reinforce the prototypically peasant "image of limited good." Given the economic reality of peasant (and military) life, one man's gain was indeed another's loss. Although this image was obviously congruent with the distribution of material goods, it also held—in the peasant's view—for the distribution of psychic goods.[21] Because the image of limited good was fundamental to the peasant way of looking at the world and was reinforced by life in the army, it is scarcely credible that military service could have done much to reshape the peasant mentality.

Officers as Outsiders

Officers, then, employed their peasant soldiers to maintain the regimental estate and to benefit themselves, and if they did not, no matter—soldiers suspected them of doing so. To complete the picture of the army as a peasant society, it remains only to consider the officer's role as outsider, a role that was, again, built in the daily routine of military life. The fact is that officers, junior officers included, spent very little time with their men. Much of their time was given over either to management and related paperwork or to verification of the management of other officers. Officers sat on countless commissions that checked the books of the various economic subunits, revolving funds, and permanent capital that made up the regimental economy. Officers were rated more for their proficiency as economic managers than for their ability to train and lead men—which, given the predominance of the regiment's economic functions, was logical enough. Little wonder, then, that the road to success lay through the company and regimental offices. It was there that junior officers came to the attention of their superiors, it was there that they could perform services genuinely useful to the regiment and its commander and could hope to reap a suitable reward. Whether or not their formal duties called for them to be in the offices, that was where they congregated at every opportunity. It was boring to spend time with soldiers—much more interesting to be involved in the social life centered on the offices. Little wonder, again, that a company commander's contact with his men was ordinarily limited to a cursory look-through (and that not every day), or that lieutenants—when forced into the barracks against their will—idled on the sidelines smoking, gossiping, and telling jokes.[22] Lack of contact between officers and men was certainly detrimental to training, but then a regiment's economic functions had priority. The economic life of the unit was routine, so only routine dispositions had to be made.

If officers were distant, periodically intrusive figures, who was in day-to-day charge of the men? Obviously the NCOs. However, after the Miliutin reforms the Tsarist army had proportionately fewer long-term NCOs than any other European army because few soldiers reenlisted after completing their appointed term. From the 1880s on there were at most the company sergeant major and perhaps one or two long-term senior sergeants—but only perhaps. All the other noncom slots were filled by literate conscripts given some extra training, but only on the company roster could these be distinguished from privates. The sergeant major was certainly the most important authority with whom soldiers regularly came into contact, but he was the *only* authority with whom they were in regular contact. The sergeant major kept no closer track of the men under him than was necessary to satisfy the company commander, or alternatively grossly abused his authority because the company commander had so little knowledge of what went on in the unit.[23]

In fact, for the most part soldiers were left to themselves, the sergeant major merely maintaining a patina of proper military order and discipline. Because soldiers were more or less free to organize themselves, it is not surprising that they fell back on the type of social organization that Russian peasants away from their villages had employed for centuries, the *artel*. (The recrudescence of familiar civilian patterns was made all the easier by the fact that most soldiers in a unit were, because of the recruiting system, *zemliaki—Landsleute*—often from the same or neighboring villages.) The company chose an *artel* leader (*artelshchik*) who was responsible for purchasing food and sundry other of the soldier's necessities with funds provided by the company commander, and it was the self-constituted soldier *artel* that concluded contacts for *volnye raboty*.[24] It seemed so natural to the soldiers that they should manage their own affairs—because that was their experience as peasants and because that was the norm in the army—that invariably the most detested officers were those who actually attempted to supervise their men. It was the very principle of officer intrusion in the barracks that soldiers resented, not the results. It made no difference that units in which officers played an active supervisory role were the best clothed, the best shod, and the best fed. Soldiers preferred and performed best for the officer who let his unit run itself, even if they suffered some privation in consequence.[25] In the soldiers' view the officer's proper role was that of an outsider; the improving officer was as much resented as the improving landlord.

Yet the Tsarist officer was not simply an outsider, he was a mediating outsider, a necessary part of the soldier's world. Only he could provide the link between the relatively autonomous, unit-level soldier community and the larger military world. And like meditating outsiders in peasant society, the Tsarist officer combined in his person the roles of sociopolitical middle man, economic intermediary, intercessor, and patron.[26] In anthropological terms, the relationship between officer and soldier was multiplex rather than single-interest (i.e., specialized)—a distinction in modes of authority that had been called the watershed between traditional and modern society.[27]

Conclusion: Was the Army a Modernizing Institution?

Other analogies can be found between peasant and military societies, but surely enough has been said to demonstrate that the Tsarist army was not a modernizing institution. In defiance of formal tables of organization and the prescriptions of training manuals, the soldier's socioeconomic experience replicated that of peasant society, the similarity extending even to types of contact with the nonpeasant (or nonmilitary) world. Though the army had on paper a hierarchy of command and discipline that had no analogue in peasant society, in practice the pattern of officer-soldier relations was familiar, even if by the late nineteenth century it was somewhat archaic by civilian standards. The peasant remained a peasant even while in uniform.

This is not to say that service in the army had no impact on individual Russian peasants. The peasant soldier was, after all, stationed far from home and in an urban environment. Still, this sort of contact with the modern urban world was itself part of the Russian peasant's ordinary experience. Millions of peasants in the late nineteenth and early twentieth centuries were engaged in migratory seasonal labor (and had been for generations), and other millions were engaged in nonseasonal but temporary labor in the cities. Yet the urban setting had a muted effect on peasant migrants because urban peasants had traditional social institutions that set them apart from the city proper.[28] If the urban peasant was in but not of the city, how much truer must this have been of the peasant soldier, whose urban experience was mediated by the peasant structure of his military unit? Whatever new experience came to the peasant soldier while in the army was being more efficiently acquired by other peasants in the civilian world. As all contemporaries reported, it was the returned peasant migrant who brought change to the village, not the ex-soldier.

In the final analysis, then, answering the question posed at the outset (Was the Tsarist army a modernizing institution?) does not contribute very much to our understanding of sociocultural change in the Russian peasantry. It has, however, been a useful way to get at what a soldier's life in the Tsarist army was really like.

We are in a better position, [too] to understand the behavior of the Tsarist army during periods of civil turmoil. For instance, the mutinies of 1905 and 1906 exhibited similarities at a number of levels to contemporaneous peasant disturbances. Allowing for differences in the organizational framework within which they occurred, mutinies and peasant disturbances had a very similar internal dynamic: the way they started and the way they worked themselves out. They also coincided in their timing (responding to the same external stimuli) and in their frequency curves (they peaked at roughly the same time in both 1905 and 1906). Finally, the ultimate objects of mutiny and peasant riot were similar. Given what we know of soldier society, it would be strange if it had been otherwise; yet the mutinies have ordinarily been treated as political demonstrations or as responses to military conditions narrowly construed.[29]

We may also be in a better position to understand the Russian soldier's performance in battle. Russian soldiers were renowned for their endurance, bravery, and stolidity but were also renowned for their lack of initiative and tendency to deteriorate into a helpless herd as soon as their officers were put out of action.[30] The virtues of the Russian soldier were characteristic of peasant society. His defects, too, were rooted in peasant social organization, which was entirely inappropriate on the battlefield. A Tsarist military unit was cohesive so long as its officers were present—but a unit without officers had lost not only its appointed leaders, it had lost as well its intermediary to the world beyond the unit. On the battlefield Russian soldiers without officers were not so much militarily as socially isolated. They had no sense of being part of an integrated military machine, nor could they have because this was not their peacetime experience. Soldiers without officers had no more notion of how to comport themselves than would a Russian village suddenly materialized in the midst of a battle.

Notes

1. A. Rittikh, *Russkii voennyi byt v deistvitelnosti i v mechtakh* (St. Petersburg, 1893), 20. Rittikh makes similar observations on pp. 38 and 263.

2. Daniel Lerner and Richard D. Robinson, "Swords and Ploughshares: The Turkish Army as a Modernizing Force," *World Politics*, 13 (October 1960): 32. Others who make much the same point are Lucian W. Pye, "Armies in the Process of Political Modernization," in *The Role of the Military in Underdeveloped Countries*, ed. John J. Johnson, (Princeton, 1962), 80–84; James S. Coleman and Belmont Brice, Jr., "The Role of the Military in Sub-Saharan Africa," in *ibid.*, 396–98; Morris Janowitz, *Military Institutions and Coercion in the Developing Nations* (Chicago, 1977), 156–58; W. Raymond Duncan, "Development Roles of the Military in Cuba: Modal Personality and Nation Building," in *The Military and Security in the Third World: Domestic and International Impacts*, ed. Sheldon W. Simon, (Boulder, CO, 1978), 77–121.

3. On the Tsarist army at the time of the Crimean War, see John Shelton Curtiss, *The Army of Nicholas I, 1825–1855* (Durham, NC, 1965). On Miliutin's reforms, see P. A. Zaionchkovskii, *Voennye reformy 1860–1870 godov v Rossii* (Moscow, 1952), and Forest A. Miller, *Dmitrii Miliutin and the Reform Era in Russia* (Nashville, 1968). P. A. Zaionchkovskii,

Samoderzhavie i russkaia armiia na rubezhe XIX–XX stoletii, 1881–1903 (Moscow, 1973), 116–17, provides figures on draftees.

4.   Required instruction was dropped in the mid-1880s and then restored, for the infantry alone, in 1902. Even when literacy instruction was required, however, it frequently (perhaps ordinarily) remained a dead letter. The officer in charge filled out and presented the proper forms during brigade inspection, and no one asked whether instruction had actually been provided. Zaionchkovskii, *Samoderzhavie i russkaia armiia*, 276–79; A. Gerua, *Posle voiny. O nashei armii* (St. Petersburg, 1907), 54–55; *V tsarstve shtykov* (Nizhni-Novgorod, 1908), 21–22; A. A. Ignatyev, *A Subaltern in Old Russia* (New York, 1944), 150; M. Grulev, *Zapiski generala evreia* (Paris, 1930), 112–13, 130–31; idem, *Zloby dnia v zhizni armii* ([Brest-Litovsk], 1911), 76, 78, reports a lack of enthusiasm for educating soldiers even after the Russo-Japanese War. A. I. Denikin, *Put russkogo ofitsera* (New York, 1953), 123, claims that at least after 1902 hundreds of thousands of Russian soldiers did become literate while in the army, but the weight of the evidence is against him.

On the instruction provided in the *uchebnye roty* for future noncoms, see A. Rittikh, *Russkii voennyi byt*, 55–56; Col. Mamontov, "Sovremennoe polozhenie unter-ofitserskogo voprosa v Rossii i za granitseiu," *Obshchestvo revnitelei voennykh znanii*, kn. 4 (1906): 82.

5.   W. Barnes Steveni, *The Russian Army from Within* (New York, 1914), 35, 44, 47, reports this as the common sentiment among Russian officers. Other officers felt not so much that the Russian army was carrying out a civilizing mission as that it should be doing so; see Captain Veselovskii, *K voprosu o vospitanii soldata* (St. Petersburg, 1900), 164; Mstislav Levitskii, *Vospitanie soldata* (St. Petersburg, 1911), 4 and passim, M. Galkin, *Novyi put sovremennogo ofitsera* (Moscow, 1906), 19, 53–55.

6.   Dragomirov's ideas on this subject are laid out in, inter alia, *Opyt rukovodstva dlia podgotovka k boiu* (many editions), especially pt. I, and *Podgotovka voisk v mirnoe vremia* (Kiev, 1906). Both are reprinted in M. I. Dragomirov, *Izbrannye trudy. Voprosy vospitaniia i obucheniia* (Moscow, 1956). Dragomirov's influence is remarked by German Miuller, "Moralnoe vospitanie voisk v Germanii, Rossii i Iaponii. Sravnitelnyi etiud na osnovanii Russko-iaponskoi voiny," *Voina i mir* no. 3 (1907), passim; Gerua, *Posle voiny*, 73–74, 100–1; and by most other contemporary commentators.

7.   In 1882 only 53.6 percent of the army was housed in regular barracks; by 1903 all field troops were quartered either in barracks or in private apartments under barrack conditions. Zaionchkovskii, *Samoderzhavie i russkaia armiia*, 270–71; Rittikh, *Russkii voennyi byt*, 138–41.

8.   Actually the introduction of conscripts to the vices began before they arrived in their regiments, as they were subject to blatant extortion by noncoms who conveyed them from the induction centers (Gerua, *Posle voiny*, 105–7). On the experience of the conscripts during their first four months of service, see *V tsarstve shtykov*, 2–4, 7, 14; M. Zenchenko, *Obuchenie i vospitanie soldata* (St. Petersburg, 1902), 71–85; Rittikh, *Russkii voennyi byt*, 38–39, 42; B. V. Rechenberg-Linten, *Russische Soldaten und Offiziere aus der Zarenzeit. Nach Selbsterlebnissen in einer russischen Garnison* (Bern-Leipzig, 1924), 8–9, 14–18; N. D. Butovskii, *Sbornik poslednykh statei* (St. Petersburg, 1910), 128, 131.

On the high rate of sickness during the first four months, see N. Butovskii, *Nashi soldaty. (Tipy mirnogo i voennogo vremeni)* (St. Petersburg, 1893), 10–11, 79, 145. Grulev, *Zloby dnia*, 241–43, points out that much of the sickness arose from the fact that many draftees went into the army "under protest"—the list of medical exemptions did not cover them, but they were not really fit for service. Grulev estimates that as many as 10 to 15 percent of all draftees were discharged on medical grounds, often after hospitalization, soon after arriving in their units.

N. N. Golovin, *The Russian Army in the World War* (New Haven, 1931), 22, also refers to the high proportion of draftees who arrived at their units "under protest."

The references to beatings, theft, and extortion are innumerable, the only question being how prevalent they were in fact. Whatever the true incidence, it is clear that newly arrived conscripts were the most vulnerable but that all soldiers considered these phenomena a normal feature of military life.

9. Rittikh, *Russkii voennyi byt*, 86–88; Gerua, *Posle voiny*, 51–52, 65–66, 103, 107–8, 111; A. P. Voznesenskii, "O voennom khoziaistve," *Obshchestvo revnitelei voennykh znanii*, kn. 1 (1906): 109–11, 118; Ignatyev, *A Subaltern*, 75; Grulev, *Zloby dnia*, 154, 229; A. M. Volgin, *Ob armii* (St. Petersburg, 1908), 114–16. A. I. Denikin, *Staraia armiia* (Paris, 1929), 1: 93, explicitly compares the running of a regiment at the turn of the century—especially in the interior—with running a *pomeste.*

10. Zaionchkovskii, *Samoderzhavie i russkaia armiia*, 272–73.

11. *Razvedchik*, no. 539, February 13, 1901. The sources on this curious practice are numerous, for it was widely discussed in the military press at the turn of the century. See John Bushnell, "Mutineers and Revolutionaries. Military Revolution in Russia, 1905–1907" (Ph.D. diss., Indiana University, 1977), 18–20 and notes. In addition, see Rittikh, *Russkii voennyi byt*, 52; Grulev, *Zapiski*, 93. *Volnye raboty* were finally suppressed in 1906; see *Razvedchik*, no. 796, January 29, 1906.

12. The two budgets (others were offered as well) are in R. Maksheev, "Zhalovane i pensii nizhnym chinam," *Intendantskii zhurnal*, no. 5 (1903): 44–47; *Razvedchik*, no. 565, August 14, 1901. On the items soldiers had to provide for themselves and the cost involved in maintaining uniforms and especially boots in required order, see Bushnell, "Mutineers," 16–18. In addition, see Voznesenskii, "O voennom khoziaistve," 105, 107. On the increase in pay and the December 1905 increase in equipment issued to soldiers, see "Ulushenie byta nizhnikh chinov," *Russkii invalid*, no. 255, December 6, 1905.

13. Bushnell, "Mutineers," 18; Ignatyev, *A Subaltern*, 146–47; Steveni, *Russian Army*, 65–66; Grulev, *Zapiski*, 94; Denikin, *Put*, 120; Rechenberg-Lenten, *Russische Soldaten*, 16.

14. The seasonal cycle is laid out in the most detail by Rittikh, *Russkii voennyi byt*, 44–47, 54, 100, 143, 146, 153. No other source offers contrary evidence. Grulev, *Zloby dnia*, comes up with a figure of twenty-five to thirty in a company after summer camp even after the *volnye raboty* had been abolished; the rest were detailed to other duties temporarily.

15. A. Denikin, "Soldatskii byt," *Razvedchik*, no. 661, June 24, 1903. On the inferior social status of Tsarist soldiers in general, see Bushnell, "Mutineers," 21–23.

16. *Golos iz russkoi armii. Razoblacheniia* (Berlin, 1902), 44, 62, provides direct soldier testimony on this point. The known behavior pattern in the army—frequent striking of soldiers and the soldiers' acceptance of same—is at least circumstantial evidence.

17. *Russkii invalid*, no. 235, October 28, 1900.

18. "Eshche o volnykh rabotakh," *Varshavskii voennyi zhurnal*, no. 1, (1902).

19. N. D. Butovskii, *Stati na sovremennye voprosy* (St. Petersburg, 1907), 62, 64; Grulev, *Zloby dnia*, 228–29, 237–38; Denikin, *Staraia armiia*, 1: 93.

20. Voznesenskii, "O voennom khoziaistve," 111–12, 122.

21. George Foster, "Peasant Society and the Image of Limited Good," *American Anthropologist* 67, no. 2 (1965): 293–315.

22. Veselovskii, *K voprosu*, 12; Gerua, *Posle voiny*, 47–51, 54, 118; Voznesenskii, "O voennom khoziaistve," 97, 112–18; Zenchenko, *Obuchenie*, 59–63; Rittikh, *Russkii voennyi byt*, 75; Galkin, *Novy put*, 49–52; Rechenberg-Lenten, *Russische Soldaten*, 13–22; Butovskii, *Sbornik*, 63–70, 120–22; Grulev, *Zloby dnia*, 54, 57–58, 155–57. There was little contact between officers and men even during guard duty because the officers and men on guard detail came from

different units; see Levitskii, *Vospitanie*, 10. Peter Kenez, "A Profile of the Prerevolutionary Officer Corps," *California Slavic Studies* 7 (1973): 129, 133–34, notes that a disproportionate number of Tsarist officers were assigned to staff work, while the ratio between officers (including staff officers) and men was the lowest of any major European army.

23. Ignatyev, *A Subaltern*, 85; *V tsarstve shtykov*, 8; Grulev, *Zapiski*, 92, 94, 98, 133; Zenchenko, *Obuchenie*, 59; *Golos iz russkoi armii*, 4–5; Rittikh, *Russkii voennyi byt*, 48–49; Mamontov, "Sovremennoe polozhenie 'unter-ofitserskogo voprosa'," 97, 101; K. V., "Sravnenie nashikh uslovii obuchenii soldata s zagranichnymi," *Russkii invalid*, no. 154, July 20, 1905; Sagatskii, "K unter-ofitserskomu voprosu," *Razvedchik*, no. 821, July 18, 1906; Zaionchkovskii, *Samoderzhavie i russkaia armiia*, 120–23; Butovskii, *Stati*, 25; Golovin, *Russian Army*, 29.

24. *V tsarstve shtykov*, 13; Voznesenskii, "O voennom khoziaistve," 110; Rittikh, *Russkii voennyi byt*, 51–52; Gerua, *Posle voiny*, 86, 88; Bushnell, "Mutineers," 20–21.

25. *V tsarstve shtykov*, 23–24. There is some indication that the "improving officer" was more common after 1905 than before and that the soldiers' perception of the proper role of their officers may gradually have been changing. But the change could only have been gradual because the bulk of the Tsarist officers were still immersed in office paperwork.

26. On the officer's role as patron (in providing special treats out of his own pocket, helping soldiers in time of need, and so on), see Ignatyev, *A Subaltern*, 86–87, 89, 144; B. V. Gerua, *Vospominaniia o moei zhizni* (Paris, 1969), 1: 58. The patron role was filled most often in the Guards, where officers were independently wealthy. It may well be that when soldiers felt that the patron role was being adequately filled, they were more likely to be loyal to their officers; this may have been one of the reasons some units did not mutiny during the epidemic of mutinies in late 1905. See Bushnell, "Mutineers," 95–97 (the evidence is therein presented, but the point is not stated in the same terms).

27. E. G. Bailey, "The Peasant View of the Bad Life," *The Advancement of Science* 23 (December 1966): 401.

28. There is a nice discussion of the peasant's place in the city in Joseph Crane Bradley, Jr., "*Muzhik* and Muscovite: Peasants in Late Nineteenth-Century Urban Russia" (Ph.D. diss., Harvard University, 1977), 98–117, 170–73, and passim.

29. Bushnell, "Mutineers," 68–97, 145–52, 295–343, discusses the mutinies of 1905 and 1906, though not quite in the same terms (the peasant analogy is suggested but not developed).

30. Representative comments from the late nineteenth and early twentieth centuries may be found in: "Report of Captain Carl Reichman," in U.S. War Department, General Staff G-2, *Reports of Military Observers Attached to the Armies in Manchuria*, pt. I, 1906, p. 244; F. V. Greene, *Sketches of Army Life in Russia* (New York, 1880), 24–25, 124–25; Steveni, *Russian Army*, 50; Grulev, *Zloby dnia*, 55, 85.

6

Peasants and Schools

Ben Eklof

The history of peasant education in Russia was shaped by the interplay of popular demands and elite notions. There is no reason to deny the virtue of studying official school policy in isolation; however, once changes in school systems are believed to flow directly and exclusively from opinions, statements, and decisions made at the top, the historical reality is grossly distorted. This, sadly, has often been the case in the writing of Russian educational history, in which the earlier predisposition of educational historians to treat their subject as a sequence of elite projects and laws has been exaggerated by the pervasive conviction that the state has been the prime mover in Russian history, that most activity has been fostered by state intervention.

The ways in which peasants could affect schooling were numerous. First, they could establish and maintain schools, hire teachers, and purchase textbooks, all on their own. Second, they could decide whether and how to participate in a system supervised and sometimes organized by others—decide if, when, and how long to enroll. They could choose whether to utilize the available educational facilities in the ways envisioned by those who shaped it or for purposes entirely incompatible with the objectives of the sponsoring or controlling elite. Perhaps most important, the very content and structure of instruction could be deeply affected by peasant choice.[1] In Russia during

Table 6.1
**The Development of Primary Education: Some Indicators of Growth
(Urban and Rural)**

	1856	1878	1896	1911
Number of schools	8,227	24,853	87,080	100,749
Number of pupils	450,002	1,065,889	3,804,262	6,629,978
Proportion of girls	8.2	17.7	21.3	32.2
One pupil for every # population	143	77	33	24.1
One school for every # population	7,762	3,299	1,443	1,449
% of pupils to population	0.7	1.2	3.02	4.04*

Source: A. I. Piskunov, ed., *Ocherki istorii shkoly i pedagogicheskoi mysli narodov SSSR* (Moscow, 1976), 518;
A. Chekini, "Nachalnoe narodnoe obrazovanie," *Novyi Entsiklopedicheskii Slovar*, 28: i–iv.

* 5.48% for boys and 2.6% for girls; if only European Russia is included, the figure is 4.43% for 63 provinces,
or 6.06% (boys) and 2.83% (girls). At the time the most common estimate for full enrollment was 9.00%.

Table 6.2
Russian Primary Education, January 1, 1915

Date	European Russia	Russian Empire
Number of 8- to 11-year-olds in population	11,171,283	15,253,758
Number of children in school	6,490,174	7,788,453
Percentage of all 8- to 11-year-olds in school	58	51

Source: Adapted from Jeffrey Brooks, "The Zemstvo and Education," in *The Zemstvo in Russia*, ed. Terence
Emmons and Wayne Vucinich (Cambridge, 1982), 270.

the last fifty years of imperial rule the peasants took advantage of all of these
opportunities to further, to guide, and to limit the schooling of their children.
The state could apply brakes or it could supply inducements, but ultimately
it was the peasantry that set the pace and determined the tone of primary
education.

The expansion of schooling in the Russian countryside after 1864 brought basic education within the reach of the majority of peasants in the European heartland by the time of World War I (see tables 6.1 and 6.2). This expansion was initiated by the purposeful self-activity of the anonymous peasant millions. The elite contribution—whether by the local *zemstvos* or officialdom—began on a large scale only after the great famine of 1891–92 when signs of social stress, dislocation, and disorder began to mount and the theme of Russian economic and military backwardness intruded into the field of popular education. Before that date it was peasants who supplied the energy, money, and effort to launch and maintain the school expansion campaign; after that date peasant pressure for more schools continued to affect the pace of school construction.[2]

Although peasant goals remained substantially the same throughout the entire half century, the tactics adopted in pursuit of these goals changed as peasants interacted with the outside world and responded to initiatives or restrictions coming from above. Until the turn of the century the strategy was one of direct actions to provide for education in what was otherwise almost a vacuum. Peasants were the sponsors and, to a large extent, the organizers of the school system established before the turn of the century.

Peasant activities forced the state to respond to persistent demand, and after the state and *zemstva* stepped in on a large scale the peasants were no longer the dominant sponsors of education. By this time it was no longer a question of whether peasants should learn their ABCs, but one of *who* should teach them, *how* they should be taught, and *what* they should learn. Elite intervention led, in turn, to the adoption of more subtle tactics by the peasantry. As the official school system gradually spread into the villages of European Russia (as peasant schools were registered and brought under *zemstvo* and then state supervision) and the state gradually assumed most of the direct costs of schooling, peasants shifted to *limiting* their children's participation in the system, to utilizing it for their own purposes while sifting out those aspects of schooling meant to intrude into, interfere with, or alter their lives and traditions.

Interfere was exactly what progressive as well as official (state) educators wanted to do. Countless comments made by educators at the time leave no doubt that they saw little purpose in teaching the ABCs if the peasants were not also liberated from the superstitions and irrational prejudices governing their lives and limiting their horizons or, in the case of the state, if they did not imbibe a heavy dose of patriotism and proper (Orthodox) religion. Progressives and conservatives differed over goals, but neither had much use for mere instruction without *vospitanie* (character education). Many peasants, on the other hand, wanted the instruction provided by the schools but fiercely resisted character molding or efforts to make them alter their way of life. Overwhelmingly, they adopted a survival rather than a profit-maximization approach to schooling. They saw schools not as a springboard to future careers but as providing tools to help cope with a world increasingly crowded with documents[3] and, in particular, to avoid being duped, cheated, or misled in a hostile and treacherous environment.

It is noteworthy that peasant initiative became most apparent soon after the emancipation (1861). When peasants learned that they had received their juridical freedom but would have to pay for the land they believed rightfully theirs, many felt that they had been duped. As one liberal landowner later recounted, when he tried to explain the emancipation terms,

> "We are ignorant," peasants told him. "But we feel things ought to be done just as the Emperor orders."
> "But this *is* what the Emperor orders, here in this document."
> "But how can we tell? We can't read."[4]

Who built the Schools?

How do we know that peasant attitudes changed little between 1864 and 1910 and that peasants consistently supported schooling? After all, in the mid-1880s the rate of industrial growth in Russia leaped from 4 to 8 percent per annum; it would seem plausible to expect a corresponding leap in peasant interest in schooling, for much of recent scholarship links the onset of industrialization with dramatic changes in popular attitudes toward schooling.[5] In the late 1880s peasant recognition of the utility of education *did* grow steadily more urgent. Peasant culture came to a realization of the utility of educating girls at this time as well. But there are several ways of demonstrating that such changes were in reality modulations of a pulse already throbbing at the time of the emancipation, not infusions of life from above.

First, between 1864 and 1890 it was peasants rather than educated elites who were the driving force behind the progress in literacy amply documented in official statistics. As late as the end of the century, noninstitutional sources continued to account for a remarkably high proportion of the total number of literates in the countryside. Historians have often referred to data showing that 36 percent of the literate factory population had learned how to read or write outside the schools—that is, from *local literates* hired individually by parents or collectively by villages to teach their children. In Saratov between one-half and three-fourths of all literates had received no formal education; in Iaroslavl the figures were 48 percent for men and 38 percent for women.[6]

Could it be that many of these unschooled literates had in fact received their instruction in the army? Minister of War Miliutin had introduced compulsory schooling for all conscripts in the seventies, and according to John Bushnell, "the Tsarist army became the single most important source of literacy for Russian peasants," with 25–30 percent of all males of draft age entering the army in the final quarter of the nineteenth century.[7] Yet many studies of the roots of literacy at the turn of the century specifically pointed to home schools as the source of instruction. Moreover, Bushnell more recently noted that in the army required instruction was dropped in the mid-1880s and then "even when literacy instruction was required [after this date] . . . it frequently, perhaps ordinarily—remained a dead letter."[8]

Undoubtedly the vast majority of "unschooled" literates had learned their ABCs in the so-called free schools, or *volnye shkoly*, which proliferated in the Russian countryside despite regulations established in 1869 to restrict private education. Until legalized in 1882, these schools lived a furtive existence and later frequently escaped documentation. Yet there are well-substantiated studies confirming their presence and testifying to their considerable popularity and support from the population.[9]

N. V. Chekhov, a prominent activist and historian, as well as enthusiast of the *zemstvo* schools, commented in 1923:

> Much more important (than the gentry-promoted schools organized by Korf, Tolstoy and others), was the independent initiative of the peasant population, expressed by the opening in the sixties of thousands of literacy schools. Despite the extremely impoverished circumstances of these schools, the barely literate teachers . . . and despite the complete absence of textbooks and amenities, or even of permanent quarters (the teacher lived and worked by moving from house to house of the parent—a form of nonmonetary tax), these schools turned out to have the greatest vitality, and formed the cornerstone for the zemstvo schools, into which they were gradually transformed in the seventies and eighties.[10]

But peasant participation was not limited to the *volnye shkoly*; until the turn of the century peasants continued to pay a hefty proportion of the direct expenditures of education in the official schools (both church and *zemstvo*). The formula worked out by many *zemstva*—that the community would pay for the purchase or rental and upkeep of a school building while the *zemstva* would provide textbooks and pay teachers, was only partially implemented before 1900. As late as the end of the eighties local communities were still funding 30 percent of teachers' salaries and outlays on books as well as meeting all expenses for facilities (except in Moscow and a few other provinces). In 1893 only one in ten *zemstvo* schools was funded exclusively by *zemstvo* monies. In 1903 the government set conditions by which *zemstva* would be

eligible for direct subsidies; among the conditions were the requirements that
zemstvo teachers receive at least 300 rubles per annum salary from the *zemstvo*
and that village communities be emancipated from all direct expenditures on
schools. Many district *zemstva* found such stipulations too burdensome and
declined government offers to help pay for the schools.[11]

When measuring the relative contribution of elite and peasant to total
school costs, one must keep other facts in mind. First, most estimates did not
include outlays on facilities, which the peasants bore solely, ordinarily as one
of many labor duties. Kulomzin estimated that the peasant contribution in 1898
was 17.9 percent, but that if labor and material obligations were included, it
was actually 43 percent. In addition, it seems appropriate to note that until
the 1890s the bulk of *zemstvo* revenues were collected through land taxes
based on arbitrary assessments by which the gentry consistently forced a
grossly disproportionate share of the tax burden upon the peasantry. Thus
in 1885 in the thirty-four *zemstvo* provinces taxes on communal allotment
lands averaged 17.7 kopeks per desiatina (equal to approximately 2.7 acres);
on nobility-held land the tax was 12.9 kopeks. Moreover, incredible as it
seems, gentry land, which was often of higher quality than allotment land,
was taxed according to estimates of size and quality of holding provided by
the individual owner himself to the *zemstvo*! For this reason large tracts of
gentry land went entirely untaxed: between 1871 and 1901 *zemstvo* statisticians
discovered over 30 million desiatinas of previously untaxed gentry land (and
many statistical boards were disbanded as reward for their zeal).[12] Except in
those *zemstvo* provinces fortunate enough to supplement their revenues with
taxes on industrial and urban property, the lion's share of money came from
peasant lands—and in many cases the *zemstvo* assemblies fought stubbornly
against efforts to prod the *zemstvo* into reassessments. Moreover, the taxes
collected from the peasantry and earmarked for education often went into
secondary rather than primary schools. In short, it would be more accurate
to say that peasants were sponsoring not only their own but also the gentry's
education, rather than the reverse: that the gentry were underwriting peasant
education.[13]

Another prominent contemporary educator, Kapterev, was very guarded
in his estimation of the *zemstvo* contribution. Recognizing that initially the
zemstvo had only limited funds at its disposal, Kapterev added:

> Initially the zemstvo showed little enthusiasm for public schooling; indeed
> many believed that the rural school was not a proper area of activity for
> the zemstvos; after all, such schools taught peasants only and should be run
> by peasants. Landowners and people of other estates did not enroll their
> children in village schools, and the zemstvo was obligated to serve all rural
> inhabitants, not just one estate. Thus, at first the zemstvo was not reluctant to

rid itself entirely of rural schools, leaving their fate largely ... to the village community.[14]

Noting that over the next thirty years the *zemstvo* gradually did become involved in rural schools, first through salary supplements and then by assuming responsibility for the teacher's entire salary, Kapterev concluded:

> Consequently, that school which today we call the zemstvo school is the product of the efforts of both the folk and the educated public. Its foundation is undoubtedly the old deacon's school, established by folk teachers and still existing even today, here and there in remote areas and among Old Believers, notably in Perm. From a private school, existing by force of individual contracts between parents and the master, it turned into a public village school, maintained by the village community. This public village school was extremely poor and inadequate, with unprepared and uneducated teachers, and without classroom materials, located in the anteroom of a bath or in a peasant hut. ... The public village school in terms of its source of funding gradually changed into the peasant-zemstvo and then into the zemstvo school.[15]

A large proportion of the expansion of the school system was in reality a process of formalization, of registration and incorporation of previously functioning peasant schools into the official network. Whereas after 1890 the expansion of formal schooling was genuine and large scale, before that date much of the expansion was in reality a conversion of informal literacy schools into *zemstvo*-supervised and partially subsidized schools. The fact is that until the 1890s it was the peasants who first set up most existing schools, peasants who continued to bear a large share of their maintenance costs, and peasants who paid the taxes applied so sparingly by the *zemstvos* to primary education.

Another way of gauging peasant attitudes toward literacy is to consider evidence of unmet popular demand for schooling. Reports by teachers indicated that peasant families were almost literally breaking down the doors of the school to gain a space for their children, even pleading for space at the back of the room if no seats were available. In many areas schools introduced a policy of opening their doors to new pupils only in alternate years in order to reduce the crush of applicants. In other areas parents who despaired of finding a place for their offspring finally gave up and hired private tutors.[16] Just how severe was the crush?

Before the 1911 Census information was only occasionally solicited on the incidence of denied admissions, and then seldom for more than one district or province at a time. According to statisticians in Vladimir and Iaroslavl, in the 1890s nearly all schools were overcrowded, which "is one of the best proofs of peasant attitudes (towards schooling)." Farmakovskii reported that "according to the unanimous testimony of school directors in the Moscow educational district, the schools are overcrowded and every school has to turn away students." Falbork wrote that "popular striving for education is growing faster than the schools are expanding; as a result a genuine struggle is taking place for the few openings in the schools."[17]

G. T. Robinson once observed how dry statistics on the number of livestock held by each rural household are for the urban-born historian, then added: how eloquently such figures really speak if we only realize that for nearly every household listed in the *zemstvo* statistics as "horseless," there was a sweating peasant man or woman harnessed to a heavy wooden plow straining to cut furrows in the reluctant soil. Information contained in the 1911 School Census yields the same kind of insight into the aspirations and blocked hopes for an anonymous, silent population; in 1910 some 999,852 (nearly a million!) children were formally denied admission to the elementary schools—this out of an estimated school-age population of 12,000,000 and an enrolled (aged 8–11) population of 6,600,000.

It is possible to assess the seriousness of the situation in different ways. Thus we may say that every year one of twelve children of school age was denied admission (for whatever reason), or that for every six children in school there was at least one who wanted entry but could not be accommodated. If we juxtapose the number of denied admissions to the total enrolled in the first grade (the most accurate reflection of unmet demand), we learn that according to the census, the chances of being rejected were even higher; the number of denied admissions was equal to approximately one-third of all pupils in the first grade. Thus for every 100 children who enrolled for the first time in 1910, there were 33 (31 boys and 34 girls, respectively) who tried but could not find a place. (Certainly many more parents, realizing there was no space, didn't even bother to apply.)[18]

Peasant initiative launched the school campaign. Together, by 1911 elite and peasantry had built an extensive school network and were sponsoring Russia's first schooled generation. But even with this successful joint effort, peasant demand for schooling considerably exceeded supply and continued to exert pressure on the state to allocate still more resources to achieve universal education. If we recall that at least one of the reasons the Russian elite became involved in school construction in the 1890s was the fear of "wild" or unschooled literacy, it follows that unmet demand would continue to add urgency to government efforts to find resources to funnel in the direction of rural schooling. This demand not only preceded but also exceeded the capacity of the elite, both official and societal; in combination with the earlier organizational efforts put into the "free" or "wild" peasant schools, it justifies arguing that the term "*zemstvo* school" is a misnomer, a historical myth, and that in some areas at least, elite intervention in Russia was a response to pressure from below rather than an effort to mobilize inert masses.

These figures must be kept in view when considering the extraordinary dropout rate pervading the school system and the fact that fewer than one in ten children managed to complete even the three-year course offered by the primary school. Why, then, at the same time were children, or their parents for them, trying to beat down the doors of the schoolhouse to gain admission? They must have known that even when they did secure a place, their children would stay for only two years or so. It seems incomprehensible that such enthusiasm would be displayed if the goal was completion of the program. Unless we assume that peasants were lemmings, blindly rushing to the schools and just as blindly leaving, at the beck of forces completely beyond their control, some strategy must have been in operation. But what strategy?

By 1914 over half of all children in the Russian Empire and six in ten children in the Russian heartland were enrolled in school. A closer look at enrollment statistics show that they understated the number of children who ever had contact with school. Studies often listed as eligible all children age seven to fourteen, but schools accepted only children age eight to eleven; thus the ratio of enrolled to eligible was artificially low. Local studies showed that because of overcrowding, too, many children were not admitted to school at age eight but later enrolled. In Moscow province up to 90 percent of boys age eleven were either enrolled in school or had already received some schooling at the turn of the century.

It can be shown through *zemstvo* statistics that attendance levels were uniformly high in Russian village schools (over 90 percent daily) but that most children of both sexes and of all backgrounds (wealthy, poor, farming, cottage industry or migrant) stayed in school only slightly more than two years and dropped out before completion of the three- or four-year program.

What impact did schools have? What were pupils learning and retaining? In the following section I argue that the schools were, despite the brevity of the program and the harsh conditions (forty children to each teacher, crowded and inadequate buildings, poor hygiene) teaching children how to read, write, and count and that peasants retained these skills some years later. Our faith in the civilizing mission of schooling has taken a beating since the early twentieth century; many in the West are less scornful of mere instruction, and recent estimates of the degree of functional illiteracy in this country (up to one-third the adult population) have produced an awareness that achieving basic literacy is no small feat.

Although poverty and illness had an effect on the dynamics of schooling, the pattern of regular attendance and early dropping out reflected parental concern both to provide a basic education and to limit the impact of schooling on children. In this interpretation, schooling represented a means of survival but not a ticket to mobility and opportunity in the outside world. A small percentage of children did complete primary schools (about 10 percent of those who enrolled), and an even smaller number continued their education. With so many million peasants, even this small number over time made up a rather sizable "peasant intelligentsia" that made its distinctive contribution to Russian culture and politics after 1900. But the result of drawing out the small minority of exceptionally talented and ambitious was often to reinforce the self-contained nature of the commune by "extruding" possible agents of change. It is also possible that peasant (parental) strategies did not always work and that children were provided broader horizons by the schools, or that intergenerational tensions mounted within the commune and family, at least partly as a result of the experience of schooling. This may be especially true for girls, who, perhaps for the first time in their lives, encountered in the person of the woman teacher (well over half of all teachers) an independent woman with views about life quite at variance with those dominant in the village.

There is much evidence to support the view that the Russian schools by and large were providing what peasants wanted: literacy without socialization. This evidence is in retention studies, all of which showed clearly, not only in mathematical tabulations but also in extensive comments sent from the countryside, that the peasants were truly learning the rudiments. Ironically, the reports gain in credibility because most teachers felt that they were *not* successful, that many of their former pupils soon regressed to virtual illiteracy. A look at their reports, however, shows that what they meant by literacy was the ability *to* learn *through* reading, whereas what the peasants were learning and retaining was the ability *to* read. The crucial "transfer" of skills, which many today see as the chief contribution of literacy to modernization, was absent, but peasants were not illiterate.[19] The universal complaints that children could not speak properly, had terrible manners, and returned to the village to become peasants is further confirmation that peasants could sift out instruction from socialization.

So what were the peasants learning? In the 1860s and 1870s scattered tests were conducted in individual schools to determine the results of schooling, and inspectors' reports in the Ministry of Education archives contain occasional descriptions of spot tests.[20] Beginning in the eighties and continuing until 1914, educators launched more systematic attempts to measure the results of a complete or incomplete primary education. The data, partially reproduced in tables 6.2 and 6.3, include studies of Korsunovsk district (Simbirsk province) in 1885, Nizhedevitskii district, Voronezh province in 1895, a compilation of surveys from ten provinces in 1887–96, a study of Kursk province in 1900, and a massive study of all *zemstvo* schools in thirty-four provinces conducted in 1911.[21] The number of pupils tested in these studies often ranged in the thousands; a convincing attempt was made to maintain impartiality; and every effort was exerted to test every former graduate of the school or district under investigation (thus preventing those who were ashamed of individual regression in reading, writing, or counting skills from avoiding the tests, thereby skewing the results).[22]

Table 6.3
Degree of Retention of Knowledge and Skills by Graduates of Primary Schools Listed by Percentage of Teachers Responding

Subject	Forgotten	Regressed	Retained	Improved
Russian	—	16.9	76.9	6.2
Arithmetic	—	23.9	74.5	1.6
Bible	0.1	43.1	56.1	0.7
Penmanship	0.3	69.4	29.7	0.6
Spelling	2.2	84.5	13.3	—

Most but not all studies investigated the retention of school-based knowledge and skills of graduates of the schools, who by definition had completed three or four years of schooling. However, only a third of enrolled pupils actually graduated; the rest dropped out after two or three years, and we would expect a higher level of regression from these dropouts. Nevertheless, there is substantial indirect evidence that the difference between graduates and dropouts was not marked and that the level of acquisition and retention of skills was similar to that of all former pupils (the tests commonly verified pupils who had graduated ten or more years previously). For example, the school commission in Voronezh province, though confining its investigation to graduates, also happened to pick up information on a number of former dropouts, and noted "that they could all read and write satisfactorily, though many had left school long ago, and some were in their thirties."[23] Well-respected educators and observers of rural life (who differed sharply on other issues), such as A. Rappoport, N. A. Bunakov, F. F. Oldenburg, and A. N. Kulomzin, all made virtually the same point.[24] Finally, detailed church inspectors' reports, located in the archives of the Holy Synod, show that the results achieved in parish schools generally matched those reproduced here.

Now consider briefly these studies. Among the interesting discoveries of the Voronezh commission was that the average reading speed of graduates was eight to thirteen lines a minute for modern Russian and six to twelve lines of Church Slavonic. (The examiners compared their own speed of twenty lines of Church Slavonic.) Also, the greater the interval from graduation, the higher the reading score. Average reading scores were 3.7 for those who had graduated ten years or more previously and 3.5 for recent graduates. (Russians use a five "ball" or point system. Five is excellent, two is failing.) Most startling, in the words of the commission report, "we didn't find a single individual who had entirely forgotten how to read and write."[25]

The retention tests of former pupils in the remote agricultural province of Simbirsk (Lenin's father, Ilia Ulianov, was the director of this school district) showed that the overwhelming majority had held onto at least the rudiments of skills acquired in the classroom. Reading and math skills had slipped the least, whereas writing had deteriorated the most. It was clear from individual reports that the measurement of reading skills was largely concerned with the *technique* of reading. That reading skills were seldom employed for learning through reading is evident from comments that the books least in demand in the Simbirsk countryside among graduates were those concerned with self-help, agriculture, and science. In fact studies of reading patterns in the Russian villages consistently showed that despite the availability of works on popular science, agriculture, and self-help, the highest demand from libraries was for entertaining literature, popular history as well as the lives of the saints, and for the stories of the old *lubki* (chapbooks) now printed in book form.

Pupils performed best of all when tested on the retention of basic math skills. As the compilers of the survey explained, the demands of the school program were very limited and attainable (the four functions, simple and compound numbers, and basic fractions); teachers knew and taught this subject best; the examiners tested with examples from daily life rather than from textbooks; and, finally, basic math skills received consistent reinforcement in the peasant's world. "Truly, the peasant practices his addition, subtraction, multiplication and division throughout his life, no matter how modest, indeed impoverished, his family circumstances, and no matter how simple and uncomplicated his social relations. He counts the strips in his field, the wood in his forest, the money in his pocket." Because of this, most reports stated that the pupils calculated rapidly and answered eagerly.[26]

A study of former pupils in Kursk province provided further confirmation that mechanics rather than abstract reasoning processes were being retained. It also suggested that pupils were causing teachers much agony by simply transcribing on paper what they heard in daily life: the result was a phonetically correct reproduction of local dialects rather than proper (formal) Russian. Lamentably, of 720 former pupils, 35 percent could not spell their own names correctly. In six to seven lines of dictation, improper knowledge of word boundaries was observed in 50 percent of the compositions, word distortion in 29 percent, omission of hard or soft signs in 34 percent. By far the worst area was with the redundant Church Slavonic elements in the orthographical system, such as the letter *jat'*, which 64 percent of the students used incorrectly. This letter and the hard *jers*, which caused so much trouble, were eliminated with the orthographic reforms of 1917.[27]

What is important here is that these troublemakers were of little or no semantic importance. Word distortion may be a sign of the persistence of significant dialects in the vernacular of the common people, and the high level of improper word separation suggests a low degree of familiarity with the written word. Perhaps the worst information was that 20 to 25 percent of the written compositions were given failing grades and judged fundamentally incoherent. However, the other side of the coin is that for the remaining 75 to 80 percent, the difficulties observed were secondary and did not involve a fundamental regression to illiteracy; according to the surveyors, of 1,028 former pupils, only 21 had completely forgotten how to read and write.

There are striking parallels here to Eugen Weber's observations concerning rural schools in France. Weber noted that schools began their work by propagating an artificial language: "the literary or written language children learned in schools was as alien to the spoken tongue as spoken French itself was to their native dialect." He observed that "the French of the schools was an alienating as well as an integrative force," but also that a key to participation in the national culture, to becoming a *citoyen*, a Frenchman and not a peasant, was the ability to use the language promoted at school, to be at ease "with the symbolism of images" and "the common points of reference" contained in this language. Weber found a vivid example of the transition from peasant to Frenchman in the files of gendarmerie reports, the language of which reflected the painful attempts of the newly literate to relate events in proper French. The result was a stilted administrative style with awkward and convoluted phrases.

Is it not plausible that the Russian peasant was simply drawing out what was useful in his own familiar world, in which no one "cared how to write it, as long as it makes sense," and that he had little interest in "participating in the national culture."[28] If the object was to communicate to a loved one in the city, to keep a record, to send a message, not to get ahead in life or leave one's milieu behind, it mattered little whether it was in formal Russian or transcribed vernacular.

A collection of surveys conducted between 1885 and 1900 produced the virtually unanimous observation that not only had former pupils not forgotten how to read, but in terms of speed and comprehension, many showed marked improvements since graduation. Even reading in Church Slavonic yielded modestly satisfying results "both in technique and in translation as well as comprehension of words and phrases." Participation in choir and church services, the cheapness and availability of the Gospels and the Psalter, played a major role in reinforcing what was learned in school. The compiler of these surveys noted that in all areas the rudimentary information provided by the school system remained firmly implanted long after graduation. He cautioned, however, that the yardstick being used was short: "The examinations touched upon the persistence of the most basic skills—reading, writing and arithmetic; concerning specific areas of knowledge and information in fields such as geography, natural science, and history, there were no questions asked."[29]

The Kursk study of 1900 repeated the same conclusion. When it came to "information on history and geography," which was included on a line on the scorecards that the examining commission was to fill out on each former pupil, more than half simply left the line blank. For the remainder the scores were the lowest of any subject.[30]

In 1894 the Voronezh district school board requested the prominent educator Nicholas Bunakov (then running a school in the district) to take part in the annual certifying examinations for graduates of the primary schools. His comments on the reading abilities of new graduates speak directly to the issue of learning *to* read and learning *from* reading:

> Reading, both in modern Russian and Church Slavonic, of print and cursive was generally unhesitating, confident and intelligent (*tolkovyi*). In almost all schools the weak side of reading was the persistence of *gross local pronunciation* and the lack of even the most primitive expressiveness. The same can be said for the manner of reading poetry aloud. The pupils of all five schools knew and had memorized poems, but by no means all showed any understanding. ... Still, when all is said and done, the results in reading, in the sense of *being able to take apart and read out loud printed text* were good in all five schools.[31]

Perhaps the most thorough study of retention was carried out shortly before the war for the All-Zemstvo Congress (1911). Over 11,000 *zemstvo* rural teachers responded in writing to the following question:

> How well have your former pupils retained, three to five years after completion of the final examinations, their knowledge and skills acquired in the following areas: reading speed; comprehension and the ability to reformulate orally what they have read; handwriting; spelling; the four functions of arithmetic; knowledge and understanding of the prayers; knowledge and understanding of the central events depicted in the Old and the New Testaments.[32]

The *zemstvo* surveyors tabulated the results, which some teachers had verified through special tests and others simply by accumulated personal observation. (The results were tabulated in terms of teachers' responses concerning their pupils in general, not the specific number of pupils falling into each category.)

Consider briefly some of the more specific responses under these general categories. Retention of language skills—whether reading speed, comprehension, or oral recitation—was uniformly high, with fewer than one in five observing a decline in skills after graduation. Retention of basic math skills was also high, but not nearly as uniform. After three to five years, pupils were considerably more adept at solving simple problems orally than at carrying out written operations; compound composite numbers and basic division seemed to give the most trouble. It was frequently observed that "adults can count out loud with much greater facility than can school children; but when it comes to solving the simplest textbook-type problem, for the most part they are completely lost." The more abstract the problem and unrelated to daily life, the less likely the peasant was to retain the ability to solve it.[33]

Not surprisingly, the worst regression took place in spelling and in penmanship. The old familiar complaints abound: "Three to four months after completing the program pupils show up for the certificate, and can hardly sign their own names without violating some grammar rule." From Viatka: "When I handed out the certificates, not one of them could write his first name, patronymic and surname correctly!"[34]

As earlier observers had noted, local dialects crept into and overran proper spelling, but for the most part, despite the evident frustration of teachers, the regression they observed did not really touch on the fundamental ability to read or write, albeit without frequent mistakes. As one teacher wrote: "Upon leaving school, the students pay no attention to spelling rules. They explain to me that such rules have no force once outside the school gates, as long as the meaning of the word and the thought of the phrase is clear. They say, 'who cares how you write it, as long as it makes sense!' "[35]

In sum, Russian schools were producing a younger generation of literate individuals capable of reading with a measure of comprehension, calculating to the degree of complexity they found useful in daily life, and communicating information and thoughts on paper. If the job of the school was to teach the basics, it was clearly successful. Certainly a degree of regression followed on graduation, and this slippage was exacerbated by shortages of books, libraries, and "culture" in the countryside. But as we have seen, this regression only rarely involved a return to full illiteracy. Much of the loss perceived was not in the ability to communicate but in proper spelling and speech. Was this not the survival of dialect and local idiom over a unified national language and a sign that the schools were not succeeding in overcoming the gap between educated society and the common working people—a gap observed by many recent historians and considered fundamental to the outcome of the 1917 Revolution? The reports explicitly stated that the former pupils could spell "phonetically," communicate their needs in writing, and make sense of (restate in their own words) passages selected from unfamiliar texts.

What teachers and others were observing was the failure of pupils to meet the standards of communication requisite for participation in privileged society. Proper writing remained a "socially privileged means of expression," but children took home with them, and kept, the tools their parents had sent them to school to acquire. If there was an educational failure in Russia, it was not in the adequacy of teacher training or in classroom instruction, but in the ability to understand that peasant needs and wants sometimes did not correspond with the aspirations that others, their betters, had imposed on them.

Notes

1. See Patrick J. Alston, "Recent Voices and Persistent Problems in Tsarist Education," *Paedagogica Historia* 16 (1976): 203–15; Allen Sinel, "Problems in the Periodization of Russian Education: a Tentative Solution," *Slavic and East European Education Review*, no. 2 (1977): 54–62; William L. Mathes, "The Process of Institutionalization of Education in Russia, 1800–1917," in *Russian and Slavic History*, ed. K. E. Rowney and G. E. Orchard (Cambridge, 1977).

A few historians in the West have noted this progress; see especially Paul Ignatiev et al., *Russian Schools and Universities in the World War* (New Haven, 1929). (Ignatiev was Minister of Education during World War I). Recently, too, Gail Lapidus has stressed the Tsarist foundations of the Soviet primary educational system; see *Women in Soviet Society* (Berkeley, 1978), 136. However, most Western and Soviet works continue to assert that before 1914 schooling had barely reached the countryside, or that when progress had been achieved, it was entirely because of the state or the local, gentry-dominated *zemstva*. For an outstanding exception, see the discussion in Allen Sinel, *The Classroom and the Chancellery: State Educational Reform in Russia under Count Dmitrii Tolstoy* (Cambridge, MA, 1973), esp. 214–52.

2. See Ben Eklof, *Russian Peasant Schools: Officialdom, Village Culture, and Popular Pedagogy, 1861–1914* (Berkeley, 1987), 252.

3. For sources, argument, and material, see ibid. The notion that in Russian peasant culture the pursuit of survival and basic welfare rather than profit maximization or risk-taking was rational, and that measures designed by outside elites to alter production cycles or to radically change peasant behavior, often carries extraordinary risks for the peasant has been eloquently presented by Teodor Shanin, Michael Confino, and Moshe Lewin in very different contexts.

4. David Footman, *Red Prelude: A Life of Zheliabov* (New Haven, 1945), 21.

5. Patrick J. Harrigan, *Mobility, Elites and Education in French Society of the Second Empire* (Waterloo, Ontario, 1980), 87–88; also see Harvey Graff, *The Literacy Myth* (New York, 1979), 1–21, 191–225, and especially 225–33.

6. See Eklof, "Peasant Sloth Reconsidered: Strategies of Education and Learning in Rural Russia before Revolution," *Journal of Society History* 14, no. 3 (Fall 1981): 362–66.

7. John Bushnell, "Peasants in Uniform: The Tsarist Army as a Peasant Society," *Journal of Social History* 13, no. 4 (Winter 1980): 565–66.

8. Thomas Darlington, *Education in Russia* (London, 1909), 192; Bushnell, "Peasant," 573.

9. On *volnye shkoly* see especially A. S. Prugavin, *Zaprosy naroda i obiazannosti intelligentsii v oblasti umstvennogo razvitiia i prosveshcheniia* (Moscow, 1890), 31–52; N. V. Chekhov, *Istoriia narodnogo obrazovaniia v Rossii* (Moscow, 1912), 28–34; and N. Bunakov, *O domashnikh shkolakh gramotnosti v narode* (St. Petersburg, 1885).

10. N. V. Chekhov, *Tipy russkoi shkoly v ikh istoricheskom razvitii* (Moscow, 1923), 35; *Sbornik postanovlenii Moskovskogo gubernskogo zemskogo sobraniia s 1865 po 1897*, 5 vols. (Moscow, 1899–1902), 5: 18.

11. V. Charnoluskii, *Zemstvo i narodnoe obrazovanie*, 2 vols. (St. Petersburg, 1910), 1: 68; B. Veselovskii, *Istoriia zemstva za sorok let*, 4 vols. (St. Petersburg, 1909–11), 1: 471, 581, 472; Ministerstvo Narodnogo Prosvesheniia, *Odnodnevnaia perepis nachalnykh shkol Rossiiskoi Imperii 18 ianvaria 1911*, 16 vols. (St. Petersburg, 1911–16), 16: 51, 117, 194.

12. A. N. Kulomzin, *Dostupnost nachalnoi shkoly v Rossii* (St. Petersburg, 1904), 44; Veselovskii, *Istoriia zemstva*, 1: 655–57; George L. Yaney, *The Systematization of Russian Government* (Chicago, 1973), 348.

13. For a more thorough discussion of taxation and school funding, see Eklof, *Russian Peasant Schools*, Chap. 3.

14. P. F. Kapterev, *Novye techeniia v russkoi pedagogicheskoi mysli* (St. Petersburg, n.d.), 21–22.

15. Ibid.

16. Pervyi obshchezemskii sezd po narodnomu obrazovaniiu, *Trudy* 6 ("Raskhody"): 65–69; P. F. Kapterev, *Novye dvizheniia v oblasti narodnago obrazovaniia; srednye shkoly* (Moscow, 1913), 90; I. Belokonskii, "Narodnoe obrazovanie v Moskovskoi gubernii," *Russkaia shkola* 2, no. 2 (1891): 139.

17. V. Farmakovskii, "K voprosu o vseobshchem obuchenii," *Zhurnal Ministerstva Narodnogo Prosveshcheniia* 345 (January-February 1903): 132: *Izsledovanie polozheniia narodnogo obrazovaniia Viatskoi gubernii* (Viatka, 1902), 52–53; *Sbornik statisticheksikh i spravochnykh svedenii Vladimirskoi gubernii*, Vypusk III (Vladimir, 1900), 39; *Nachalnoe obrazovanie v Iaroslavskom gubernii po svedeniiam za 1896–1897 uchebnyi god*. Vypusk I (Moscow, 1902), 6.

18. *Odnodnevnaia perepis*, vol. 16, table 20, p. 69.

19. See also Harvey J. Graff, ed., *Literacy and Social Development in the West: A Reader* (Cambridge, England, 1981); idem, *The Legacies of Literacy: Continuities and Contradictions in Western Culture and Society* (Bloomington, 1987); Daniel P. Resnick, ed., *Literacy in Historical Perspective* (Washington, DC, 1983); and Jeanne S. Chall, *Learning to Read: The Great Debate* (New York, 1967). Chall has identified three stages of *learning to read* and two more of *learning from reading* (comprehensive literacy). On the notion of "transfer," see especially Sylvia Scribner and Michael Cole, "Cognitive Consequences of Formal and Informal Education," *Science*, November 1973: 9, 553–59.

20. See, for example, Nikolai A. Korf, *Nashi pedagogicheskie voprosy* (Moscow, 1882), 144–209; this work summarized a number of earlier investigations.

21. See Evgenii A. Zviagintsev, *Narodnaia zhizn i shkola*, 2 vols. (Moscow, 1912–13), vol. 1, for a summary of some of these tests and a discussion of their reliability. The Voronezh test is from Nikolai F. Bunakov, *Selskaia shkola i narodnaia zhizn: Nabliudeniia i zametki selskago uchitelia* (St. Petersburg, 1906), 175, 184–85. The Simbirsk study can be found in S. Krasev, "Chto daet krestianam nachalnaia narodnaia shkola," *Russkaia mysl*, 11, nos. 1–2 (1887): 49–72 and 110–30.

22. Zviagintsev, *Narodnaia zhizn*, 1: 14.

23. Bunakov, *Selskaia shkola*, 182.

24. Ibid.; also see F. F. Oldenburg, *Narodnye shkoly evropeiskoi Rossii v 1892–1893 godu: Statisticheskii ocherk* (St. Petersburg, 1896), 3–4; Kulomzin, *Dostupnost*, 15–16.

25. Bunakov, *Selskaia shkola*, 175–76, 184–85.

26. Krasev, "Chto daet," no. 1, 67–70.

27. Zviagintsev, *Narodnaia zhizn*, 1: 17–24.

28. Eugen Weber, *Peasants into Frenchmen* (Stanford, 1976), 337, passim.

29. Zviagintsev, *Narodnaia zhizn*, 1: 21.

30. Ibid.

31. Bunakov, *Selskaia shkola*, 187, italics added. See also *Sbornik statisticheskikh svedenii*, 3: 222–30.

32. Pervyi obshchezemskii sezd po narodnomu obrazovaniiu, *Trudy:* vol. 5, *Anketa*, 63–79.

33. Ibid. Numeracy—the ability to count and to do basic calculations—has traditionally drawn less attention than literacy. This is regrettable because its potential impact was enormous. The teacher was being asked to carry out a minor revolution in peasant perceptions if students were to pass examinations at the end of three years, for traditionally the Russian peasant had little use for official weights and measures, relying instead on complicated local systems of measurement. Yet both the Official Program and the Military Regulations (providing a reduced term of service for graduates) required knowledge of these weights and measures. If the reports are correct—that in most areas pupils were learning the program and were capable of problem solving at the daily level using standardized measures—a new skill with broad ramifications had indeed been introduced. A survey of math textbooks in use can be found in *Voprosy i nuzhdy uchitelstva*, 6: 10–34, and 9: 6–80; also see M. I. Demkov, *Nachalnaia narodnaia shkola*, 2d ed. (Moscow, 1916), 304–15.

34. *Anketa*, 63–79.

35. *Ibid*, 67.

7

Popular Justice, Community, and Culture among the Russian Peasantry, 1870–1900

Stephen P. Frank

Agrafena Ignatieva was known as a sorceress and a fortuneteller in the village of Vrachev (Tikhvinskii district, Novgorod province). An impoverished widow with no means of livelihood, she was forced to beg for her daily subsistence. Unfortunately for "Grushka," as the peasants called her, an outbreak of "falling sickness" in the locality where she lived brought suspicion on her. Most people knew that such an illness resulted from a spell, or *porcha*, and Ignatieva appeared to be the most likely culprit. Early in January 1879 Grushka had asked her fellow-villager Kuzmina for some cottage cheese but was refused; shortly thereafter Kuzmina's daughter fell sick and began crying out that Grushka was the cause. With this episode still fresh in everyone's mind, the illness reached Katerina Ivanova, whose sister had died from the same affliction, also "hexed" by Grushka. Ivanova attributed her sickness to the fact that she had once forbidden her son to chop firewood for the sorceress; Grushka was obviously seeking revenge. Ivanova's husband even lodged a complaint against Ignatieva with the local constable (*uriadnik*), but few villagers expected that she would be punished.

Because of the number of misfortunes attributed to her, the peasants of Vrachev decided to burn Grushka. They made their decision during a meeting of the village assembly, which had gathered to divide the property of four peasant brothers. After settling this case, the villagers reached an agreement among themselves, took some nails, and set off to "seal" Grushka, as they put it. On reaching Agrafena Ignatieva's hut, they found the entrance shed locked and broke down the door. Four peasants entered the storeroom in search of charms and potions while six others went into the house itself. After parleying for some time with the woman, they proceeded to "seal" the house. First a pole was set into the entranceway and nailed in place. Next they nailed a plank against the larger window and sealed off two small windows with logs, so that all exits were completely blocked. At about five p.m. they set fire to a bundle of straw and rope in the entrance shed, and the hut burned to the ground while nearly 200 people from Vrachev and a neighboring village looked on. Though certain they had done the right thing to protect their village, the peasants nevertheless sent the local constable 22 rubles so he would forget the case, but he declined their offer. Those most guilty in the burning of Grushka—sixteen persons—were brought before the circuit court, where three confessed their guilt and were sentenced to church penitence, while the others went free.[1]

Community or "mob" violence of this sort frequently found its way into the pages of Russia's urban and provincial press. It was by no means limited to persons accused of sorcery; thieves were commonly subjected to community reprisal, as were those who transgressed certain village norms of conduct. Nor was the phenomenon peculiar to backward, isolated regions. Although cases in urban centers had become rare by the late 1800s, we find numerous reports of extrajudicial retribution carried out close to large provincial or district towns.[2] Still, available evidence suggests that *samosud* (literally, self-adjudication), as educated Russians called it, was primarily an activity of rural villagers and occurred most often in areas where the effects of capitalist development had been least felt, for there the presence of police and other agents of state coercion was weak and traditional peasant institutions retained greater strength. It existed in nearly all provinces of the empire and remained widespread throughout the nineteenth century and after, accounting for as much as 1 percent of all rural crimes tried before the circuit courts.[3]

Samosud in the Russian countryside was a far more complex phenomenon than contemporaries believed it to be. Most of Russia's educated elite saw *samosud* as little more than mob violence or lynch law, and the greatest attention was paid to just these types of extralegal reprisal. The best dictionary of the period, however, took a broader view, defining *samosud* not only as willful punishment but also as arbitrariness and "adjudication of one's own affairs."[4] In fact, many instances of *samosud* did not involve violence but bore close resemblance to the *charivaris*, "rough music," and shivarees of Western Europe and North America. Although peasants rarely offered definitions to investigators who questioned them about their juridical beliefs and practices, they did include such nonviolent acts in their conception of *samosud*.[5] In addition, although they did not categorize the types of *samosud* practiced in the village, close examination of the acts themselves reveals that peasants distinguished sharply between punishments inflicted on community members and those used against outsiders. With fellow villagers *samosud* took on a highly ritualized character; violent forms were reserved almost exclusively for outsiders whose crimes posed a threat to the community.

This distinction between punishing members of the community and outsiders is perhaps the most useful framework for analyzing the nature and function of *samosud* in rural Russia and for understanding such acts from the perspective of the villager rather than of the urban elite. For this reason I will consider three frequent forms of popular justice, all of which were termed *samosud* by the participants: ritualized disciplinary action such as *charivari*, in which villagers inflicted shame and public disgrace on the guilty party, usually without resorting to violence; punishment of theft, particularly the theft of horses; and, briefly, violence directed against those suspected of witchcraft.

These types of popular justice reveal the range of peasant actions commonly lumped together under a single heading by representatives of the dominant culture. More important, they provide excellent examples of the complexity of *samosud* by showing why peasants turned to specific extralegal actions to punish very different crimes and how such decisions were based on the status of the offender as well as on the nature of the infraction.[6] The study of *samosud* allows us to explore one of the vehicles through which the reproduction of village social relations and peasant culture occurred, while offering insights into the larger conflict between peasant and elite culture at the lowest level of late nineteenth-century tsarist society.

The Variety of Samosud

One reason educated Russians had difficulty characterizing *samosud* is that it did not constitute a homogeneous category of crimes. No section of Russia's criminal code dealt with summary justice or even referred to *samosud* by name. Rather, the burning of Agrafena Ignatieva or beating a horse thief to death had to be treated under articles 1449–71 on murder, and cases in which death did not result, would be prosecuted as torture, bodily injury, insult, or arbitrariness.[7]

Even greater confusion is found in ethnographic descriptions of peasant juridical beliefs. For Petr Efimenko and E. Kartsev, *samosud* was any case not brought before the official courts but settled instead by popular, unofficial courts. Such cases involved petty theft, injury, fights, quarrels, infliction of damages, and numerous civil suits, though Efimenko did include the murder of horse thieves in this group.[8] Viacheslav V. Tenishev, by contrast, distinguished clearly between popular courts and extrajudicial punishment. *Samosud*, he wrote in 1907, could be characterized by the implementation of judicial authority not recognized by official law and carried out willfully and, in the majority of cases, violently. This violent implementation of a judicial decision set *samosud* apart from popular courts, "which also are not recognized by law, but are voluntarily accepted by the litigants themselves."[9] Yet litigants did accept certain types of *samosud*, not all of which were violent in nature. Villagers did little to clarify matters. When asked by outsiders about *samosud* in their locality, villagers often failed to mention violent incidents at all (for obvious reasons), speaking instead of such innocuous matters as the punishment of children or the public humiliation of petty thieves.[10]

What are we to make of this diversity of opinion? It is well known that violence was no stranger to the Russian countryside, and that a large proportion of criminal and civil cases arising in village communities never reached the officially sanctioned township (*volost*) courts.[11] But violence and the ignoring of official courts were not features of *samosud* alone. We must therefore seek out those elements of *samosud* that set it apart from other forms of popular justice.

Writing in 1880, the jurist Petr Skorobogatyi argued that *samosud* displayed the exclusive rights of society in the moral control of its members, while its strength derived from "the peasantry's respect for the authority of the commune; [from] that moral dependence upon the commune which the offender fully recognizes; and ... the close acquaintance and tight bonds which all fellow-villagers have among themselves."[12] In this way the authority of the commune stood in place of state authority, which villagers recognized only selectively. Invoking the commune's moral authority was one of the most notable features of *samosud*. Peasants usually brought a case before the village assembly before inflicting punishment, especially if the offender was a community member, and the assembly frequently sentenced the guilty party to some form of *samosud*. In this way the assembly sanctioned what outsiders would deem an illegal action and lessened the chance that a criminal would complain to the authorities or seek revenge, considering that to do so challenged a decision of the assembly as well as the authority of the community itself.

Other distinguishing features of *samosud* included community participation in the punishment, a real or perceived threat to local norms or to the community's well-being, and an attempt to prevent repetition of a crime through ritualized public humiliation of the offender or, in more serious cases, by ridding the community of a criminal altogether. Because the presence of these characteristics in a given act of *samosud* depended on the nature of the crime and the offender's status as villager or outsider, they helped both to differentiate the various forms of *samosud* and to join them together in a common meaning, as we shall now see.

Charivaris

At its simplest level, *samosud* might be inflicted for a multitude of petty infractions such as *potrava* (damage caused to another's crops by one's livestock); it was also used to discipline minors if the case warranted serious attention.[13] One of the most widespread types of *samosud* in rural Russia, however, was called "leading of the thief" (*vozhdenie vora*, or simply *vozhdenie*)—a punishment that had the ritualistic character of *charivari* and, unlike other acts of *samosud*, was visited only upon members of the community. Known by various names throughout Europe and North America, *charivaris* were a traditional means of public criticism or punishment in which the entire community could participate and a disciplinary technique by which family or community members were forced to follow collective rules. A strong, formal similarity existed between *charivaris* in Russia, where the practice endured as late as the 1920s, and in countries such as England, France, and Germany.[14]

The typical Russian *charivari* consisted of parading an offender through the street either on foot or in a cart, in some cases wearing a horse collar, while villagers followed along playing *paramusique* by beating upon oven doors (evidently the most favored instrument), pots and pans, washtubs, and other domestic or agricultural implements, sometimes carrying signs, mocking the victim, and singing songs. Women were often stripped naked or had their skirts raised before being led around the village; men might first be stripped, then tarred and feathered.[15] Apart from minor differences of detail, the similarities here with European examples are striking.

Yet the kinship between *charivaris* in these countries remained largely one of form. As Edward Thompson argues, "these forms are of importance not—as Levi-Strauss has suggested—as universal structures but precisely because the immediate functions of the rituals change. The kinds of offender subjected to rough music are not the same, from one country to another, or from one century to another."[16] It is, in fact, with the function of the rituals and the victims themselves that Russian *charivaris* differed from those in other countries. The *charivari* in England and France most often expressed disapproval of marital mismatches or conjugal relations considered to be deviant, such as marriages between people of great age difference, socially ill-matched marriages, or a recently widowed villager marrying a single, younger person. Sexual offenders were also common victims of *charivaris*, as were cuckolded husbands, unwed mothers, persons (usually women) who committed adultery, wife-beaters, and household members deviating from accepted sex roles—for example, men who performed women's work or whose wives beat them.[17]

In postreform Russia we do find cases of *charivaris* involving adulteresses (and occasionally adulterers too), unwed mothers, and "immoral" women, but they account for only a small proportion of collective community actions that can be termed *vozhdeniia*. Nor did I find reports of cuckolded husbands or husbands beaten by their wives being subjected to rough music. The apparent scarcity of such cases in Great Russia suggests that other matters occupied a higher priority when it came to the collective enforcement of local norms. Chief among these was petty theft.

Russian peasants treated many kinds of theft and pilfering quite leniently. Both unofficial and township courts used reconciliation far more than punishment in cases of petty theft. In the Volga region, for example, a peasant who perpetrated such a crime was not always viewed as someone capable of real harm to the community—a perspective clearly expressed in the popular saying, "The thief is not a thief, but a half-thief." Yet despite their apparent leniency, villagers did not simply dismiss the crime; in many instances *charivari* was a typical punishment, and its magnitude was determined above all by the seriousness of the crime, and especially by the value of the stolen item.[18] During *charivaris* involving petty theft, offenders would be marched through the village with the stolen object hung on them. In the village of Zabolonia, Smolensk province, for example, one peasant was caught stealing another's goose. Hanging the goose from his neck, villagers led the thief three times around the hamlet, pounding all the while upon oven doors. After this procession the thief begged forgiveness, bought drinks for everyone, and there the affair ended.[19] In another case a woman from the village of Kozinkii, Orel province, stole a sheep from her neighbor and butchered it. She was discovered and brought before the village assembly, which sentenced her to a *charivari*. Village women gathered together with sickles, oven doors, and other "instruments," hung the sheep's head around her neck, and amid songs and banging, led the woman three times through the town before letting her go.[20] A. F. Brandt found that petty thieves in parts of Mogilev province were led along the streets by a rope tied to the neck.

Sometimes the thief might be forced to wear a horse's collar or one fashioned from straw especially for the occasion.[21] With little variation, similar accounts appear in descriptions from nearly every province examined by government commissions, jurists, and ethnographers.

The additional humiliation of being stripped for a *charivari* was reserved mainly for women. In one village of Novgorod province, Cherepovets district, a woman named Drosida Anisimova was caught picking berries before the time agreed on by the village assembly. A village policeman brought her before the assembly, where they stripped her naked, hung on her neck the basket of berries she had gathered, "and the entire commune led her through the village streets with shouts, laughter, songs, and dancing to the noise of washtubs, frying pans, bells and so on. The punishment had such a strong effect on her that she was ill for several days, but the thought of complaining against her offenders never entered her mind" (or so the report claimed).[22] Likewise, Katerina Evdokimova, a peasant from the village of Ermakov, Iaroslavl province, was accused in 1874 of stealing linen. The assembly found her guilty and decided to undress her, wrap her in the stolen linen, and lead her through the streets. Evdokimova, however, pleaded not to be completely disrobed, so the assembly accommodated her by uncovering her only to the waist, then wrapping her in linen and leading her in public with her hands tied to a stake as everyone rang bells and beat upon oven doors.[23]

Charivaris could also result from a refusal to obey the assembly's decision in a criminal case. In Orel province a peasant named Mikhail was found guilty of stealing a sheep and ordered to buy the village elder and his friends a half-bucket of vodka. This they quickly drank and demanded another, promising to forgive Mikhail afterward. But while consuming the second bucket the peasants continued berating Mikhail for his crime, and becoming concerned for his safety, he fled to his home. When they finished their vodka and noticed Mikhail's absence, the irate villagers went to the thief's house led by the elder. Demanding more vodka, they became even angrier when he called them drunks and robbers. For this new insult they took a wheel from his wagon and sold it for vodka, after which they seized Mikhail, tied a large sack of oats onto his back, and led him around the village accompanied by other peasants who beat upon oven doors while laughing and insulting the victim. When the *charivari* ended, Mikhail was forced to pawn clothing at the local tavern in order to buy the men still more vodka. With this they finally agreed to forgive him, but sternly warned that things would go much worse if he ever stole again.[24]

Mikhail got off lightly, having not been beaten. Refusal to obey the will of the assembly could lead to more severe retribution involving violence and even expulsion from the community. To her misfortune, a peasant from the village of Meshkova, Orel province, learned this the hard way. Anna Akulicheva had been found guilty of stealing canvas, and the assembly decided to subject her to a *charivari* and then sell her own fabric for vodka. First the villagers knocked off her kerchief (a grave insult among Russian peasants) and dirtied her holiday shirt. Next they tied her sack-cloth on her back, bound her hands behind her, hitched her up, and led the woman through the village. Two peasants walked ahead beating with sticks upon oven doors while Anna followed in harness with the reins held by two others. The entire village turned out to watch and laugh, and children threw clods of dirt at her. Finally they brought her home and untied her, taking only the cloth they had placed on her back to purchase vodka. At this point, however, Anna attacked her tormenters with a chain seized in the shed and then fled the village to avoid further punishment.

On the suggestion of peasants from a neighboring village, Anna lodged a complaint with the local land captain. He summoned the elder from Meshkova, who confessed in detail and was forbidden to do such a thing again. Furthermore, the land captain sentenced him to two days' arrest. When he returned home, the elder immediately summoned the assembly and told them what Anna had done. The members wasted little time in responding to this latest offense. They ruled that Anna should be whipped in public by her husband, Sergei, and that some of her clothes would then be taken to sell for vodka, after which she would undergo all sorts of public ridicule. The woman was brought before the assembly but resisted her husband's efforts to force her to lie down for the beating. Finally, other peasants threw her to the ground and held her there while Sergei administered thirty blows with a knout. Following this severe punishment, he went to fetch his wife's clothes, but Anna had already taken all of her things to her family in Balasheva. As a result, Anna was ostracized. She fought with her husband daily. Worse, the community held her in contempt and mocked her, and village children pelted her on the street with clods of earth to shouts of "hurrah." At last she decided to leave Meshkova. With her husband's approval she received a passport and set off, first to the city of Orel and then to Odessa.[25]

In all of these examples the obvious function of *charivaris* was to shame thieves so that they would not steal from fellow villagers again. With its wealth of symbolism and ritual, public humiliation of a wrongdoer brought both crime and criminal before the offended community for judgment, and it was the community that oversaw conformity to established rules, thereby asserting the primacy of its authority. At the level of symbolic discourse, the *charivari* held out a threat of greater sanction, for it acted as a ritualized, though temporary, expulsion of an offender from the community and reminded all villagers—not only the thief—that expulsion could be permanent if someone repeated his or her crime or perpetrated a more serious infraction. Petty thieves were allowed to return to the collective fold only after publicly acknowledging their guilt and begging the community's forgiveness. Hence the equally symbolic payment in vodka which villagers demanded at the conclusion of a *charivari*. In "treating" the community to drinks, a thief won forgiveness and, more important, readmittance.

Beyond their immediate purpose of discipline, then, *charivaris* were a constituent element of village culture and an important means of social regulation. They played a significant role in governing behavior, regulating daily life, and ordering conduct "in a highly visible and comprehensive way." In this respect the *charivari* was only one of the tools in a village culture's arsenal of regulatory customs and rituals.[26] *Charivaris* also helped to preserve local solidarity by preventing the taking of sides in a dispute and a subsequent development of open feuding, which would otherwise disrupt activities and social relations crucial to the peasant economy. The punishment thus acted to soothe ill feelings and hostilities by involving an entire village, often with the elder's authorization and active participation.

In the majority of recorded cases peasants first brought a thief before the local assembly for sentencing, though eight to ten assembly members together with an elder or a township headman were deemed sufficient to reach a decision.[27] It is here, in fact, with the villagers' use of their assembly as a judicial organ, that we find the basis of the commune's exclusive right in the moral control of its members referred to earlier by Skorobogatyi. The assembly's decision legitimated a *charivari* in the eyes of all villagers and made revenge on the victim's part unlikely, because to seek retribution against the participants was tantamount to challenging the authority of the commune itself. The escalation of punishment during a *vozhdenie* resulted from just such a challenge. Similarly, escalation occurred when a demand for "payment" in vodka went unmet and the offender thereby refused to reach reconciliation with the community.[28]

Charivaris directed against persons other than thieves do not fit so neatly into the conclusions drawn thus far. Many forms of *charivari* worked in a manner similar to the French *charivari* so often held up as a model for comparison—to maintain community norms of morality and to exert community control over sexual behavior and conjugal relations. To give one example, Evgenii Iakushkin reported in 1875 that if a bride in Olonets province had not preserved her virginity until marriage, villagers would stick a peg over her door, hang a horse collar on it, and lead both her and her mother under it.[29] Adulteresses, too, might be subjected to *charivaris*. Such events included all the common elements of *charivari*: leading offenders through the village, public derision, humiliation, and paramusic.[30] Yet in some cases of adultery, the element of violence was used even when a victim offered no resistance; the process of escalation did not function because violence seems to have been inherent to this type of *charivari*. Thus a woman named Oksana Vereshchikha was suspected by peasants in her village of Poznanka (Volynia province) of carrying on an illicit affair with the township clerk. For this they stripped her naked, placed her in irons, and tied her to a post, where she stayed all night. In the morning the villagers returned and ordered her to buy them a pail of vodka, even though they had already pawned her kerchief and sheepskin jacket for one pail on the previous day. Because she had no money, a *charivari* was organized with "musicians" marching in front, followed by Vereshchikha, the elder, and the villagers. This was a particularly creative procession in which a garland of straw and burdocks was placed on the victim's head, and she was forced to dance before the crowd. They led her seven times along the street, beating her with fists and flogging her with the birch, all the while passing vodka around. At last they took her home, beat her again, and let her go.[31]

Charivaris of adulteresses or of housewives who somehow had failed in their domestic duties reveal the ability of communities "to compel individual family members to follow collective rules," as well as the public control to which "the deviant relations of husband and wife are subject."[32] As with cases of theft, collective responsibility and supervision constituted the basis of *charivaris*. Yet in the Russian village, communal authority was less concerned with punishing adultery than with punishing theft; adultery involved a different set of property and power relations that rested on the generally accepted position of male domination and the husband's customary authority to punish his wife with almost complete impunity. Neighbors rarely intervened to quell domestic violence between husband and wife.[33] Thus few *charivaris* were directed against adulteresses by Great Russian peasants because villagers usually left it to a husband to mete out appropriate punishment. The expectation of corporal punishment, in turn, may account for the use of violence in those instances when villagers did subject an adulterous woman to *charivari*, for here the community symbolically took on the role of offended spouse and punished as custom dictated. Though signs of change can be found in some areas, the persistence of such punishments helps to explain the relative scarcity of incidents in which adulteresses were victims of *charivaris*. Marital violence was especially likely to occur when a wife had committed adultery or left her husband; both deeds could disrupt the household economy and bring a loss of honor to the husband.[34]

Evidence from township courts shows that women tried to escape domestic violence or to seek justice through formal litigation. Yet peasant judges ruled in a woman's favor primarily when they found no justification for a beating, or when they deemed that the punishment had been overly cruel.[35] In cases of adultery or "abandonment," however, litigation had little chance of success; the husband was within his rights to punish his wife as he saw fit. Community leaders sometimes intervened to support the husband and to bring matters to a close. Thus in the early 1880s, a justice of the peace from one northern province heard the following complaint, lodged with the district constable by a woman named Ferapontova:

> I complained to the township court that my husband beat me, but the court did not resolve the case according to the law; instead, the village elder gathered some people together, came to the home ... where I was staying, and amidst a din and shouts they seized me, and ordered my husband to tie my hands with a saddle strap, which is just what he did. Then I was pushed out of the house and, while I was tied up, he thrashed me down the entire street and up to our house, and ... he dragged me inside and there, where people had already gathered, threw me on the floor ... and, though he didn't beat me further, he mocked me in all kinds of ways, cursing with every possible word. I implore you to carry out an investigation quickly, otherwise I will have to endure still more torture from my husband. Is it possible that they can order people to be tortured and mocked? Save me, for the sake of God, I haven't the strength to bear this torture.[36]

Russian court records are replete with similar stories of women being sent back to their husbands, who would beat them again for complaining to the authorities. When adulterous behavior led to neglect of the household economy and threatened the village with the possibility of a greater tax burden, a community might intervene to punish the guilty couple, often using the courts to do so. But township courts generally declined to hear other cases of adultery because they did not recognize this crime to be under their jurisdiction.[37] Rather, the husband was expected to reassert his authority and display his ability to control and master a recalcitrant wife.

The element of public supervision remained active in many instances, however, and therein lay a resemblance to *charivaris*. In order to distinguish between a *charivari* and the punishment of adulterous or disobedient wives, we need to note the absence of ritualized processions, symbolic expulsion, and the purchase of vodka for reconciliation. Most important, the infliction of punishment was reserved for the husband. When Anna Akulicheva stole a piece of cloth, villagers organized a *charivari*; but when she resisted their collective discipline and thereby insulted the community, it was her husband whom they ordered to flog her. So, too, with Ferapontova, whose husband tied her up and dragged her home while beating her, with no assistance from the elder or the boisterous crowd of supporters accompanying him.

These punishments functioned as explicit, often public acts of repression directed at women whose behavior threatened the authority or honor of their spouse, as well as important cultural norms of the village. They served to define the very boundaries of male authority and to reproduce relations of domination and subordination within rural society.

Russian *charivaris*, then, differed in important respects from those in many countries of Western Europe. Great Russian peasants used rituals of public shaming far more to punish theft than sexual and conjugal misconduct, perhaps because of the increased significance of property relations in the postemancipation period and an attendant weakening of the primacy of kinship. When villagers did punish sexual misconduct, their attention focused primarily, apart from unmarried girls, on adulteresses whose husbands were absent or, in the community's view, required assistance in controlling their wives. Finally, the Russian *charivari* sought to bring offenders back into the community rather than drive them out altogether, using the symbolic threat of expulsion together with the forced purchase of vodka (i.e., symbolic reconciliation) as its main instruments for reestablishing normal intravillage relations. This fact helps to distinguish the *charivari* from other types of *samosud*, in which ritual was largely absent, violence was prominent, and expulsion constituted the overriding objective. It is to these manifestations of *samosud* that we now turn.

Samosud *and Property Crime*

A second form of summary justice that clarifies the peasants' distinction between *charivari* and *samosud* brings us back to property crime, though this time to crime of a serious rather than a petty nature. Such acts were especially likely to meet with harsh penalties if the criminal was an outsider or had repeatedly committed theft in a given locality. Popular retribution involved beatings, myriad gruesome and often lethal tortures, and outright murder. These acts were almost always carried out by a crowd but lacked the organized, ritual character of *charivari*. Although an elder might direct the violence, meetings of the village assembly were not necessary before punishing a criminal.

Peasant reprisals could be merciless, especially if their aim was to rid the community of the criminal once and for all. In one part of the Mid-Volga region, for instance, a gang of six peasants had long caused trouble among their fellow villagers by stealing property and money, but attempts by the local population to catch the thieves met with no success. When the gang turned to highway robbery, villagers grew particularly enraged and selected three men to kill them, which they finally did. One thief in Kazan province was beaten savagely and then, before a large crowd on a riverbank, he was killed by the village elder and buried in the sand.[38] Elsewhere a peasant named Vasilii Andronov had been exiled to Siberia by communal decree from his village of Grigorev, Samara province. In 1872 Andronov escaped and returned to Grigorev seeking revenge. Once there he committed theft and arson and threatened murder. On December 3 the peasants summoned their assembly and decided to end the matter by doing away with him. "At dusk the entire assembly, led by the village elder, surrounded the house where Andronov was hiding. He was caught and killed."[39]

Here we have cases of straightforward, premeditated, collective murder by a community. Yet summary justice also included ingenious tortures, all described in great detail by the urban press, popular writers, and scholars. In Vetluzhskii district of Kostroma province, according to one report, "this is what they do with thieves: they drive the handle of a whip into his rectum and shake up everything there. After this the peasant weakens and dies."[40] Variations of this punishment could be found in other areas as well, where a jagged stick might be used so that it could not be removed. Some thieves and arsonists had nails driven into their heads or wooden pins behind the fingernails; others were stripped naked in winter and drenched with cold water until they died.[41]

Horse thieves inspired the greatest fear and hatred in the Russian countryside. They usually operated in gangs, sometimes composed of several hundred members who formed networks or "societies," dividing a territory among themselves to carry out their trade. With organizations stretching into several provinces and controlling many officers of the rural police force, horse thieves worked with little fear of capture, wielding great power among the populace. Villagers knew that revenge was likely to follow if they reported the thieves' activities in their locality.[42] Yet for peasants a horse represented the most valuable piece of property, without which farming would be impossible, as countless sayings attest: "Without a horse you're not a ploughman"; "Without a horse you're another's worker"; or "A peasant without a horse is like a house without a ceiling."[43] Thus villagers encountering horse thieves confronted a situation in which they were prey to a parasitic gang that stole their major means of subsistence, and all too often the peasants could take no measures to prevent this loss.

When a horse thief did fall into their hands, peasants let loose an elemental fury with often deadly results. Ivan Stepanov, for example, was a well-known thief in one of Russia's central provinces. As a fellow villager later told the court investigator, hardly a person in the village had not suffered some loss from Ivan's trade. He had been publicly whipped on numerous occasions, and the last time he was caught the village assembly warned him that if he stole again, he would be exiled to Siberia. Many peasants shouted in protest that it was not worth it to spend community funds to send him away; it would be far easier just to kill him. After this Stepanov disappeared for eight months; rumors circulated that he had taken up work as a horse thief in another locality and had even sneaked into town several times to bring his wife some money. Following one of these nocturnal visits, Stepanov was leaving the village early in the morning when he spied a foal in Dmitrii Petrov's meadow, jumped onto the horse, and rode it into the nearby forest. Unfortunately for him, Stepanov was caught by a group of peasants who grabbed him and brought him back to the village, where a search had already begun for the foal. On learning of the thief's capture, a crowd gathered and started beating Stepanov. "They beat him for a long time, and Dmitrii Petrov beat him most of all. When Stepanov already lay motionless, Dmitrii cruelly kicked him in the back and sides. Seeing that he was dead, the assembly came together to discuss the matter. Petrov, a well-to-do farmer, begged them not to ruin him by turning him in, promising to help Stepanov's widow for the rest of his life. Because the murdered man was hated by all as a thief, whereas Petrov was a young man and a good worker, the assembly took pity on him. They asked the widow, who agreed to the deal, and the assembly voted unanimously to conceal the murder from officials."[44]

Peasants reserved their worst punishments for horse thieves, who, if caught, were castrated or beaten in the groin until they died, had stakes driven into the throat or chest, were branded with hot irons, and had their eyes put out. Two punishments appear to have been particularly widespread. In one peasants first nailed a pully high onto a gatepost. Then the thief, with his hands and feet tied together, was raised into the air by a rope running through the pully. When he hung at a sufficient height, they released the rope. "He falls to the ground, striking the lower part of his back in a terrible way. This is repeated many times in succession, and each time the snap of the poor devil's vertebrae can be heard." The punishment might continue long after he had died.[45] Another torture consisted of stripping a thief and wrapping his torso with a wet sack. A plank was then placed on his stomach and peasants beat on it with whatever they could find—hammers, logs, or stones—"gradually destroying the unfortunate's insides." The utility of such a punishment was that it left no external signs, so whoever found the abandoned body would suspect no crime. With the introduction of coroners as part of the court investigator's office in the late nineteenth century, however, the practice became far less foolproof.[46]

Peasants treated horse thieves with such severity because of the real economic threat they posed to individual farmers and to the community as a whole. To steal a horse was to take away someone's ability to farm, forcing him to rent a draft animal or, worse, to rent out his labor. Without a horse a peasant would also be hard-pressed to pay taxes, and this was a serious concern for the commune. With no police protection to speak of, villagers were forced to take their own countermeasures to ensure that a thief, when caught, was rendered incapable of stealing again.[47]

Given the availability of courts for punishing these crimes, why did peasants continue to employ *samosud* knowing that, if discovered, they too could be punished? One reason was their conviction that the official courts did not punish severely enough. Even in those instances when villagers turned a criminal over to the authorities, they first inflicted their own penalty. Horse thieves and arsonists might be sentenced to several years of incarceration or exile, but eventually they regained their freedom and often took up their old trade. None knew this better than villagers who had to deal with the criminals again, especially if they returned seeking revenge, and a few years in prison did not seem a just punishment. Furthermore, peasants could never be certain the thief would be punished. The overburdened, understaffed, and inefficient rural police, even if honest, were no match for professional thieves working in large groups and living secretly in prosperous, well-protected settlements. Peasants also mistrusted the official courts and attempts by outsiders to meddle in local affairs, feeling that they best knew how to treat criminals who threatened their community. They showed particular reluctance to turn a fellow villager over to an alien authority, for as one saying went, "He's *our* criminal and it's up to us to punish him."[48]

Witchcraft

Russian peasants also had ways of dealing with persons whose magical powers endangered the health and welfare of community members, crops, and livestock (recall Agrafena Ignatieva!). Belief in sorcery and maleficent spells remained an active element of peasant culture throughout the period, and villagers frequently utilized practitioners of magical or healing arts for many purposes. But when some disaster such as plague, epidemic, or crop failure befell the community, blame might be placed on the very people whose powers previously had appeared beneficial. Somehow, it was believed, they had been offended and were seeking revenge on the entire village or certain of its members. It proved difficult to accuse these people in court, for official law no longer recognized witchcraft as a criminal offense and often punished the complainants themselves while the sorcerer went free.[49] As with horse theft, then, villagers confronted with maleficent spells felt that they were unprotected by state law and had to take matters into their own hands. When the "culprit" was identified, peasants meted out punishment of similar brutality to that suffered by horse thieves, and their justice often resulted in the murder of the accused.[50]

The link between peasant culture and *samosud* appears most dramatically in instances of popular reprisal against suspected practitioners of magic. *Samosud* of sorcerers and witches could not be written off as an aberration as long as epidemics and other natural phenomena were explained within a framework of supernatural causation, and the ease with which devious charlatans and criminals exploited peasant beliefs merely confirms that such a mode of explanation continued to operate in the countryside throughout the late nineteenth century.[51] Cases I have examined conform to the general, Western pattern of witchcraft accusations in which the main victims were impoverished elderly persons, itinerants, and the socially isolated. Despite peasants' traditional generosity toward wanderers and beggars, when such a person depended on others in the community for daily subsistence, she or he might come to be seen as a burden and, under the proper circumstances (such as an outbreak of disease), could easily become the target of hostility. Other cases might arise from a grudge held by one villager against the "witch." Having little or no say in community affairs because of their economic (and, hence, social) position, these people were particularly vulnerable to any accusation—a fact well known to neighbors and other villagers, who may have used it to their advantage.[52]

None of this is to say that accusations of witchcraft were only pretexts for settling preexisting conflicts in the village. Persons who accused a "witch" may have known the charge was false. Still, despite such incidents, most peasants who leveled witchcraft accusations, and those who punished the accused, were directed by their belief in the supernatural. Evidence of the widespread persistence of such belief is far too convincing for us to conclude otherwise.

It is all too easy to attribute the brutality of such punishments to the peasants' lack of "culture" or "legal consciousness" and to overlook the interaction of peasant and elite cultures that was involved. Earlier criminal codes provided for severe punishment, mutilation, or execution of horse thieves (as well as other criminals), and these punishments were carried out in public settings. Even more important was the often brutal punishment of serfs on gentry estates, which certainly contributed to the peasants' concepts and practice of justice in the village (though this influence must have worked in both directions). Official codes such as that of 1839 made corporal punishment one of the few penalties that peasant courts could impose in practice. If not directly modeled on official and gentry treatment of offenders, the punishments employed by peasants had developed as a complex mixture of official and popular forms of retribution.[53]

In the three areas discussed in this article *samosud* was a response to threats against the community or challenges to village norms and authority. It was not "lawless violence," as outsiders claimed, but action aimed at suppressing particular forms of behavior and criminal activity that could disrupt social relations or seriously harm the village economy. With little protection against danger other than that offered by their own local rules and institutions, peasants responded with the weapons available to them: *charivaris*, public beatings, ostracism, and murder.

These weapons, however, differed in both form and purpose. Directed against village members, the *charivari* employed an array of symbols and rituals designed to reconcile criminal and community and to restore peaceful relations among villagers. Only if reconciliation was rejected did peasants resort to harsher measures, for in such cases the offender became an outsider by spurning the community itself. Violent *samosud*, in contrast, focused on outsiders—defined either as nonmembers of the community or those who, through the harm caused by their crime or because of their social isolation, removed themselves from the community, thus the absence of ritual "processions" with their symbolic expulsion and reconciliation. Outsiders, by definition, could not be brought into the community except through bonds of marriage or kinship, and when they threatened the well-being of the village, mechanisms of reconciliation did not function. The purpose of punishments used against them, therefore, was to ensure that they would pose no further threat.

Samosud also forced peasants to defend their juridical beliefs and practices before the dominant culturé. Educated Russia viewed such acts not only as violations of the criminal code but as proof of the ignorance and low level of civilization in which the rural population was immersed. Villagers rejected official law on this matter, as they did on many issues that touched their lives, and continued to behave as necessity dictated, resorting to *charivaris* or violence when necessary and accepting the risks accompanying their collective actions. Peasants were clearly aware that state law forbade *samosud* because they frequently attempted to conceal the results of their popular justice, and probably succeeded more often than we would imagine. Yet their views of justice did not draw the same delimitations as official law with regard to which crimes they could and could not punish.[54] Infractions punished by *vozhdeniia*, for example, concerned the community alone, and outsiders had no business meddling in such affairs regardless of what their law might forbid. Similarly, official courts did not punish crimes such as horse theft as severely as peasants believed they should; and in cases of witchcraft the state had ceased to regard this serious problem (as villagers saw it) to be a crime. Official law punished crimes according to an entirely different set of criteria from those used by the peasantry—criteria that often took little account of local needs and concerns; and participants in the murder of a horse thief or a witch may have found no alternative to their own methods of justice.

Peasant juridical beliefs, like *samosud* itself, were most concerned with protecting the community from disruptive and harmful forces. Their juridical practices thus developed as a body of ideas incorporating norms of behavior, rules, and principles that could best serve to maintain and preserve the community. Through the continual assertion of its principles in juridical practice, the rural community asserted and reproduced not only its worldview but also the social, economic, sexual, and cultural relations by which this very community took on meaning.[55] Although certain types of interaction with the dominant culture could be incorporated, transformed, or at least made manageable by the village population, other efforts to force changes on peasant views of law, crime, or justice threatened to disrupt basic mechanisms through which the reproduction of the community took place. *Samosud* was one such mechanism, and efforts to eradicate the practice highlights the larger clash between peasant and official culture. When the community's ability to preserve and reproduce itself appeared threatened by government laws or regulations, peasants resisted, rejected, or simply ignored them. No such reaction was seen when the state tampered with the township court, for its reform did not impinge on villagers' lives in significant ways. The survival of *samosud* well into the Soviet period should be viewed not merely as an indication of the tenacity of Russian peasant culture in an era of major socioeconomic change but as the continued viability of an important, local, and spontaneously generated institution designed to regulate and protect village society.

Notes

1. L. Vesin, "Narodnyi samosud nad koldunami. (K istorii narodnykh obychaev)," *Severnyi vestnik*, no. 9 (September 1892): 64–66.

2.   See A. A. Levenstim, *Sueverie i ugolovnoe pravo* (St. Petersburg, 1899), 39.

3.   See, for example, A. N. Trainin, "Prestupnost goroda i derevni v Rossii," *Russkaia mysl*, no. 7 (June 1909): 20–21, 23. Data can be found in Ministerstvo Iustitsii, *Svod statisticheskikh svedenii po delam ugolovnym* (St. Petersburg, 1872–1914), sec. 2.

4.   Vladimir Dal, *Tolkovyi slovar zhivago velikorusskago iazyka* (St. Petersburg and Moscow, 1882), 4: 135.

5.   V. V. Tenishev, *Pravosudie v russkom krestianskom bytu* (Briansk, 1907), 33–35; idem, "Obshchie nachala ugolovnago prava v ponimanii russkogo krestian," *Zhurnal Ministerstva Iustitsii*, no. 7 (September 1909): 125–27, 135, 138–39.

6.   Apart from accounts in newspapers and legal journals, the major sources are the *Trudy komissii po preobrazovaniiu volostnykh sudov*, 7 vols. (St. Petersburg, 1873–74); and materials gathered by the amateur ethnographer Prince V. N. Tenishev on peasant life in central Russia, now held in the State Museum of Ethnography in Leningrad. His program was published as *Programma etnograficheskikh svedenii o krestianakh Tsentralnoi Rossii* (Smolensk, 1897). Tenishev's son published several works based on this material. See V. V. Tenishev, *Pravosudie*; idem, "Obshchie nachala"; and *Administrativnoe polozhenie russkogo krestianina* (St. Petersburg, 1908).

7.   See, for example, A. L. Saatchian, *Svod zakonov ugolovnykh* (St. Petersburg, 1911).

8.   P. S. Efimenko, *Sbornik narodnykh iuridicheskikh obychaev Arkhangelskoi gubernii.* (Trudy Arkhangelskago gubernskago statisticheskago komiteta za 1867–1868 g., fasc. 3) (Arkhangelsk, 1869), 277–78; and E. Kartsev, "Selskoe pravosudie. Iz zhizni russkoi derevni," *Vestnik Evropy*, January 1882: 333. See also Skaldin, *V zakholusti i v stolitse* (St. Petersburg, 1870), 144–45; and Petr Skorobogatyi, "Ustroistvo krestianskikh sudov," *Iuridicheskii vestnik*, no. 6 (June 1880): 309–46.

9.   Tenishev, *Pravosudie*, 33.

10.   Tenishev, "Obshchie nachala," 138–39; Efimenko, *Sbornik narodnykh iuridicheskikh obychaev*, 227; E. I. Iakushkin, *Obychnoe pravo. Materialy dlia bibliografii obychnogo prava* (Iaroslavl, 1875), 1: xxxviii–xxix; and Skorobogatyi, "Ustroistvo," 343–45.

11.   M. F. Zamengof, "Gorod i derevnia v prestupnosti," *Zhurnal ugolovnogo prava i protsessa*, no. 1 (1913): 79; M. N. Gernet, "Statistiika gorodskoi i selskoi prestupnosti," *Problemy prestupnosti*, no. 2 (1927): 15–24. Stephen P. Frank, "Cultural Conflict and Criminality in Rural Russia, 1861–1900" (Ph.D. diss., Brown University, 1987), chaps. 3–4; and Peter Czap, Jr., "Peasant Class Courts and Peasant Customary Justice in Russia, 1861–1912," *Journal of Social History* 1, no. 2 (Winter 1967): 158–59.

12.   Skorobogatyi, "Ustroistvo," 343.

13.   See, for example, Tenishev, *Pravosudie*, 34–35; idem, "Obshchie nachala," 127, 138–39.

14.   A. Kistiakovskii, "Volostnye sudy, ikh istoriia, nastoiashchaia ikh praktika i nastoiashchee ikh polozhenie," in *Trudy etnografichesko-statisticheskoi ekspeditsii v zapadno-russkii krai*, ed., P. P. Chubinskii, (St. Petersburg, 1872), 6: 18–19; and Edward Shorter, *The Making of the Modern Family* (New York, 1975), 218, 224.

15.   Tenishev, "Obshchie nachala," 134; Iakushkin, *Obychnoe pravo*, xxxviii–xxxix; and Skorobogatyi, "Ustroistvo," 344. Compare European descriptions in E. P. Thompson, "Rough Music: le charivari anglais," *Annales E.S.C.*, (March-April 1972): 285–312; Jacques Le Goff and Jean Claude Schmitt, eds., *Le Charivari* (Paris, 1981); and Martine Segalen, *Love and Power in the Peasant Family* (Chicago, 1983), 43–47.

16.   E. P. Thompson, "Folklore, Anthropology, and Social History," *Indian Historical Review* 3, no. 2 (1977): 259.

17. Segalen, *Love and Power*, 43–49; Shorter, *Modern Family*, 218–27; Thompson, "Rough Music," 297; and Eugene Weber, *Peasants into Frenchmen* (Stanford, 1976), 402–3.

18. E. T. Solovev, "Prestupleniia i nakazaniia po poniatiiam krestian Povolzhia," in Russkoe Geograficheskoe Obshchestvo, Otd. etnografii, *Zapiski Russkogo geograficheskogo obshchestva po otdeleniiu etnografii*, vol. 18, fasc. 1: *Sbornik narodnykh iuridicheskii obychaev*, vol. 2, ed. S. V. Pakhman (St. Petersburg, 1900), 227, 286 (hereafter cited as Pakhman, *Sbornik*).

19. S. V. Pakhman, "Ocherk narodnykh iuridicheskikh obychaev Smolenskoi gubernii," in Pakhman, *Sbornik*, 93.

20. Tenishev, *Pravosudie*, 44.

21. A. F. Brandt, "Iuridicheskie obychai krestian Mogilevskoi gubernii," in Pakhman, *Sbornik*, 116; Skorobogatyi, "Ustroistvo," 343; and Iakushkin, *Obychnoe pravo*, xxxviii.

22. Tenishev, "Obshchie nachala," 135.

23. Iakushkin, *Obychnoe pravo*, xxxviii–xxxix.

24. Tenishev, *Pravosudie*, 39–40. See also Iakushkin, *Obychnoe pravo*, xxxix.

25. Tenishev, *Pravosudie*, 41–43.

26. On the ordering and regulation of conduct within a "folkloric culture," see Michael R. Marrus, "Folklore as an Ethnographic Source: A 'Mise au Point,'" in *The Wolf and the Lamb: Popular Culture in France from the Old Regime to the Twentieth Century*, ed. Jacques Beauroy et al. (Saratoga, CA, 1976), 115–18; and Jan Vansina, *Oral Tradition as History* (Madison, 1985), 94–136.

27. Solovev, "Prestupleniia i nakazaniia," 280–81.

28. Compare here the striking similarity with rituals of Christmas caroling (*koliadki*), in which reprisals of various kinds were meted out to those who did not "pay" the singers with coin or food. See Frank, "Cultural Conflict and Criminality," 86–89.

29. Iakushkin, *Obychnoe pravo*, xxxxi. See also P. A. Dilaktorskii, "Sviatochnye shalosti v Pelshemskoi volosti Kadnikovskogo uezda," *Etnograficheskoe obozrenie* 10, no. 4 (1898): 134.

30. For examples, see Skorobogatyi, "Ustroistvo," 344; Efimenko, *Sbornik*, 277; and Iakushkin, *Obychnoe pravo*, xxxix–xxxx.

31. Iakushkin, *Obychnoe pravo*, xxxx.

32. Shorter, *Modern Family*, 218, 227. See also Segalen, *Love and Power*, 44, 46; and Shorter, "The 'Veillée' and the Great Transformation," in Beauroy et al., eds., *The Wolf and the Lamb*, 127–40.

33. Pakhman, "Ocherk," 95–96.

34. Equally important, such acts also challenged traditional power relations in the community. On the problem of defining and delimiting female and male spheres of power, see Jill Dubisch, ed., *Gender and Power in Rural Greece* (Princeton, 1986), 12–26.

35. Ilia Shrag, "Krestianskie sudy Vladimirskoi i Moskovskoi gubernii," *Iuridicheskii vestnik*, nos. 7/8 (1877): 74–77.

36. Ia. Ludmer, "Babi stony. (Iz zametok mirovago sudi)," *Iuridicheskii vestnik*, no. 12 (1884): 670.

37. Shrag, "Krestianskie sudy," 77; and A. A. Titov, *Iuridicheskie obychai sela Nikola-Perevoz, Sulostskoi volosti, Rostovskogo uezda* (Iaroslavl, 1888), 101. Adultery was tolerated in cases of women whose husbands were away for long periods, either in the army or working as migrant laborers. See Solovev, "Prestupleniia i nakazaniia," 291–92.

38. Solovev, "Prestupleniia i nakazaniia," 282.

39. Iakushkin, *Obychnoe pravo*, xxx; and Tenishev, *Pravosudie*, 47. See also "Narodnyi samosud," *Novosti*, no. 266 (1879); and F. Shch—n., "Narodnyi samosud i raspravy," *Nedelia*, no. 23 (1879): 781–87.

40. Tenishev, *Pravosudie*, 47.

41. Cited in Valery Chalidze, *Criminal Russia* (New York, 1977), 12–13. See also Solovev, "Prestupleniia," 281.

42. G. N. Breitman, *Prestupnyi mir: ocherki iz byta professionalnykh prestupnikov* (Kiev, 1901), chap. 9. Also useful are F. Shch—n., "Organizatsiia konokradov i skotokradov v Kubanskoi oblasti," *Nedelia*, no. 26 (1879): 627–46; L. Vesin, "Konokradstvo, ego organizatsiia i sposoby borby s nim naseleniia," *Trudy Imperatorskago volnago ekonomicheskago obshchestva* 1, no. 3 (1885): 350–68; and Tenishev, *Pravosudie*, 47–54.

43. A. S. Ermolov, *Narodnaia selskokhoziaistvenaia mudrost v poslovitsakh, pogovorkakh i primetakh*, vol. 3, *Zhivotnyi mir v vozzreniiakh naroda* (St. Petersburg, 1905).

44. M. F. Chulitskii, "Tolpa. (Iz vospominanii byvshego sudebnogo deiatelia)," *Istoricheskii vestnik*, 110, no. 12 (1907): 294–95. See also Shch—n., "Narodnyi samosud," passim; and *Saratovskii listok*, no. 186 (September 1, 1906): 3.

45. Breitman, *Prestupnyi mir*, 129.

46. Ibid., 129–30; Chulitskii, "Tolpa," 292.

47. See Breitman, *Prestupnyi mir*, 122; and D. S. Fleksor, *Okhrana selskokhoziaistvennoi sobstvennosti* (St. Petersburg, 1904), 193–94.

48. Breitman, *Prestupnyi mir*, 118; Pakhman, "Ocherk," 93; Solovev, "Prestupleniia," 287–89; Shch—n., "Narodnyi samosud," 786; and Brandt, "Iuridicheskie obychai krestian Mogilevskoi gubernii," 116.

49. See Vesin, "Narodnyi samosud nad koldunami," 61–63. Township courts were the only exceptions, for they did treat witchcraft accusations seriously.

50. For examples, see A. Kirpichnikov, "Ocherki po mifologii XIX veka," *Etnograficheskoe obozrenie*, no. 4 (1894): 1–42; Vesin, "Narodnyi samosud," 66–69; Ludmer, "Babi stony," 658–59; *Novoe vremia*, no. 7116 (December 19/31, 1895); and A. A. Levenstim, *Sueverie i ugolovnoe pravo* (St. Petersburg, 1899), 36–37.

51. Indeed, Russell Zguta has suggested that at least in the Ukraine, the practice of swimming witches increased during the nineteenth century. Zguta's finding would confirm Keith Thomas's argument that an escalation in the number of witchcraft accusations indicates changing social and economic conditions—certainly a plausible explanation for nineteenth-century rural Russia, where population pressure and land shortage must have eroded traditional patterns of charity and support for impoverished members of the community. Russel Zguta, "The Ordeal by Water (Swimming of Witches) in the East Slavic World," *Slavic Review* 36, no. 2 (June 1977): 228. See also Keith Thomas, *Religion and the Decline of Magic* (New York, 1971), 535–69.

52. See Vesin, "Narodnyi samosud," 76–77; P. A. Tulub, "Sueverie i prestuplenie. (Iz vospominanii mirovogo sudi)," *Istoricheskii vestnik* 83, no. 3 (1901): 1084–87; and Levenstim, *Sueverie i ugolovnoe pravo*, 36.

53. See Efimenko, *Narodnye iuridicheskie obychai*, 278–79; M. N. Dukhovskoi, *Imushchestvennye prostupki po resheniiam volostnykh sudov* (Moscow, 1891), 41–43; D. N. Zhbankov and V. I. Iakovenko, *Telesnye nakazaniia v Rossii v nastoiashchee vremia* (Moscow, 1899), 165–67; and Richard Hellie, *Slavery in Russia, 1450–1725* (Chicago, 1982), 9–10.

54. See Frank, "Cultural Conflict and Criminality," chap. 4.

55. Including relations of domination and exploitation. For exemplary studies of the reproduction of social relations within the domain of culture, see Gerald M. Sider, *Culture and Class in Anthropology and History: A Newfoundland Illustration* (Cambridge, 1986).

8

Popular Religion in Twentieth-Century Russia

Moshe Lewin

Religion is a key component of the peasants' social and cultural world, an important factor that allowed them to survive and to retain their identity as well as to manifest enormous resilience and resistance to change whenever "change" looked menacing. The industrial and cultural impulses for change coming from the cities, still weak and accompanied as they were by insatiable demands for squeezing resources from the countryside, made change so costly to peasants that their resistance can be understood in more sympathetic and comprehensive terms than just by alluding to their being "benighted" (*temnye*).

Rural Religions

Russian peasants were always described as very "pious," a trait they manifested by frequent genuflections, crossing themselves, praying, prostrating themselves, fasting, confessing, and repenting. Asked who they were, they would say, "We are the Orthodox." They did not need to add, "We are Russians." Orthodoxy was the state religion, and until 1905, when the relevant legislation was changed, every Russian was considered Orthodox, and opting for a different religion was forbidden. Many did switch, of course, despite interdiction and persecution. Nevertheless, the statement "We are the Orthodox" is not to be taken lightly. Some authors (for example, Belinsky, Chekhov, Lenin) said that the Russian peasant was not really as pious as he was "superstitious." He was too practical to be truly and deeply religious. But many authors, including Dostoevsky and some of the later "god seekers," claimed the opposite: the peasant was deeply Christian. Pascal would add that they—or, more nearly, their popular Orthodoxy—actually represented Christianity par excellence, pure and undiluted, the epitome of Russian religiosity, more so than the official Orthodox creed. At the same time, the peasant was not "clerical" and not dependent on the church. Against it, Kravchinsky would argue that the peasant was not really Orthodox at all but rather pagan, or at best practicing a dual faith, a mixture of Christianity and paganism.[1] Such opposing views have persisted well into our times.

Sociologists and ethnographers taught that religious beliefs and systems are products of societies and of status groups (or social classes). If they are right, then we can assume a priori that official denominations never express reality in matters so complex. We are therefore allowed to hypothesize that as long as peasants live in conditions and an environment that set them apart from other social groups in society, they will certainly develop and stick to their own way of believing. The idea that they should fully share a religious system and outlook with the higher clergy and other upper layers of city dwellers can safely be discarded. The same applies equally to, say, Catholic Poland or Italy, certainly so in past centuries and more than probably still today. In fact all the great religions, eager as they have been to conquer popular allegiance, have had to conduct a protracted warfare against, as well as agree to compromise with, the old, pre-Christian beliefs of the masses, who were predominantly peasant. In the words of Max Weber, "Neither the prophet nor the priest can afford to reject all compromise with the traditional beliefs of the masses."[2] The same applies equally to the pre-Christian era, as well as our own, but no doubt to political systems too.

Considering the deep-seated specific traits of their society, mentality, and culture, city-made and state-imposed Christendom (at least in Russia in the tenth century) had somehow to be assimilated and become a peasant (*muzhik*) religion—otherwise it was bound to lose out in the countryside. Historically this was in fact the way it happened. The church adopted many of the pagan festivals, rites, and rituals and adapted them to its needs and symbols. All rural religions are deeply dependent on magic, and the church was particularly virulent in fighting this expression of heathendom. Yet at the same time the church itself introduced, though in its own form, some of the magic it so bitterly opposed. It did practice, often or occasionally, exorcism in order to compete with popular healers and quacks; it claimed credit for miracles in order to eliminate magicians; it persecuted witches for having sold their souls to Satan—thus admitting that Satan was active in everyday life and that witchcraft existed, though we know that much of this was officially disavowed from the eighteenth century on.

Be that as it may, the coexistence of the "miracle" (by saints) and magic (by witches and sorcerers) is an important component of popular religion, in our cultural area and elsewhere, and we can see here a continuation of the historical compromise, this time in the minds and imagination of the peasants themselves—even if the official church in our century would disagree.

This leads us to another preliminary assumption: the process of adaptation during the compromise certainly worked both ways. The church adapted itself and adopted popular customs in order to rule and to maintain its monopoly over the supernatural and the sacred as defined in its own terms. In turn, the rural world did its part from the other end. They accepted, selectively, the official new creed but chewed up and transformed many of its elements. The peasants also preserved many components from their own old religion and carried them down through the centuries into our time in a peculiar symbiosis with official Christendom. Thus like much else in their life—culture, popular law, social organization—it was a popular religion very much of their own making, a religion they have practiced even into the twentieth century.

The Christianity of the Muzhik

The majority of Russian peasants, well into the late 1930s, were Orthodox Christians and said so. On the whole the *muzhik* did believe in God and, probably even more, in Christ. Although he was never polled on this question, it is safe to say that deity and Christology were enmeshed in his mind, strongly seconded by the veneration—very special to the Orthodox creed—of Mary as a kind of supersaint. He accepted the sacraments and was a churchgoer—not for daily services on the whole but for the more important holidays, especially Christmas, Easter, and the Pentecost. He also fasted fervently, knew of life after death, and had some hope for salvation, though some claim that this aspect of his creed was not central to him. After all, if salvation depends on heaven, the salutary effects of a rain falling at the right time for crops to succeed could overshadow other blessings. He might have felt differently at the "supreme crisis," when facing death, but here too one expects reactions different from those of other social strata. Peasants also followed and probably were impressed by much of the ritual and liturgy. Altogether, they had a good deal in common with the church. There are, however, "buts," and many of them.

First, the peasant (except, to some extent, the sectarian, who is not our topic here) knew nothing of dogma; he could not explain many of the church's principles, assuming he ever heard of them, and—quite pertinently when dogma is mentioned—like most, he could not read. But when there are no constraints of dogma, much more freedom is left for the imagination and all kinds of deviations. The peasant shared with the church the veneration of icons. They were his Bible. He could not read, so he followed the biblical stories as depicted on the icons assembled on the iconostasis in the church. At the same time, the icon that was displayed in his hut in the place of honor—the "red" corner above the family table—was also his physical and symbolic link to his ancestors, from whom the icon was inherited, and a shield against adversities. The role of the icon in the peasant's mind is often debated. Some say that it is just a symbol, a Christian symbol; others that it is the real person of saint, not a symbol but a source of magical protection, pre-Christian in character.

The cults of the saints were also shared with the church. But here, too, a strongly accentuated adoption and adaptation—or, to put it plainly, ruralization—occurred. According to some researchers, many of those saints were local pagan deities appropriately "rebaptized." Perun, the god of lightning and thunder, became Elijah, also "responsible" for the same forces of nature. Volos became Saint Vlas. Many other local idols became saints. Saint Nicholas, for example, was both a national saint and a local namesake.

Many of the numerous saints (the Orthodox church has about three hundred of them), insistently and predictably were supposed to serve the special needs of a rural consistency, namely, the whole agricultural calendar. A saint patron existed for the most minute agricultural function and action: Vlas was responsible for cattle; Frol and Lavr for horses; Elijah for rain and thunder. Those were some of the national saints. Locally there were other patron saints, such as Peter Polukorn (fodder), Vasilii Kolesnik (wheeler), Irin Rassadnitsa (planter), Ermolai Zapriagalnik (harnessman); Muchenitsa (the martyr) Paraskeva was patron of flax and yarn and was called, appropriately, a woman's saint (*babia sviataia*). The list goes on and on.

Thus the peasant's Orthodoxy was a very special rural version of the official creed, as was the parish priest (*pop*), who came from the peasantry himself and, unlike the Catholic priest, was not very much respected. The wretchedness of the *pop* was proverbial and their drunkenness notorious. So was their greed, a direct result of their poverty and low level of education.

The peasant often despised the *pop* and bargained hard over the price of religious services, the main source of the priest's income. Peasants were not generous in either the sacred or the profane spheres. The priest was often an object of superstitious fears (it could be ominous to stumble upon him in the dark when he was not on duty), but he was welcome to the huts to secure different services and sacraments as well as to participate in processions around the household, with icons and incense, to protect cattle and the fields against parasites and epidemics.

The *pop*, who had no fixed salary, depended entirely on his flock. He also squeezed them, if he could, and the flock defended themselves as best they could. But all this did not necessarily diminish their attachment to their faith, even though such a priest could to be powerful enough to solve all the problems befalling a peasant community. The numerous saints did their share better, but they too (probably) had limited power, and it was to be expected that a vigorous and needy social class would look for more support elsewhere to cope with those aspects of life that were out of the church's competence.

Without as yet overstepping the limits of the official faith, the peasant, Pierre Pascal suggests, had at his disposal more than just the rural church as his religious forum. His own house, his *izba*—the focus of his life cycle, the basis of the productive and reproductive family unit—was heavily sacralized and served as the breeding ground for an elaborate mythology. Here was placed the icon, which elevated the hut to a minishrine, more potent than and probably of equal status with the road shrines often found at country crossroads. The main ceremonies that related to birth, marriage, and death took place in the hut, and here too was located the cult (or, shall we say, numerous remnants of the cult) of the ancestors, shared, of course, with the local cemetery. This aspect of peasant beliefs was shared only partly with the official church, which celebrated memorial days and otherwise remembered the dead (who, as a matter of Orthodox dogma, were all included in the church community). But the peasants went well beyond their common ground with the church: they preserved ceremonies and customs from time immemorial. Those were especially prominent in the traditional festivals, which were a real treasury of old pagan rites. Peasants left food for their dead parents after ceremonial meals, "invited" them to come and join them at their table, went to the cemeteries at Easter time to place triple kisses on ancestors' graves, offered them *bliny* (ritual pancakes), exchanged thoughts, and had chats with them at their graveside. The rural funeral, a solemn ceremony permeated with ancient customs and marked by the heartbreaking laments of relatives or of professional mourners, would normally end later in monumental feasts in the homes or at the cemeteries, with much heavy drinking for a better and fonder remembrance and to celebrate life.

We know how important the family is in the village. This key institution led all too often so precarious an existence that its survival and well-being needed all the support it could marshal. Ancestors, especially parents, certainly could be relied on as benevolent spirits. And their souls were never too far away from their huts, which they too, somehow, still needed very much. Thus the extended family was actually more extended than met the eye; it included past generations and a network of relations.

This, of course, was already beyond the pale of official teachings. But this "deviation" is only the beginning. Around the peasant hut much more was going on than the occasional visit of a defunct parent. In fact, there was a whole population there, in and around the hut, which no census ever counted, all belonging to the kingdom of "evil spirits" or "forces."

Rural Demonology

"The priest goes his way, the devil his own" is a common peasant saying. In the countryside the two worlds—the church and the demons—coexisted, each with its own sphere and rules. The peasant, actually believing in and dealing with both, operated between these two complicated and opposing poles of their sociomythical system. However, there was more than a simple duality in that religious world. Not just the church versus the Devil but also the church versus the peasant hut. The church provided (and accepted) the Devil, and the peasants, of course, accepted him and his cohorts as well. But the hut was an independent breeding ground of its own mythology, one that coincides only very partially with that of the church. In this peasant mythology there are about forty names for various devils and evil and not-so-evil spirits.

Again, not unlike the saints, these are divided into categories and functions dictated by the realities of rural life. Thus we find, first, the house and household spirits, who reside in the house as well as in the barns and other farm buildings. Among them are the house spirit and his spouse (probably), the farm spirit, the bathhouse spirit, and the one in the grain dryer.

Next are the spirits causing (and explaining) illnesses, such as the one who causes widespread female hysteria, called *klikushestvo*, and the spirits causing different forms of febrility.

Finally, there are the spirits from the fields and the natural environment. In the fields you find a female spirit "active," appearing mainly at midday and very vicious if she meets anyone. There is also a "specialized" devil of the fields. The forests are the domain of "wood spirits"; the rivers and lakes shelter the menacing water spirit.

On crossroads, especially in the forest, and many other places where they can meet one alone and at night, a variety of all-purpose devils engage in various forms of mischief, misleading people—especially drunks, of whom they are particularly fond. They also like women, and as they can transform themselves into almost anything, they come to the villages and visit all kinds of maidens, wives of soldiers, and widows. Many a pregnancy becomes explainable in this way, but so do ailments and especially mental illnesses. You had better put two pieces of wood in the form of a cross on your water receptacle and cross your mouth promptly after a yawn—they penetrate everywhere, given the chance.

Obviously these spirits are unseen, and yet so many peasants somehow meet them. The stories of such encounters are legion, not only in folklore but also in literature and theater, evoking awe and laughter simultaneously. Relations between the peasants and the mythical population, especially the *cherti*, are complicated. These devils are both joke and menace, but this paradox is only apparent. The peasant was reacting to something very familiar, something he believed in, was worried about, but also knew quite well. Devils can be communicated with, not only through spiritualism but in more direct ways. The Devil can be bribed; like most of us, he is not infallible; he can be placated, persuaded, even frightened off. There is a whole arsenal of means—Christian and magical—for chasing him away, and it is all available in amazing, practical detail, like recipes in a cookbook or a medical prescription: take such and such herbs, say a certain formula three times, put the cross on your back, and so on.

It is interesting that the Devil can be outsmarted. Toward a creature so powerful and so concrete the peasant must develop a sense of combat. The *muzhik* has a self-image like everybody else. He is not learned, but he can be smart. And only he (certainly not the other classes) can outsmart the Devil (as well as representatives of those other classes, all of whom are more powerful than he).

The "evil ones" are numerous. There are swarms of them. They have servants and families, tails and horns, and their behavior ranges from rather friendly to murderous, with the gamut of nuances in between. There is also an intermediary category on which we cannot now dwell, people whom devils or sorcerers have transformed into a wolf or other creature, the mythical Russian *oboroten*, who leads a tragic and frightening existence and is very dangerous.

There are special days in the year when devils are allowed to roam freely everywhere and are very angry. They prey on humans, snatch newborn babies (and substitute a *chertenok*) from mothers who happen to curse the baby when overtaken by pain.

The descriptions of this "population" are so concrete that the saying about the priest and the Devil becomes very clear to us, as is another version of the same saying, which uses the term "God" instead of "priest." Peasants, to my knowledge, believe in God but do not describe him. This means they don't even try to imagine him—they find enough material for their imagination elsewhere.

Considering the massive evidence of the vitality of belief in these various demons, it becomes obvious that the church never succeeded in uprooting this ancient layer of spirits or "lower demonology" (which are somehow related to ancient polytheisms) or in assimilating and thus legitimating them. Had it tried, it would have had to condone the widespread belief in the "evil eye," without which the peasant could not explain all kinds of everyday trouble. Telling him that this all resulted from his "sins" would probably be counterproductive.

"Outcast Souls"

The *zalozhnye*, or "outcast souls," are yet another interesting category of mythological creatures that bring us back to the souls of the ancestors. A serious study published in 1916 by D. K. Zelenin, an ethnographer and student of religion, showed that in popular belief the dead—or rather their souls—were divided into two categories: "ancestors" and those who died prematurely of unnatural causes. The latter included children who died before they were christened, people who drowned, and suicides (a particularly reprehensible act in the rural view). The "outcast souls" were supposedly not accepted by "mother earth"—that is, they would not, if buried normally, rot away and would damage crops. They were therefore not buried in the regular manner but "put away" into a crevice or swamp, or at least not in any decent burial places. The problem with these souls was that they would become "evil." That is, the "evil ones" or devils would take them over to serve as their slave, courtesan, or wife. Another term for these dead and dead souls (somehow body and soul is not clearly separated in the evidence peasants offer on these matters) is *mertvyaki* or *upyri*—ghastly corpses, as pernicious as vampires.

Thus far this category sounds rather sinister, and it is. These souls must remain in limbo around their unpleasant graves for as long as necessary to use up the balance of time between their premature demise and what would have been their normal time of death. What happened next is unclear. The peasants are not certain about this, and neither is the Orthodox church, which does not recognize the concept of purgatory but does accept life after death. Cases are mentioned of dead who were salvaged and returned, though rarely, to the living world. Some of these are prematurely deceased children plagued by the unwitting curses of their own mothers. They haunt their families, moan, and beg their mothers to save them. Something can perhaps be done if the demon has not yet taken full possession of them.

One special and complicated subcategory of "outcast souls" is worth singling out: women, old or young, who fall into this category of "irregularly" dead became *rusalki*—water nymphs who live in rivers and along shores. Although they evoke an image of mermaids and sirens, they are actually very Slavic, and there is a great deal of information about them. They are either young and extremely beautiful (mostly in southern Russia) or old and ugly. They walk around naked, of course, have large breasts (most sources agree), are very playful, like to dance and prance around, and use tree branches for seesawing. Their enchanting voices affect the passer almost fatally, and they enjoy playing with men by tickling them to death. They can do the same to women. On hearing their voices it is best not to respond. If one does stumble on them, it is prudent to draw a circle around oneself with one's cross and not move at all, because the angry water nymphs will crowd around the circle and throw stones at the irritant. To move in this situation could prove fatal. . . .

A special, very ancient festival called *rusalnitsa*, taking place around the Pentecost complex of holidays, is dedicated to accompanying the water nymphs back to their streams after time off on land. The name, incidentally, does not stem from *rusyi* (red or ginger) but from the Latin *rosalia*, the name of a Roman festival. The water nymph had red hair in the south but green (and green eyes) in the north of Russia. It is obvious that here was an outlet for peasant sexual fantasies, and one in which girls as well as boys were interested. That they could attract the attention of writers is also quite understandable, and Gogol can be quoted describing the enchanting creatures as the epitome of amorous temptation and feminine attraction. Some Russian ethnographers, too, writing about rural mythology, would inescapably append to their articles a verse by Pushkin in which water nymphs are prominently featured dangling on tree branches, their favorite pastime.

Magic and Sorcery

We have examined, as S. V. Maksimov put it in 1903, the Christian as well as the "evil" force. There remains, however, a third source of beliefs and mythological production: the "mysterious force" (*nevedomaia sila*). This included remnants of ancient cults based on veneration of the forces of nature (sun, water, wind, storm, and the earth) that were heavily present, together with remnants of fertility cults, in the rural festivals, especially in obviously pagan ones such as *maslenitsa* (Shrovetide or Carnival, falling in late winter or early spring) or Ivan Kupala (summer), as well as in official Christian festivals such as Easter. In all of them specialists discern amazingly well preserved vestiges of the ancient agricultural belief systems, with their Dionysian, orgiastic, phallic elements interposed with later Christian symbols and rites.

If the family dwelling and the village are so heavily populated and surrounded by mythical yet familiar creatures causing problems to crops, cattle, and humans (drought, famine, fires, illness—especially mental illness—and suicides), there is an urgent and obvious need to deal with them. Presumably the official church and the strictly Christian component of the creed did not satisfy all the demands of rural life and imagination. With so many spirits lurking everywhere trying to block the smooth flow of seasons, tampering with rainfall, interfering with the fertility of women and the soil, remedies could be found at the same source that begot the demons in the first place. Tilling, sowing, and hard labor alone were not enough. Magic was needed precisely in order to help the seasons flow unhindered, to ensure good health to men and cattle, and for all to breed abundantly and to escape the ravages of epidemics.

The use of magic was considered by Max Weber and others as the trait par excellence of rural religions. We have already seen how peasants adapted many Christian symbols and rites to this purpose, especially the icon, but also candles, processions, and holy water. In addition, they had at their disposal a great choice of their own prescriptions and of the ever-present divinations. All the many needs of a peasant household were taken care of by magic rites, formulas, potions, herbs, all helping to find the thief and recover the stolen goods, to ensure a successful birth (including that of domestic animals), to protect the newlywed (and everyone else) from the "evil eye," to preserve the family from ominous influences that a corpse in the house awaiting funeral could create. All the stages of the cycles of nature and of life required protection.

It was unthinkable that peasants could engage in such intense magical activity without "professional" help. They had no choice but to appeal, albeit very reluctantly and fearfully, to the sorcerer or the witch—fearsome, mean creatures who were the heirs to the ancient magicians and shamans. Only an evil eye cast by them could explain why a cow's udder suddenly dried out or why a young girl began to languish, and only another sorcerer could undo the mischief one of his kind had wrought.

The strength of the sorcerer was shown by his ability to operate magic, an ability one could possess only at a price. In order to acquire such powers they had to sell their souls to the Devil and thus become themselves part of the *nechist* (demonic world). And the price they paid was indeed terrible: protracted and painful agony before dying (described in great detail by numerous informers); becoming outcast souls after their death (and hence, no decent burial, with all the consequences this entailed); numerous outbursts of peasant wrath against the sorcerers (who would be crudely mobbed on such occasions; from the eighteenth century on, the church—and the state—forbade this as "an act of superstition" and hence it became criminally punishable).

But more often than attacking them, peasants used the sorcerer's and witch's services widely, as well as those of more benign alternatives—healers, fortunetellers, and diviners. Networks of such practitioners, competing to some extent with the church, were widespread in the rural world, which produced religious and semireligious figures of other types too. Out of the countryside came a plethora of "wanderers," saintly hermits and "elders," (who were sometimes acknowledged but often ignored by the church), and the very intriguing figure of the "God's fool," an interesting and picturesque personality of Russian national and religious life that became part of folklore, art, history, and belief. In addition, the world of the sects produced a plethora of "Jesuses" and "Marys" and all kinds of prophets and other religious leaders, all testifying to the significant fact that the religious life of the Russian peasantry was richer and more complex than is sometimes realized.

A Magico-Religious Amalgam?

The term "dual faith" may be misleading. Given the coexistence in the Russian rural religious universe of different subsystems, all equally interesting and most very ancient, one would do better to talk of a *system* of antipodes, not only pagan versus Christian but also church versus the peasant hut, miracle versus (or complemented by) magic, Orthodox versus Christian anti-Orthodox, and more. Influences from Asia, the Classical world, the Middle Ages, the modern world, old Slavonic creeds, and Manichaean and Cathar and other old heresies all converged in shaping this rural religion. The peasantry absorbed them and preserved them, chewed them up or "lost" them, sometimes only temporarily, for they always left traces in the popular cultural treasury, a living museum and a laboratory of cultural and religious synthesis and innovation. We remember the main "subsystems" described earlier: the Christian one, heavily "ruralized," as we have shown; the Orthodox and anti-Orthodox versions, some even anti-Christian; the elaborate demonology, the "evil spirits," in a specific conjunction with remnants of the cult of the ancestors, as well as the subcategory of the "outcast souls" and remnants of cults of fertility and other forces of nature, all put to good use through the working of either the miracle or the less saintly forms of magic.

Even if some of these components were rudimentary and already on the wane in our century, they were present, and whether in full force or on the wane, they contributed to the web of beliefs still in actual use. What remains unclear is whether we can talk here of a "religious system" or of coexisting and quite different structures and disjointed elements. Do we have here basically a Christian system (Orthodox) tinged with the unavoidable dose of "superstition"? Or perhaps a basically pagan creed with a Christian veneer?

The first proposition has many adherents, who sometimes offer an additional argument that the Orthodox church, more than the Catholic, is a popular religion in its own right. Many factors argue in favor of this interpretation: the "communality" (*sobornost*) of this church; the rural character of its parish clergy; the prevalence of liturgy over dogma in Orthodoxy; the preponderance (or, at least, equal standing) of the icon over written texts. Such students would ignore the rich demonology and relegate most of the non-Christian elements (we think they were more than "elements") to the realm of "superstition," a term that would evoke sharp criticisms from other scholars who would claim that if one uses it, one had better stop studying religion at all.

Provisionally, I would abstain from claiming to make an interpretation of the material at hand and would group the popular religions of the

Russian peasantry into three streams. First of these are the sects, which in the early 1920s had millions of adherents, and are here lumped in one "stream," though they exhibited a great variety of creeds, from Protestant of several denominations to the non-Christian "Sabbatarians." Second, the Christian Orthodox church in its ruralized version could be called a popular religion in its own right, and many peasants adhered to just this approach.

The third stream, the most widespread still in the early decades of this century, is the popular creed, which interests us here: a unified construct felt and practiced by the peasants as one system. Despite the seemingly conflicting polarities that analysis can discern, priest and the devil, church and hut, miracle and magic, the Holy Trinity and the multitude of spirits and demons were quite tightly knit in a cultural-religious synthesis expressing the age-old traditions and interests of a rural community and class. A changing but still distinct agricultural civilization (undestroyed as yet by industrial and urban development) was weaving its beliefs from a variety of often very ancient roots, deeply modified by Christianity but again remodified by peasant life and imagination.

We can thus call this religion "rural Christianity," which, not unlike rural Islam, is especially an amalgam of Christian symbolism welded onto a bedrock of an old agricultural civilization. The fact that this civilization could withstand crises and upheavals can be attributed not to one particular institution, such as the church (although it played its role), but to various factors inherent in the social reality of the village itself, with its powerful mechanisms of conflict resolution and solidarity, neighbor and family networks, which act as very efficient socializers, and the family itself, supported by its ancestors and by its household spirits, all trying hard to cope with, placate, and outsmart the legions of evil spirits swarming between the hut and the church.

Such an amalgam does create what some Russians call "the existential (*bitovaia*) religion," meaning one that emerges from and merges with the crucial functions of everyday life and helps to explain its longevity. I would add, to strengthen this last point, that peasant women, with their special role in and around the family household, were and continue to be the (sometimes sole) carrier and mainstay of this rural Christianity and ensure its vitality.

But the official church can in this context be dispensed with, and peasants can fall back on other resources when they find the church wanting or persecuted and when the churches are being closed. It is so with peasant societies in most spheres of life. When in crisis or under pressure, they can retreat into their own shell, opt out of the "larger society," ensconce themselves in their own "world" (*mir*), which has at its disposal a self-contained economy, a system of law, and a religion.

This potential of the traditional peasantry is always feared by rulers and intellectuals, and with good reason. The peasants can effect a retreat from the market economy through the "naturalization" of their needs; turn away from the official world of culture, of courts and tax assessors, and back to a more primitive stage. It could indeed be a catastrophic course, both the cause and result of some social cataclysm.

In such or similar circumstances, the home shrine, the magic, and the mythology are sufficient to preserve present religious integrity without, or against, the official church. At such times their own religion can offer what religions are supposed to offer: the spiritual resources to compensate for deficiencies of material life; solace and support in times of crisis and catastrophe when religious feelings are heightened in the effort of survival; the strength needed to cope with individual life cycle dramas. The supernatural forces available, sacred or evil or both, will come to play their role and supply additional symbolic resources when it is necessary to fight the state or the combined forces of church and state. Russian peasants did produce and use powerful mythical mobilizers when engaging in a contest with the state, and this left an indelible memory in the consciousness of every ruler of Russia. The obvious example is the revolt of the "Old Believers" (seventeenth century), who challenged the state and *its* church as manifestations of the Antichrist and the emperor as the Antichrist in person.

Notes

1.   Sergei Kravchinsky, *The Russian Peasantry: Their Agrarian Conditions, Life and Religion* (Westport, CT, 1977 [reprint of 1888 edition]).
2.   Reinhard Bendix, *Max Weber: An Intellectual Portrait* (London, 1966), 92.

9

Images and Ideas in Russian Peasant Art

Anthony Netting

A close look at Russian peasant art yields two divergent impressions. The profusion of styles and techniques is amazing, testimony to the ready creativity of peasant craftsmen. But throughout this wealth of invention a constant tone prevails: the images portrayed are few and everywhere much the same.[1]

Two images predominate: the sun, at times accompanied by flowers, birds, and animals; and a flowering tree (*drevo zhizni*: literally "tree of life") or a woman raising her arms, with two figures, often armed men on horseback, at either side. Most designs in peasant art involve one of these persistent images.[2] The concern of the present paper is to explore what they may have meant.

Both basic images are ancient. B. A. Rybakov and other archaeologists have shown that virtually identical designs appeared on artifacts of the Sarmatian and Scythian periods in South Russia.[3] The same images continue in various forms in the decorative art of pre-Mongol Rus. The female figure flanked by horsemen appears repeatedly from the sixth century A.D., the beginning of the historical Slavic period in Russia.[4]

In later centuries the old images were sometimes much disguised. They became overgrown with decorative detail, or receded into a corner of the design. But their place in the pattern should not be taken as the only measure

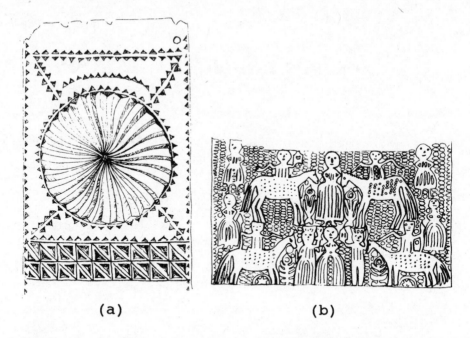

(a)   (b)

Figure 9.1. (a) *Prialka, Shenkurskii uezd,* Arkhangelskaia guberniia. After Iurii Arbat, *Puteshestviia za krasotoi* (Moscow, 1966), illus. following p. 176. (b) *Naboinaia doska.* After V. S. Voronov, *Krestianskoe iskusstvo* (Moscow, 1924), 25.

of their significance. Too idolatrous to openly dominate the art of a Christian people, they may still have operated as secret signs, which invested an entire picture with a familiar value.

Where the old forms do remain central to the design, they commonly come clothed in modern dress. The erstwhile goddess wears a crinoline skirt. Horsemen stand in their traditional pose, decked out in the fashions of the Alexandrine era, with three-cornered cockades or top hats, and muskets in hand. Or the whole tableau is domesticated: husband and wife face each other across a samovar. Through all these mutations, which the plasticity of the original forms facilitated, the modern designs are visibly akin to the old. As late as the Revolution and for some years after, it was only stray works of folk art that wholly lost touch with the old circle of images.

The presence of the old forms has raised a major problem of interpretation. Since Gorodtsov first pinpointed the persistence of archaic emblems in peasant embroidery over forty years ago, Soviet scholars have recognized the widespread survival in modern peasant art of forms and images from the distant past. But almost in one voice, and with some asperity, they have concluded that the peasants had forgotten the old meaning of these elements and repeated them purely out of habit or for decoration.

But the viability of the traditional forms casts doubt on this interpretation. At first glance cut and dried, the old forms come to life when followed through a series of designs. They are not merely copied but playfully rearranged in new costumes and new settings.[5] And the images themselves change, shifting places, growing and dissolving into each other through myriad transitional forms. Suns put out petals, blossoms align into a tree, horses turn into roosters. The apparently fixed motifs flow together, as though all were regarded as avatars of a single spirit.

So the peasants saw their art not as select objects set in a museum case but as a host of images in motion. On ceremonial occasions especially they

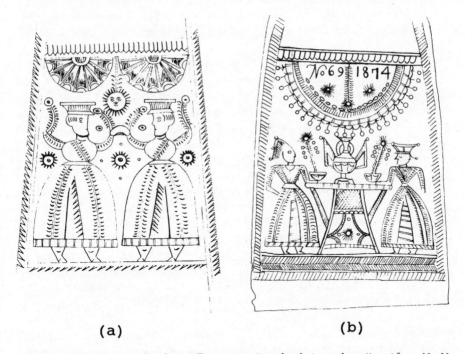

(a)   (b)

Figure 9.2. (a) Detail of *prialka-terem*, Iaroslavskaia guberniia. After N. V. Taranovskaia and N. V. Maltsev, *Russkie prialki* (Leningrad, 1970), plate 24. (b) Datail of *prialka-terem*, Iarovslavskaia guberniia. After V. S. Voronov, *Narodnaia rezba* (Moscow, 1925), illus. 5.

had before them an array of kindred designs, theirs and their neighbors', new and worn, expert and homemade. The variations fused into a montage, delivering a composite impression.

Continually turning in the peasant imagination, the ancient forms in later art never look old. Whether done by a master craftsman or crudely by a local imitator, they come out clear and fresh. They endured because the peasants took care that they should.

Undoubtedly peasant artists, to some extent, did work by habit, following conventions handed down to them. But habits, as diverse schools of psychology agree, fade unless they are continually reinforced. Erik Erikson has put it well for the historian: "Values do not persist unless they work, economically, psychologically, and spiritually."[6] The old peasant images, persisting through a kaleidoscope of styles and techniques, must have continued to work—to have meaning.

Indeed, in certain instances where a given style was stabilized for a generation or so, contemporary motifs began to dissolve while the old forms took on new life. The intricately carved distaffs from northeast Iaroslav province, the *teremkovye*, or tower-house distaffs, provide a clear example of this process.

The earliest distaffs, dating from the end of the eighteenth century, show a clock tower carved in close detail. It was presumably the tower of the Peter and Paul Fortress, which impressed the Yaroslav peasant craftsmen (*pitershchiki*) who came to work in St. Petersburg, the new capital. Below the tower were carved two scenes, usually of figures at a table sipping wine or tea.[7]

Before long the tower began to lose this sharpness, eventually eroding down to a mere outline. The parlor drinking scenes persisted, though in the area around Danilov the cavaliers at their wine were supplanted by roosters facing a tree. But these tableaux began to be intruded on by the natural world. Little suns pierce the walls, blaze from between curtains, flash from under tables and stools. The tea drinkers sit holding leafy branches. Fronds and florets sprout from the table and dangle from the ceiling. More sprigs shoot up from the tower, or what is left of it, and little birds perch on the spire. Like castles in a jungle, the urban structures, the aristocratic chambers with their classic decor, are gently but irresistibly pervaded with sunshine, vegetation, and flowers.

In this way the peasant imagination gradually, without effort, digested urban experience.[8] The Iaroslav tower-house disaster show that the old images had not lost their resilience and vitality. Far from encumbering the peasant artist, they gave him the power to decompose startling urban novelties into the world he understood.

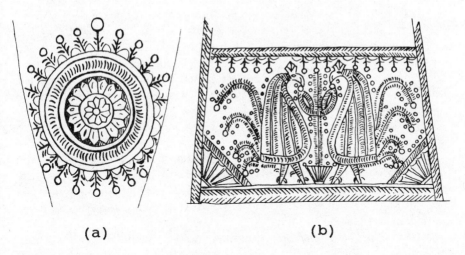

(a)   **(b)**

Figure 9.3. (a) Detail of *prialka-terem*, Iaroslavskaia guberniia. After Taranovskaia and Maltsev, *Russkie prialki*, plate 25. (b) Detail of *prialka-terem*, Iaroslavskaia guberniia. After Voronov, *Krestianskoe iskusstvo*, 45.

But peasant art, geared to generations, turned slowly. Most craftsmen, as Zhegalova has shown, stuck to the designs worked out in youth.[9] Although new impressions were raining in on the peasantry throughout the nineteenth century, not many found their way into peasant art.[10]

By the early twentieth century, however, the old forms were losing their grip. They could no longer contain the rush of new experiences. The Russian village was coming apart, as peasants were pulled further into industry and modern institutions. Finally two decades of war and social upheaval, culminating in collectivization, destroyed the autonomy of the villages, leaving the peasants helpless to respond as a group to their condition. Peasant art, an outgrowth of collective peasant experience, soon withered away. The waning of the ancient forms did not free the peasants for a new artistic flowering. It signaled the demise of that peasant culture which had held its own for centuries, only to be finally overwhelmed by the urban world.

The old images were not the whole of peasant creativity, but they anchored it. They were like a man's native village, which he might leave for the better part of his life yet belong to always. These forms remained at the heart of the peasants' apprehension of the world. No history of peasant art is possible without understanding them.

By the nineteenth century the old images in peasant art did not come clothed in explanations. When questioned by educated observers, the peasant could not or would not explain them.[11] Possibly these pictures were never put into words, for words do not blend together in an unbroken circle of meaning as these images do. Most likely they arose as a way of directly visualizing belief. If so, the old pictures are no more mute than they ever were. And though the historian has no hieroglyphics to assist him, the images have also not been shattered or eroded. Renewed by each generation of peasants, they come down to us pristine.

First, the sun. A picture of the sun can hardly be misunderstood. The question is, how deeply can we comprehend that image? It is easy to take the sun for granted, to note the "solar disks" in Russian peasant art, and pass on. But then the sun stays flat: the big northern distaffs, carved with many suns, remain blank and dumb.

"Solar disk" is not a term peasants would have understood; we have missed what impelled them. We have to try to see with their eyes. They did not see a circle. They saw a full sun high above them, a huge dome on the horizon, segments of light from trees and houses, rays of sunlight shooting out from behind clouds. They saw no disk but a mass that flashed and whirled and blazed, and in the flickering light of their oil lamps and tapers, their carved suns also sparkled. For them the sun was everywhere, rising and sinking, warming and fading. They saw a procession of suns, following in a cycle that made days, and years, and time. They were constantly turned to the sun, for they lived mainly out of doors, depended on sunlight and heat, fed on plants the sun grew and ripened. June and November, sprouting and harvesting, basking and shivering, color and blindness—year after year in these experiences the peasants saw the sun. They saw the exploding energy that Blake and Van Gogh saw. They saw the source of life on earth.

To say that the sun in peasant art is a symbol is to set up a screen where none existed. The peasants could not easily gaze at the sun. Its brilliance hurt their eyes; labor bowed their heads. But through the intricate carvings they could look at the sun to their heart's content. Pictures of the sun were a way of discharging an emotional debt, built up over years of utter dependence on solar light and warmth. They were a heightening of attention and a simple expression of reverence.

The sentient multitude of flowers, animals, and birds portrayed in peasant art expand the central vision of the sun. They embody the streaming solar energy. Flowers were mostly abstract, possibly because the artist,

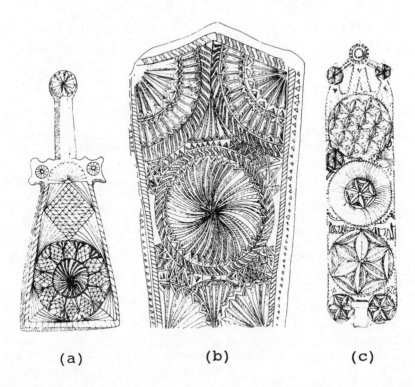

(a)   (b)   (c)

Figure 9.4. (a) *Valek*, probably Iaroslav region. After V. M. Vasilenko, *Russkaia narodnaia rezba i rospis po derevu XVIII–XX vv.* (Moscow, 1960), 148. (b) *Rubel*, Vladimir region. After Vladimir-Suzdalskii muzei zapovednik [G. Shamrai], *Narodnaia dekorativnaia rezba po derevu* (Vladimir?, 1969). (c) *Prialka*, 1855, Purnema, Onega peninsula. After N. V. Maltsev, "Ornamentalnaia rezba po derevu na Onezhskom poluostrove," in *Russkoe narodnoe iskusstvo severa* (Leningrad, 1968), 73.

working usually in winter, had only the memory of summer blooms before him. Still the painted blossoms possess a vitality—the twining, unfolding vigor of living plants—which distinguishes them from the set floral motifs of urban decorations.

Rootless radiant blossoms easily merged with the image of the sun. On late nineteenth-century distaffs the meticulous carvings of the sun were mostly replaced by brightly painted flowers. But where the flowers are carefully drawn, the solar image clearly reemerges. Living surrounded by flowering plants, the peasants continued to see in them the life-creating energy of the sun. In a more earthy form, they shared Shelley's vision:[12]

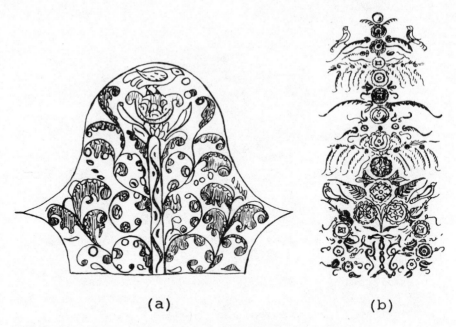

(a)   (b)

Figure 9.5. (a) Detail of *prialka*, early twentieth century, Puchuga, Northern Dvina, Arkhangelskaia guberniia. After Arbat, *Puteshestviia*, illus. following p. 48. (b) Mural, *selo* Topolnoe, Soloneshenskii raion, Altai. After Iurii Arbat, *Russkaia narodnaia rospis po derevu* (Moscow, 1970), 106.

> Life, like a dome of many-colored glass,
> Stains the white radiance of infinity.

Birds and animals were nearly as prominent in peasant decoration. The peasant artist put little songbirds everywhere in treetops and flowering foliage. He caught the distinctive shapes of water and game birds with laconic accuracy. But his favorite birds were poultry, especially roosters. He drew them in their proudest moments, strutting and crowing. By stressing the arch of neck, the plumed tail, he magnified the scrawny backyard cock into an almost regal bird.

Along with idealized domestic fowl, the peasant artist portrayed a fabulous bird, the *ptitsa-sirin*. This creature, with the body and plumage of a bird and the head, sometimes the breasts, of a woman, is known from Kievan times, where she turned up on pottery and cloisonné.[13] In late centuries she joined various heraldic animals in stone reliefs on churches.[14]

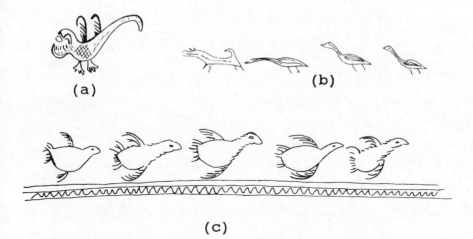

Figure 9.6. (a) Goose alighting, detail of *prialka*, Palashchele, Mezen, Arkhangel-skaia guberniia. After Arbat, *Puteshestviia*, illus. following p. 80. (b) Detail of *dontse* (*prialka* base), Nizhegorodskaia guberniia. After Voronov, *Krestianskoe iskusstvo*, 49. (c) Water birds, apparently *Alcidae* sp., detail of *prialka*, Palashchele. After Taranovskaia and Maltsev, *Russkie prialki*, plate 54.

From the seventeenth century the Sirin remained a favorite image, not only in purely peasant art but in Russian folk culture generally. She frequently posed for popular prints (*lubki*). A set caption explained that the Sirin dwelled in the east, in paradise, but occasionally flew out to earth singing so beautifully of future bliss that any mortals who heard her were smitten senseless and died.[15]

Despite the allusions to God and the saints in these captions, written no doubt for the censors of the Holy Synod, the Russian Sirin is clearly sister to the sirens of classical mythology.[16] She also bears a family resemblance to the mermaids who tempted the northern European sailors. Indeed in the carvings on peasant houses along the upper Volga, inspired by the decorations on river barges, the Sirin was often replaced by a mermaid, known as *rusalka* or *beregin*.[17] These names take us to the roots of this widespread image in Slavic folk culture.[18] The *rusalki* and *beregini* were water maidens who dwelled in rivers and streams, often thought to be the restless spirits of unchristened children and young women who had drowned. In early summer these nymphs emerged and romped through forests and fields, grass and grain springing up lushly in their tracks.

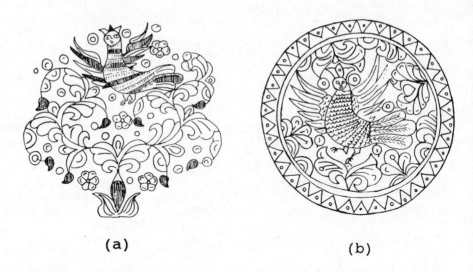

Figure 9.7. (a, b) Details of *prialki*, Permogore, Northern Dvina, Vologodskaia guberniia. After Arbat, *Puteshestviia*, illus. following p. 48.

The *rusalki*, like mermaids and sirens, were equivocal creatures. Youthful and lovely, with long bright hair and beguiling voices, they threatened to ensnare lone mortals who encountered them. Perhaps these playful spirits embodied memories of a time when people wandered hunting and gathering, before they were peasants rooted to one place and fastened in a chain of

Figure 9.8. (a) Detail of house carving, Middle Volga, probably Nizhegorodskaia guberniia. After Voronov, *Krestianskoe iskusstvo*, 12. (b) Detail of house carving, *selo* Shchekino, Nizhegorodskaia guberniia. After S. Agafonov, *Gorkii, Balakhna, Makarev* (Moscow, 1969), 149.

agricultural toil. Significantly, the *rusalki* were exorcised in June, just before the gladness of early summer gave way to the intense period of haying and reaping. In a ceremony similar to the other spring festivals,[19] the girls and women fashioned a straw *rusalka*, clothed in finery or ribbons, and with laughter, song, and dances conveyed her *out* of the village, strewing her on the field to encourage the heading rye, or casting her back into the water.[20]

The joyous mock funerals of the *rusalki*, like the captions for the Sirin prints, reflect the ambivalence the peasants felt toward such creatures. In one print the assembled people are blasting away at a lovely Sirin with a cannon.[21] In some festivals, the escort divided into two groups, mourners and mockers, who struggled for possession of the effigy, reuniting in general merriment when she was finished off.[22]

A similar mockery surfaces in the pipe-smoking *rusalki* on a few of the Volga friezes. But in most peasant woodcarving and painting—done, of course, by men—the Sirin or *rusalka* is shown in a benevolent light. The Sirin is invariably portrayed crowned, hovering in the air or alighting on a tree, as if she had just flown down from her heavenly abode.[23]

At Permogore, where she was a favorite subject, the Sirin usually floats benignly over scenes of domestic well-being. Sometimes she poses inside the sun in all her splendor; at other times with flopping wings and comblike crown she hobnobs with the local chickens: only her face gives her away. On certain distaffs it is possible to see a progression from scrawny pullets through showy roosters to the paradise bird.

The Permogore artists painted the most realistic pictures of everyday peasant life. It seems strange that they included the Sirin bird in their scenes, almost as a member of the family. That strangeness should tell us that the peasants did not see the world as we do; they did not feel obliged to draw a line between reality and fantasy. To them the *ptitsa-sirin* belonged to the natural world.

Common birds, like roosters, also had their fabulous side. At times they displayed a color and verve that in Permogore painting literally raised them out of the barnyard, joining them to the Sirin and the sun. And this reveals another peculiarity of peasant imagination: the urge to associate far overrode the impulse to classify. Peasant art, lore, and ceremony are an unending spider web of associations as fecund and fragile as dreams.

No being had a sharp boundary; each thing tended to flow over into something else, and the more creatures were charged with solar energy, the more fluid they became. The *rusalki* and *siriny* radiated a freedom, beauty, and pleasure too strong for single mortals to bear. Only the village collective, through its organized ceremonies, could harness this unearthly energy: lead the *rusalki* out to fertilize the grain; call down the Sirin to bless the marriage union.

Returning to the stream of peasant imagination—but shifting from birds to mammals—natural, exotic, and fabulous creatures mingle. The deer, dogs, cows, pigs, goats, cats that populate the background spring from a few sure lines, drawn by those who knew them thoroughly. Even unicorns, griffins, and other heraldic beasts, though traced at times from patterns, possess a rough vitality, the gift of artists who lived with animals and respected them.

Of the exotic animals, only lions appear with any frequency. The peasants pacified them. They smile down from the Volga cabins, their pliant bodies twisted like vines into the narrow spaces on the boards, their tails blossoming, their manes spreading like rays of sun or luxuriant foliage. Though tamed, the peasant lions radiate vigor and energy. And this may have been part of the appeal of strange and wonderful creatures—they revealed the boundless creativity of life.

But the most important animals in peasant art were horses—or better, steeds (*koni*). Dostoevskian nags never appear; only spirited mounts and carriage horses. The fascination with horses spread beyond decorative art into every corner of peasant life. On old Russian cabins the butt end of the scooped log that capped the roof was carved into a horse's head (*konek*). The carved heads apparently replaced horse skulls, which the early Slavs had once fixed to the rooftop.[24] In places in the upper Volga region the top log was still sometimes called the "skull log."[25] Smaller *konki* cropped up everywhere: on barn roofs, apiaries, cemetery and memorial crosses; porch newel posts, benches, partitions, flareholders, looms and spindles; combs, mirrors, cleavers, salt-holders, bowls and cups for ceremonial brew.[26]

(a)   **(b)**

Figure 9.9. (a) Detail of house carving, *derevnia* Sharypovo, Gorodets district, Nizhegorodskaia guberniia. After Arbat, *Puteshestviia*, illus. following p. 128. (b) Detail of house carving, probably Vladimirskaia or Nizhegorodskaia guberniia. After [Shamrai], *Narodnaia dekorativnaia rezba po derevu.*

In pictorial art the peasant drew a proud horse—neck and tail arched, foreleg raised high—champing at the bit or racing away. Often the horses were painted white or red and clad in fancy trappings to emphasize their remove from the dull bony beasts who dragged carts and plows. The lines of these epic animals were not left to chance. Birds might be lumpy, human figures awry, but ungainly horses are rarely to be seen. All strongly resemble the horses of icon art, especially the folk icons of northern Russia.[27] In other words, the portrayal of horses was stylized to stress certain key characteristics: strength, mobility, verve.

We now happen on a curious link. At their most stylized, horses come to resemble birds, and vice versa. The two animals were paired with each other: birds carved on rafter ends with a *konek* on the roof, a horse on one side of a Gorodets distaff base, a matching bird on the other. At times the two almost fuse into one archetypal animal. Evidently peasants sensed qualities in horses and birds—pride, flamboyance, free movement—which set them above the other domestic creatures.[28]

Both animals, moreover, shared a special relationship with the sun. In the depth of winter and in the dark of every night, the crowing cock heralded the return of the sun, a fact made much of in peasant lore and custom.[29]

There was also the widespread legend, dating perhaps from neolithic times and persisting in Russian folklore, that the sun was carried across the sky in a horse-drawn chariot.[30] Descending into the Western Ocean, the

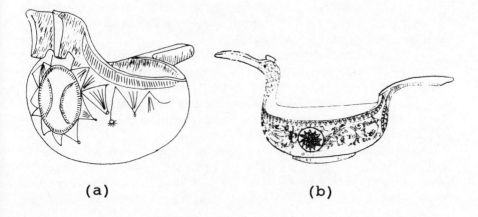

(a)   (b)

Figure 9.10. (a) *Kovsh*, Nizhegorodskaia guberniia. After Voronov, *Krestianskoe iskusstvo*, 50. (b) *Kovsh*, Permogore, Northern Dvina, Vologodskaia guberniia. After *Muzei narodnogo iskusstva* (Moscow, 1968).

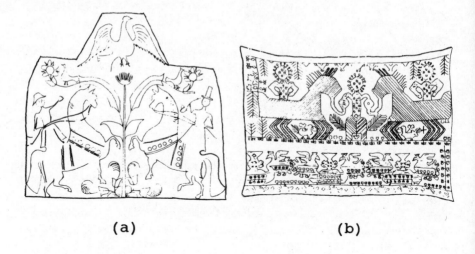

(a)   **(b)**

Figure 9.11. "Homage" motif, classic forms: (a) *Dontse*, Gorodets district, Nizhegorodskaia guberniia. After Voronov, *Krestianskoe iskusstvo*, 37. (b) Embroidery, North Russia. After T. M. Razina, *Russkoe narodnoe tvorchestvo* (Moscow, 1970), 137.

horses were transformed into water birds, who drew the sun around to the dawn.[31] In Russian peasant art this legend is illustrated by the elegant wooden drinking boats, with prow-handles shaped like the heads of horses or water birds and floral suns on the side,[32] and by rough-hewn red toy carts, each loaded with a sun-wheel.[33]

As birds and horses, pared down to visual epithets, converge, they move away from the peasant's awareness of the natural world. That awareness centered on the sun. The artist's first concern was to evoke the experience of sunlight and the burgeoning of life beneath it. But the cock-steed silhouettes lose the look of natural creatures. They take on the cast of symbols, standing for something present but not visible.

As symbols, stallions and roosters lead in to the second circle of images. Here the dominant form is a vertical figure flanked by two lower creatures. Traditionally the central figure was a woman with upraised arms; later it was often a tree with flowers, fruit, or birds. The adjoining creatures might be humans, especially mounted horsemen, horses, or rooster-birds.[34]

What are we to make of this basic image as persistent as it was mutable? The archetypal quality of the animals and other figures involved suggests that we are looking not at a picture of nature objects but at a

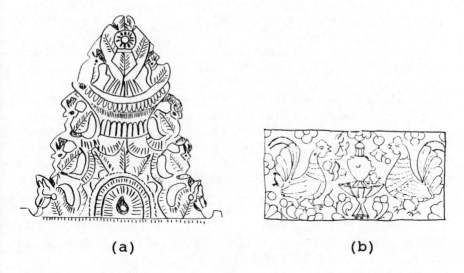

(a)   **(b)**

Figure 9.12. "Homage" motif, occluded variants: (a) Top of *prialka-terem*, Iaroslavskaia guberniia. After Taranovskaia and Maltsev, *Russkie prialki*, plate 25. (b) Detail of *prialka*, Permogore, Northern Dvina, Vologodskaia guberniia. After Voronov, *Krestianskoe iskusstvo*, 94.

representation of something invisible though no less real. To the peasants the one reality that could rival nature in importance was society and human relationships.

What does this image reveal about the social world of the peasants? To begin with, it is a picture of harmony, not conflict. The design is balanced, the figures in repose. They appear to be involved in a ceremony of obeisance or homage.

Homage involves a willing submission to an authority deemed legitimate. In this respect the image is curious. For the figure in the position of power is a woman, or a flowering tree with birds. Those doing reverence are commonly men, often armed men on horseback. Thus the pattern of authority so painfully conspicuous in Russian peasant society is reversed: men do homage to a woman, and analogously, roosters and stallions yield up their speed and power before a flowering tree.

But neither woman nor tree is treated as final authority. There also is an air of being open to something from above: the ancient goddess raises a chalice, the trees open their blossoms, the birds their wings. And often enough the higher power deigns to show its face: the sun, or some solar avatar, shines down on the whole scene. Thus not only is the ordinary social order turned upside down: it is revealed to be a part, a subordinate part, of the greater natural order.

At first glance the image also invites a sexual interpretation. The central form appears phallic, aiming toward a solar womb. Yet this "phallic" shape is often represented as a flower or a woman, with male figures—horsemen, stallions, roosters—in attendance at either side. Again the facing pair may be a couple: bride and groom, husband and wife.

Peasant art, like village society, kept the differences between men and women continuously in view.[35] Yet these differences were regarded less as an absolute dichotomy than as the phases of a single vital rhythm. The phallus was called forth by woman, dissolved into her, was again revived by her, and new males given birth. The sense of male-female as an oscillation of sexual energy is echoed—in fact experienced—in peasant designs. Male and female aspects, both explicit and subliminal, are intermingled and superimposed, so that the attention of the viewer swings from one to the other. The sexes are visibly distinguished only to be fused in a living union.

Significantly, scenes of a harmonious balance between man and woman decorated especially those objects—distaffs, embroidered towels, ceremonial dishes—closely connected with the work of women and with the marriage ceremonial. The continual spinning-courting bees that absorbed village youth from October on, the consecutive fall festivals devoted to a female goddess in Christian disguise, culminated in marriage and the recreation of human life on the one hand, and, on the other, in solstice and the rebirth of the life-giving sun.[36]

Peasant art thus served in a great undertaking that required as intense a concentration of human energies as planting and harvesting the crops. In this effort women took the lead: the ceremonies they created were partially wishful, conjuring sunlight and fertility, but they were much more. They were also practical, a carefully orchestrated perpetuation of human life despite the cold and dark. The winter marriage was a human triumph over death. The undertones of sexuality in the image of the goddess and her guardians reflect the fact that this was an emblem of sublimated sexuality, of sexual impulses put to social uses to create family and social order. The pictures were not idle: the scenes on distaffs at the courting parties illustrated how young people should behave.

Finally, we should not ignore the political implications in the homage motif. In peasant art it was usually not peasants who paid homage to the goddess or flowering tree but men at arms: the mounted warriors, nomads or lords, who for two thousand years had controlled peasant society on the Russian plain.

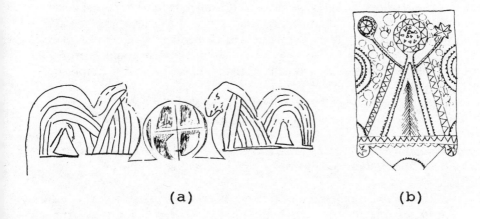

(a)   (b)

Figure 9.13. "Homage" motif, spontaneous variants: (a) Top of *prialka, derevnia* Iarygino, *Staritskii uezd*, Tverskaia guberniia. After Taranovskaia and Maltsev, *Russkie prialki*, plate 20. (b) Detail of *prialka*, Kenozero, *Kargopolskii uezd*, Olonetskaia guberniia, ibid., plate 37.

The peasants thereby denied that their rulers ruled the earth, or even established the social order. Proud and powerful as the lords appeared to be, they too paid reverence to the force of life.[37]

Should we conclude that the peasants were idealists, that they portrayed their society—family, village, state—not as it was but as they wanted it to be? Or should we say that they saw social relationships not as they seemed to be but as they truly were? For peasant art can hardly be called Romantic. It does not have the bitter sense of schism, the spurning of the corrupt world at hand while pining for another, brighter realm. There is no accusation, no despair.

Peasant art is invariably bright, serene, and joyous—*zhizneradostnyi*, as Russian observers aptly say. Considering the squalor of Russian village life, such a vision was an extraordinary culture *tour de force*. Compare peasant art with the abysmal existence sketched by Chekhov in *The Peasants*. In conditions that struck the sensitive, educated observer as utterly degrading, peasants were able to perceive life as joyous.

The cultural vitality of the Russian peasantry shows up still more sharply in the ability of peasant artists to assimilate alien elements. In drawing their masters the peasants recorded with laconic accuracy, almost as in a cartoon, the changing fancies of the elite in arms and conveyance, costumes and poses. The mansions of the boyars, classical drawing rooms, the clock tower of Peter and Paul Fortress and the paddle-wheel steamers all make their appearance on peasant distaffs. When urban fashions began to trickle into the village in the nineteenth century, samovars and chandeliers assumed the place of honor in the traditional homage scene. And the peasant couple came to the evening gathering in their boughten finery; he in his patent leather boots, she in her kerchief and ribbons.

As suggested earlier, the attention the peasants devoted to the culture of the elite may be read two ways. One can say, as is usually done, that nineteenth-century peasants were fascinated by the changing world around them and tried to portray it *realistically*. And undoubtedly peasant art often reflects the wonder of the rustic, the admiration of the muzhik for his betters.

But this admiration was not abject. The village artist looked closely at only a few elements of the high culture, and he deliberately arranged these in the old designs. He did not show peasants bowing down to their masters, but those warriors reined in before the tree of life. Marveling at tower and steamer, he saw that the great clock and the paddle wheel were only new faces of the eternal sun. The samovar that came onto the tables of the fortunate radiating warmth and comfort, with its big belly and upraised arms—was it not a new incarnation of the goddess awaiting the old reverence?

These contemporary scenes in ancient poses are ambiguous. Are the figures in an embroidered landscape water nymphs with flippers flanking a sacred tree, or cavaliers with wide sleeves boating in a park?[38] Was a modern world coming alive for the peasant within the husk of the old forms? Or did ancient beliefs endure, camouflaged in modern dress?[39] Many designs contain an unavoidable ambivalence that the artists had no wish to resolve, which they lovingly cultivated and sharpened. This ambivalence was a source of the tension and power in peasant art and part of the strength of peasant culture.

For peasants did more than register fashions and forces imposed on them from without. They persisted in seeing things their way, as part of the natural order. Art was one way of taking cultural control. Incorporating what attracted them into their designs, the peasants disavowed the pretensions of the high culture. Despite new-fangled towers, ships, and fancy garments, the mounted warriors did not rule the universe. They brought their marvels as tribute and testimony to the tree of life.

The peasants did not openly reject existing authority: they sought to transcend it. Their response was essentially religious. But the religion involved was not Christianity. The virtual absence of Christian symbols in peasant art is striking.[40] Peasant artists paid little attention to Orthodoxy, though many learned their skill painting icons or illustrating Old Believer manuscripts.[41]

What explains the indifference to things Christian, even among the avowedly pious? Apparently Christianity remained in their eyes a parochial though powerful cult advanced by the state for its own ends. The peasants used this imposed faith to express reverence, to sanction certain rituals, or to solicit aid from on high without believing that Christianity had the sole view of the truth. The chapels, the icons, the carved wooden crosses and statues of North Russia show that Christianity had a place in the religious feelings of the peasants. But that place remained on the outskirts of the village, on the periphery of communal and family ceremonies.[42]

In this light the Old Believer movement seems less of a dead end.[43] Overt religious dissent in Russia was rooted in the web of counterbelief we have been exploring. The conjunction between known strongholds of Old Believer faith and conspicuous centers of peasant art (Borok, Semenov, Gorodets, Nizhnii-Tagil, the Altai) is indicative.

Peasant artists often got training and assurance from the underground dissenter tradition. But inspiration flowed even more strongly the other way.[44] To take only two examples, an elaborate print from the Vyg workshops shows the spiritual clan of Andrei Denisov as solar medallion flowers on a spreading "tree of life," with a pair of Sirin birds above and the dissenter monastery-convent far below.[45] Only the tiniest of crosses on the wooden domes marks the tie to Christianity. Equally instructive are the splendid Sirin birds painted by Vyg artists with the device *Vidom i Glasom*—"by appearance and by voice"—that is, by beauty seen and heard. To clarify this image, one eighteenth-century panel juxtaposed the Sirin to an imperial eagle, captioned *Silom i Zrakom*—"by force and by vigilance."[46]

The dissenter movement may be seen as a new, more conscious, and more bitter phase of the long struggle between Christian practice and folk belief. The rigid doctrine and ritual of the old believers, so aggravating to the elite, served as a fortified barrier. Behind these defenses the religious awareness of the peasants pulsed with heightened brilliance.

To call this religion pagan is to think of it as sub-Christian, enmeshed in "primitive" rites and superstitions. The belief of the Russian peasants, as it gleams through popular art, belongs rather with the great Oriental religions, with their insistence on the oneness of life in all its forms and their reverence for life-energy. In the immediate sense this outlook counseled acceptance of things as they were, for everything that happened was part of life. But in the long run, stubbornly, slyly holding to this faith, the peasants refused to submit, for they denied the claim of the existing powers to absolute and rightful authority. And their view of life was after all the broader one. They observed the antics of the masters with benign clarity, putting them in their place in the great cycle of life that fused with the sun. It was the peasants, those "dark people," who were the more conscious of the world they lived in.

Notes

1.   V. S. Voronov, *Krestianskoe iskusstvo* (Moscow, 1924), 43; I. Ia. Boguslavskaia, "O transformatsii ornamentalnykh motivov, sviazannykh s drevnei mifologiei, v russkoi narodnoi vyshivke," Report to the Seventh International Congress of Anthropological and Ethnographic Sciences held at Moscow, 1964, p. 8.

2.   The primary material for this essay was the decorations on articles of wood, bast, or bark formerly used by the peasants of north and central Russia—notably some six hundred *prialki* (distaffs) examined directly or through photographs and descriptions. Some use was also made of peasant designs in other materials: weaving, embroidery, woodcuts (*lubki*), enamel and metalware, bone carving, and so forth.

3.   See the seminal essay of V. A. Gorodtsov, "Dako-sarmatskie religioznye elementy v russkom narodnom tvorchestve," *Trudy goudarstvennogo istoricheskogo muzeia* (Moscow, 1926), 7–36; and the later studies of B. A. Rybakov, "Drevnie elementy v russkom narodnom tvorchestve," *Sovetskaia etnografiia*, no. 1 (1948): 90–106, and his "Prikladnoe iskusstvo i skulptura," *Istoriia kultury drevnei Rusi: Domongolskii period*, vol. 2: *Obshchestvennyi stroi i dukhovnaia kultura* (Moscow-Leningrad, 1951), 396–464; L. A. Dintses, "Drevnie cherty v russkom narodnom iskusstve," in ibid., 465–91; A. K. Ambroz, "O simvolike russkoi krestianskoi vyshivki arkhaicheskogo tipa," *Sovetskaia arkheologiia*, no. 1 (1966): 61–76, translated in *Soviet Anthropology and Archeology*, 6, no. 2 (1967): 22–37. [Rybakov's work—its honesty as well as accuracy—has been challenged recently in the USSR. —BE]

4.   Rybakov, "Prikladnoe iskusstvo," 399. In the peasant art of neighboring Poland some similar images appear, but much subdued, obscured by Christian and secular urban themes. See O. A. Gantskaia, *Narodnoe iskusstvo Polshi* (Moscow, 1970). But neither image was limited to the Slavic cultural area. Ambroz (p. 69) notes the goddess motif on archaic Greek vases, and I came across a similar design in the folk weaving of modern Bihar, hardly surprising considering that the mother or tree goddess has been prevalent in Indian art as far back as Harappan times. See Richard Lannoy, *The Speaking Tree* (New York, 1971), xxv, 9, 22, plate 7, and passim. The image appears most conspicuously in the art of the ancient Fertile Crescent as far back as the earliest Babylonian dynasties. See Goblet d'Alviella, *The Migration of Symbols* (New York, 1956 [Reprint of 1894 ed.]), 118–76. Whether the goddess-tree with her acolytes came to Russia from the Near East or arose indigenously is a moot point. Clearly she appealed to a wide range of agrarian cultures.

5.   Compare this insouciance in peasant art with formal Christian symbols, and especially with the official conventions of icon painting and the rigid *mestnichestvo* of the *ikonostas*.

6.   Erik Erikson, *Childhood and Society* (New York, 1950), 121. Both the obvious freshness of the ancient images in later peasant art and the impossibility of their surviving as mere habits without meaning have been recognized by recent Soviet researchers. See T. M. Razina, *Russkoe narodnoe tvorchestvo* (Moscow, 1970), 136–38. But even Razina, hampered by an outlook more aesthetic than historical, slips back into the groove and concludes that

the peasants were overcoming the old images, transforming them into decorative motifs or into more realistic designs (ibid., 138–42, 146).

7. S. K. Zhegalova, "Khudozhestvennye prialki," in *Sokrovishcha russkogo narodnogo ishusstva: Resha i rospis po derevu*, Zhegalova et al. (Moscow, 1967), 137.

8. For another example of this process, compare the "artistic folklorization" of the *rusalki* in the nineteenth-century Volga housecarving. V. M. Vasilenko, *Russkaia narodnaia resha i rospis po derevu* XVIII–XX vv. (Moscow, 1960), 44–46.

9. Zhegalov, "Khudozhestvennye prialki," 136.

10. See the 1863 Iaroslav *prialka* in the State Historical Museum depicting a train chugging out of a station, or the midcentury series by an unknown master with fashionable "classical" scenes elegantly carved in low relief (for example, the 1868 *prialka* in Zhegalova et al., *Sokrovishcha*, illus. 137–38.

11. M. P. Zvantsev, *Nizhegorodskaia rezba* (Moscow, 1969), 14.

12. The contact between Romantic and peasant art is more than tangential (as the Romantics themselves divined). The Romantic artist, intellectually and emotionally, was trying to escape the walled city, which shut the peasants out. But the Romantic, beginning with his individual consciousness, sought a transcendent fusion with the universe which would leave his self unimpaired. That was one worry Russian peasants were free of; they would not have understood the regret in Shelley's "stains."

13. Z. P. Popova, "Raspisnaia mebel," in Zhegalova et al., *Sokrovishcha*, 50–52; Tamara Talbot Rice, *A Concise History of Russian Art* (New York, 1963), 92.

14. See the decorations on the Church of St. George (1120–28) at Iuriev-Polskii (Rice, *Russian Art*, 33), and on the gates of the Church of the Resurrection in the Forest (*na Debre*) at Kostroma (1652) in V. Ivanov, *Kostroma* (Moscow, 1970), 84–86, 98–101.

15. D. Rovinskii, *Russkiia narodnyia kartinki*, 5 vols. (St. Petersburg, 1881), 1: 484–87, 5: 140–41; Iu. Arbat, *Puteshestviia za krasotoi* (Moscow, 1966), illus. following p. 48.

16. The Greek sirens were originally birds. Those portrayed beguiling Odysseus on a fifth century B.C. vase from Vulei look almost exactly like the Russian *ptitsy*; Michael Grant and John Hazel, *Gods and Mortals in Classical Mythology* (Springfield, MA, 1973), 367. For classical representations of the sirens, see John Pollard, *Seers, Shrines, and Sirens: The Greek Religious Revolution in the Sixth Century, B.C.* (South Brunswick, NY, 1965), 137–41.

17. For an indication that the *ptitsy-siriny* and *rusalki* were related, the writer B. V. Shergin recalls from his native Arkhangelsk province gingerbread depicting either *ptitsy-siriny* or *rusalki*, there called *beregini* (recounted by Vasilenko, *Russkaia narodnaia*, 40). They were also called *farunki*, from an obscure but tenacious pseudo-biblical legend that identified them with the pharaoh whom Jehovah had drowned in the Red Sea, or with the pharaoh's daughter. It is hardly possible to trace the twists of popular imagination which resurrected the persecutor of the chosen people as a mermaid. Possibly the association was with the compassionate princess who had found the baby Moses floating in the rushes, or conceivably the Russian peasants felt some affinity between their own river nymphs and other pagan spirits submerged by the mighty Judaeo-Christian God, particularly since the story, according to Vasilenko, "arose in Old Believer circles"; *Russkaia narodnaia*, 36.

18. Zvantsev, *Nizhegorodskaia rezba* 14–16, illus. 63–86, and especially Vasilenko, *Russkaia narodnaia* 35–52. On the classical derivation of the word *rusalka* and the solstice ceremonies associated with her, see S. A. Tokarev, *Religioznye verovaniia vostochno slavianskikh narodov XIX nachala XX v.* (Moscow, 1957), 87–94; V. Ia. Propp, *Russkie agrarnye prazdniki* (Leningrad, 1963), 77–81.

19. Propp, *Russkie agrarnye prazdniki*, 68–77, 81–89. Such ceremonies generally fell in the solstice period between the week before *Troitsa* (*rusalnaia nedelia*) and the end of

June (*Petrov den*). It should not be supposed that they were all observed everywhere. Each locality, even each village, elaborated its own unique seasonal festivals.

20. Propp, *Russkie agrarnye prazdniki* 77–81; Tokarev, *Religioznye verovaniia*, 90–91; Vasilenko, *Russkaia narodnaia*, 49–54.

21. Iu. Ovsiannikov, *Lubok: Russkie narodnye kartinki XVII–XVIII vv.* (Moscow, 1968), 81.

22. Propp, *Russkie agrarnye prazdniki*, 81, 88.

23. Ovsiannikov, *Lubok*, 80.

24. A Belov, "Konki: Istoriko-etnograficheskii ocherk," *Zhivopisnaia Rossiia*, no. 98 (1902): 556–58; V. V. Stasov, "Konki na krestianskikh kryshakh," *Sobranie sochinenii*, 3 vols. (St. Petersburg, 1894), 2: 105–14.

25. S. K. Zhegalova, *Russkaia dereviannaia rezba XIX veka: Ukrasheniia krestianskikh izb Verkhnego Povolzhia* (Moscow, 1957), 38.

26. See, for example, Arbat, *Puteshestviia za krasotoi* 64 ff.; 176 ff.; M. I. Milchik, *Po beregam Pinegi i Mezeni* (Moscow, 1970), 21, 35, 108, 120, 135; Dintses, "Drevnie cherty," 467–68; S. M. Prosvirkina, *Russkaia dereviannaia posuda* (Moscow, 1957), 143.

27. See especially the numerous icons of Flor and Lavr, and of St. George and the Dragon; F. M. Smirnova, *Zhivopis obonezhia XIV–XVI vekov* (Moscow, 1967), 72, 88, 174.

28. Dintses, "Drevnie cherty," 475.

29. Tokarev, *Religioznye verovaniia*, 55.

30. The finest early representation of this legend is the elegant sun chariot from Trundholm (ca. 1300 B.C.), now in the Danish Museum. The conveyance of the sun by chariots and bird-ships is abundantly represented in rock carvings and metalwork from the Scandinavian Bronze Age. See Peter Gelling and Hilda Ellis Davidson, *The Chariot of the Sun* (New York, 1969). For additional evidence on prehistoric sun worship, see E. Anati, *Camonica Valley* (New York, 1969). By comparison, occasional references to sun chariots in classical mythology, though well known, are much less compelling; in the Mediterranean such ideas were "swamped in a sea of Hellenism" (Gelling and Davidson, *Chariot of the Sun*, 123). Still, in the irrepressible idolatry of Palestine, sun chariots were prominent enough to provoke Jehovah's wrath (2 Kings 23: 10–11).

31. Vasilenko, *Russkaia narodnaia* 48–51, 97–99; Prosvirkina, *Russkaia dereviannaia posuda*, 32–33.

32. See also the bowls illustrated in O. V. Kruglova, "Severodvinskie rospisi," in *Russkoe narodnoe iskusstvo severa* (Leningrad, 1968), 32; Voronov, *krestianskoe iskusstvo* 50–51; Razina, *Russkoe narodnoe tvorchestvo*, 47.

33. Dintses, "Drevnie cherty," 479, 482.

34. Ibid., 470–71, 473.

35. Compare the deliberately asexual quality of Christian art, in Russia and elsewhere.

36. See the brilliant description of the fall ceremonials in V. I. Chicherov, "Zimnii kalendar," in his *Zimnii period russkogo narodnogo zemledelcheskogo kalendaria xvi–xix vekov* (Moscow, 1957), 25–63.

37. The horsemen were often shown impregnating a female symbol or trampling their enemies (Ambroz, "O simvolike russkoe," 69–72). Thus the whole design stressed male sex and power, within the social and natural balance.

38. Dintses, "Drevnie cherty," 472–73; Ambroz, "O simvolike russkoe," 75.

39. Kievan figurines dressed like the Scythian-Sarmatian earth goddess suggest that the Slavic peasantry was long accustomed to putting on the costumes of its rulers (Dintses, "Drevnie cherty," 483–84).

40.   In the few instances in which Christian themes enter peasant art, they are all but submerged, as in the needlework in which an onion-domed chapel is deftly transformed into the familiar goddess (ibid., 488–90). In peasant art the substitution of Christian symbols never took hold. In pre-Petrine Russia, when cultural communication between peasant and high culture was still vigorous, the influence was more the other way: the artisans who made fine objects for the elite came mostly from the peasantry and used peasant themes in their decorations (Rybakov, "Prikladnoe iskusstvo," p. 416).

41.   See K. A. Bolsheva, "Krestianskaia zhivopis Zaonezhia," in *Krestianskoe iskusstvo SSSR* (Leningrad, 1927), 53, 57; M. A. Reformatskaia, *Severnye pisma* (Moscow, 1968), 16.

42.   Peasants did not sharply segregate Christian and folk practices. In the spring ceremony of *kumlenie*, girls kissing through wreaths of braided birch also exchanged the crosses they wore as tokens of loyalty (Propp, *Russkie agrarnye prazdniki*, 129–32). But crosses and blessings by the priest served only to add additional authority to non-Christian beliefs.

Christianity also had no more than a toehold in the intricate marriage ceremonial, with which peasant art was closely connected. N. P. Kolpakova, "Otrazhenie iavlenii istoricheskoi deistvitelnosti v svadebnom obriade Russkogo Severa," in *Slavianskii folklor* (Moscow, 1965), 259–83.

43.   "A living fossil," as Treadgold put it. His essay "The Peasants and Religion" articulates the prevailing pejorative attitude toward the Old Belief; see Wayne Vucinich, ed., *The Peasant in Nineteenth-Century Russia* (Stanford, 1968), 72–107.

44.   Peasant designs and symbols soaked into Orthodox Christian art too. See Ambroz, "O simvolike russkoe," 65–67. But Ambroz errs in stressing roundabout borrowings from "Eastern" art via Byzantium and discounting the direct impact of folk images through peasant artisans.

45.   Ovsiannikov, *Lubok*, 78.

46.   Popova, "Raspisnaia mebel," 59–60, illus. 58–59.

10

The Russian Peasant Movement of 1905–7: Its Social Composition and Revolutionary Significance

Maureen Perrie

The significance of the Revolution of 1905 lay in the fact that it represented, for the first time in Russian history, a simultaneous attack on autocracy from all levels of society—sectors of the professional and commercial middle class, the radical and liberal intelligentsia, the urban workers, and the peasantry. The causes of such widespread discontent were to be found in the complex of interrelated social and economic changes that followed the emancipation of the serfs in 1861. By the beginning of the twentieth century, the impact of Witte's policy of rapid industrialization at the expense of agriculture was making itself felt in a wave of agrarian disturbances in the south and a militant strike movement in the towns. In the face of a growing domestic political crisis, the Russian government in 1904 engaged in war with Japan, believing, in the words of Pleve, that "in order to hold back the revolution, we need a short victorious war."[1] The disastrous course of the war in the Far East precipitated a revolutionary situation in which the Russian peasantry was to play a major role. This paper will attempt to assess that role in terms of the social composition of the participants in the peasant movement, and the extent to which they were influenced by the revolutionary forces in the towns.

The Peasant Movement

By the provisions of the Emancipation Act, the Russian peasantry received less land than they had previously used under serfdom.[2] An unprecedented increase in the size of the rural population in the second half of the nineteenth century intensified the problem of "land hunger." Heavy redemption payments on their communal holdings, in addition to an onerous burden of taxation, increased the impoverishment of the peasantry. The inadequacy of his allotment to meet his obligations forced the peasant either to rent or purchase land from the gentry or to seek off-farm wage labor in agriculture or industry. The pressure of population increase, however, pushed up land prices and rents and kept wages low. The economic dependence of the peasantry on the gentry landowners was therefore on the increase in the decades after emancipation. Those of the gentry who retained their land at the end of the century[3] either rented their estates to the neighboring peasantry or went over to more capitalistic methods of farming. In areas where this transition to capitalist agriculture was taking place, the peasants were deprived not only of the opportunity of renting land but also, in many cases, of their traditional rights of access to resources such as forest and pasture. The overall effect of these developments was the same: the progressive impoverishment and pauperization of the mass of the Russian peasantry.

In the postemancipation period, industrialization and the creation of an industrial labor force went hand in hand with the development of the agrarian crisis. The government's policy of financing industrialization through fiscal pressure on the peasantry forced million of peasants to find work in the towns. The phenomenon of the "peasant worker" played an important role in channeling urban ideas and attitudes to the country-side. A general improvement in communications in the second half of the nineteenth century was helping to break down the isolation of the peasants in their communes and to extend their experience beyond the immediate horizon of the village. The professional employees of the *zemstva* constituted a new "rural intelligentsia" of teachers, doctors and nurses, lawyers, agronomists, and statisticians, often sharing a populist ethos of service to the people through "cultural enlightenment," who introduced the peasants to secular urban intellectual values, which were very different from those traditionally conveyed by the priests and local state officials.[4]

The generation that participated in the peasant movement of 1905 was therefore somewhat different in outlook from that which had responded so apathetically to the Populist "movement to the people" of the 1870s. There was a growing awareness and resentment of the fact that emancipation had brought not the longed-for "land and liberty" but a progressive deterioration in the economic condition of the peasantry. At the same time, the traditional values of religion and loyalty to the tsar—which had, with a few exceptions, made passive resignation to fate the major characteristic of the Russian peasantry throughout the nineteenth century—were gradually losing their hold on the peasant imagination. The economic independence the young attained through wage work was eroding the patriarchal structure of the household and village, with obvious implications for the equally patriarchal structure of church and state.[5]

It is difficult, however, to assess the extent and significance of such changes in peasant attitudes. Certainly the mood of the countryside was rebellious: the revolutionaries who went to the peasantry at the beginning of the twentieth century were gratified to find a ready response to their advocacy of direct action to achieve land and liberty, which contrasted with the passive millenarian expectation of "the tsar's favor" encountered by their Populist predecessors.[6] Yet the events of 1905–7 were to show that the old ideas were still strong; many agrarian disturbances were triggered by rumors of the appearance of an Imperial Manifesto granting a general redistribution of the land.[7] The Russian peasantry in 1905 was still very much a "traditional" peasantry, but one that was increasingly being affected by the modernization of Russia—a process of which they were the first victims. If its causes lay in the process of modernization, however, the forms the peasant movement assumed were essentially traditional, directed primarily against the traditional enemies of the peasantry at the local level rather than at the national center of power embodied in the tsar.

The agrarian unrest of 1902–3, which had died down somewhat in 1904, flared up again at the beginning of 1905 sparked by the wave of strikes that followed the "Bloody Sunday" massacre in St. Petersburg, and continued throughout 1906 and 1907.[8] Tables 10.1–10.3 show the main forms of the movement and its regional distribution. The movement was predominantly directed against the landowners: conflicts with police and troops usually developed as a consequence of their intervention in the movement against the landowners. In many areas the peasants replaced with their own freely elected representatives village and rural district (*volost*) elders and other officials whom they considered to be simply the puppets of the state bureaucracy. Refusals to pay taxes were also common. The movement against state intervention in peasant affairs was particularly strong in Georgia, where virtual anarchy reigned in the countryside for much of 1905 and 1906.[9] The forms assumed by the movement against the landowners were determined primarily by the system of land tenure and

Table 10.1
Forms of the Peasant Movement in Russia in 1905–7*

Form of movement	No. of Instances	Percentage of Total	Total No. of Instances	Percentage of Total
Action against landowners:				
Arson	979	18.1		
Destruction of estates	846	15.7		
Illicit wood-cutting	809	15.0		
Strikes by agricultural workers	723	13.4		
Seizure of meadows, pasture, etc.	573	10.6		
Withdrawal of labor from estates	474	8.7		
Seizure of foodstuffs and fodder	316	5.8		
Seizure and tillage of arable land	216	4.0		
Rent conflicts	211	3.9		
Conflict with landowners and estate officials	205	3.8		
Conflicts over boundaries	52	1.0		
Total	5404	100.0	5404	75.4
Conflicts with state officials, police, and troops			1041	14.5
Conflicts with *kulaks*			97	1.4
Conflicts with clergy			33	0.5
Other (attacks on traders, usurers, liquor shops, etc.)			590	8.2
Grand total			7165	100.0

* The table covers all regions of European Russia except the Baltic and Transcaucasian provinces. The table is based on data in S. M. Dubrovskii, *Krestyanskoe dvizhenie v revoliutsii 1905–1907 gg.* (Moscow, 1956), 65, 67.

agrarian relationships in each given locality. The movement was strongest in those areas—such as the Central Black Earth, the Volga, and the Ukraine—where the exploitation of the peasant renters by the gentry landowners was greatest, or where the severest hardships had been caused by the transition from renting to large-scale capitalist farming. Here the predominant form of the movement was the attack on the landowner's estate. This often involved the destruction of the manor house and outbuildings to ensure that the "master" would never return, and the seizure of estate lands and property by the peasants. In some areas, such as those in the west, where the estates

Table 10.2
Regional Distribution of the Peasant Movement of 1905–7*

Region	No. of Instances	Percentage of Total
Central Black Earth	2196	30.6
South-West	985	13.7
Little Russia	850	11.8
Mid-Volga	724	10.3
Belorussia	655	9.1
Central Industrial	482	6.7
Novorossiia	468	6.5
Lower Volga	244	3.4
Lakes	235	3.3
Lithuania	168	2.3
Urals	104	1.5
North	54	0.8
Total	7165	100.0

* Source: S. M. Dubrovskii, *Krestianskoe dvizhenie v revoliutsii 1905–1907 gg.* (Moscow, 1956), 60.

were worked by an agricultural proletariat, strikes for better wages and conditions were common.[10] The aims of the movement therefore ranged from straightforward demands for the amelioration of economic conditions, as in the strike movement, to a much more far-reaching social goal, "black repartition," involving the total abolition of gentry landholding and the de facto implementation at local level of the deeply rooted peasant belief that only they, who worked the land with their own labor, had any right to it.[11]

Differences in the social structure of the countryside were reflected in the composition of the peasant movement in its various manifestations. In spite of the widespread prevalence of the repartitional commune with its equalizing tendencies,[12] the peasantry was far from being a homogeneous mass, and the sectional interests of the various strata often came into conflict in the course of the movement. The most obvious example of such conflict was the case of the *kulaks*, or rich peasants, whose farms were sometimes the object of attacks similar to those on the gentry estates.[13] The problem of the "true" nature of the peasant movement was the topic of much lively debate among contemporaries, especially within the rival socialist parties, who believed that the sociopolitical character of the revolution would be determined by the aspirations of the peasantry. The Social Democrats saw the peasant movement as essentially a conflict between the peasantry as a

Table 10.3
Regional Distribution of Forms of Peasant Movement of 1905–7*

Region	Total No. of Districts	No. of Districts Affected	% of Total	Destruction of Estates		Forms of Movement										
				No. of Districts	% of Districts Affected	Illicit Wood-cutting		Strikes		Seizure of Pasture and Fodder		Illicit Tillage		Seizure of Grain from Fields		Rent Conflicts	
						No.	%	No.	%	No.	%	No.	%	No.	%	No.	%
Central Black Earth	75	68	90.7	54	76.5	45	66.2	46	67.6	47	69.1	7	10.3	18	26.5	28	41.2
South-West	36	35	97.2	9	25.7	19	54.3	31	88.6	22	62.9	8	22.9	5	14.3	8	22.9
Little Russia	41	41	100.0	26	63.4	28	68.3	35	85.4	29	70.7	5	12.2	11	26.8	26	63.4
Mid-Volga	51	45	88.2	30	66.7	39	86.7	16	35.6	26	57.2	18	40.0	14	31.1	12	26.7
Belorussia	43	39	90.7	6	15.4	33	84.6	25	64.1	6	15.4	5	12.8	—	—	—	—
Central Industrial	71	45	63.4	4	8.9	38	84.4	8	17.8	19	42.2	7	15.6	—	—	3	6.7
Novorossiia	39	32	82.1	19	59.4	16	50.0	17	53.1	13	40.6	17	53.1	7	21.9	22	68.8
Lower Volga	17	9	52.9	7	77.8	6	66.7	1	11.1	7	77.8	4	44.4	2	22.2	4	44.4
Lakes	34	23	67.6	3	13.0	20	87.0	10	43.5	12	52.2	2	8.7	2	8.7	4	17.4
Lithuania	23	17	73.9	—	—	18	76.5	14	82.4	10	58.8	4	23.5	2	11.8	—	—
Urals	29	11	37.9	1	9.1	10	90.9	—	—	2	18.2	—	—	—	—	—	—
North	19	9	47.4	—	—	9	100.0	1	11.1	2	22.1	1	11.1	—	—	2	22.1
Totals	478	374	78.2	159	42.8	281	75.1	204	54.5	195	52.1	78	20.9	61	16.3	109	29.1

*Based on a table in A. Shestakov, *Krestianskaya revolutsiia 1905–1907 gg. v Rossii* (Moscow, 1926), 52.

whole and the gentry landowners, a conflict that contained within this first antifeudal bourgeois-democratic stage the seeds of the future class struggle between the rural proletariat and the peasant bourgeoisie.[14] The Socialist Revolutionaries, on the other hand, considered the movement to be both antifeudal *and* anticapitalist, part of the general struggle "of the poor against the rich, of those who labor against those who do not, of the exploited against those who extort surplus value,"[15] which united the peasantry with the urban proletariat and the socialist intelligentsia in the "working people's revolution." In order to assess the relative merits of these rival views and to achieve a better understanding of the complex character of the Russian peasant movement and its relationship to the revolutionary movement as a whole, a detailed study is required of the degree of participation in the movement by the different social groups within the peasantry, and also of the extent and nature of external influence.

Observing the Peasant Movement

Probably the most valuable source for any study of the peasant movement is the survey conducted by the Imperial Free Economic Society, a learned body with broad liberal and even radical sympathies. About 20,000 copies of a detailed questionnaire on the nature, causes, and effects of the movement were sent in 1907 to correspondents and contacts of the society in forty-seven of the fifty provinces of European Russia. Of the 1,400 replies received, 702 contained positive information concerning the existence of peasant unrest in the correspondent's locality. According to the editors of the survey, these correspondents were

> representatives of very heterogeneous strata of the population, various political tendencies and social trends, peasants and landowners, teachers and estate stewards, priests and state officials, extremists of the left and of the right, participants in the movement and police officers, victims of political repressions, and victims of agrarian destruction.[16]

The question on the survey form included detailed requests for information on the participation of peasant and nonpeasant elements in the movement; for example:

> Was there any influence from outsiders? How was it expressed?
> Which strata of the village took part in the movement: poor peasants, middle peasants, or the prosperous? What was each stratum's attitude toward the movement? What was the attitude of the peasants who had purchased land?

Was any part played by peasants engaged in off-farm wage work in factories and towns? If so, what?

Was any part played by soldiers and reserves returning from Manchuria? If so, what?

What part was played by the young men? By the old men?

What was the attitude of the women?[17]

The form in which the results of the survey were published makes it difficult to attempt a precise analysis of the informants' answers to these questions. The compilation of a digest of the returns for each region was entrusted to separate editors, who were granted considerable freedom in their approach to the materials. The quality of the editors, like that of the informants, varied considerably: some provided much more detailed and systematic analyses than others.[18] No attempt was made in the published results to present an overall picture of the movement in any of its aspects: what follows represents my personal analysis of the evidence in the regional digests concerning the social composition of the participants in the movement.

Although external influence was frequently cited by correspondents as a factor contributing to the outbreak of peasant unrest, it was by no means a universal factor. Agitation and propaganda in the countryside by nonpeasant elements often served as a precipitating factor for the movement, but there were also other precipitants, of which news and rumors of the revolutionary events in the towns and the occurrence of peasant disturbances in neighboring localities were probably the most important.[19] Even if the movement was sparked by external factors, however, it was usually fueled by grievances that were peasant and often purely local in character. As Groman noted in his introduction to the reports from Novorossiia, the influence of "outside agitators" was more likely to be claimed by correspondents hostile to the movement than by sympathizers.[20] This phenomenon would appear to be a reflection of the conservative predilection for the "conspiracy theory" of history, with its corresponding reluctance to admit that social unrest might have its roots in genuine problems and hardships. This is not to say, of course, that "outside agitation" was simply a figment of the imagination of reactionary tsarist officials and landowners. Revolutionaries of all parties—or of none—flocked to the countryside from the early summer of 1905. Their influence, however, was not always inflammatory; in some cases they tried to divert the violent direct action of the spontaneous movement into more peaceful political channels. The outsiders were usually described in the reports only generically as "agitators" or "revolutionaries." Sometimes the party organizations they represented were specifically mentioned: the Social Democrats, Socialist Revolutionaries, the Jewish Bund, or the Peasant Union.[21]

The social groups from which the agitators were recruited were rarely mentioned, or mentioned only in terms—such as "Jews and long-haired students"[22]—which for the Russian conservative were virtually synonymous with "revolutionary agitators."[23] The influence of local factory workers was rarely mentioned: nor was it always welcome. Striking railwaymen in Pskov province who tried to enlist peasant support suffered severe beatings for their efforts.[24]

In addition to this predominantly urban category of complete outsiders, frequent mention is also made of the role of the rural intelligentsia as agitators and conductors of revolutionary ideas to the peasantry. The groups most often cited in this connection were village teachers, members of the clergy, medical workers, and employees of the local *zemstvo* organizations. In some cases a literate stratum of "peasant intellectuals," especially peasant artisans, performed a similar function to that of the nonpeasant intelligentsia.[25] It was reported from Kursk that "in this locality there were no agitators, but the peasants themselves frankly pointed to their own literate fellows, who had read to them from the 'Russian Word', a newspaper widely distributed in our district, the proceedings of the Peasant Congress in Moscow."[26]

An important part in the movement was played by those peasants who had experience of the world outside the village, as seasonal workers in agriculture and industry. In some cases these peasant workers, returning to their villages in the course of 1905 to help with the harvest, or because of unemployment and the strike movement in the towns, served simply to spread the general revolutionary mood from the factories to the countryside; in other cases their influence was more consciously political. The editor of the reports from the Central Black Earth region described the nature of their influence as follows:

> The "ferment" or "brain" of the movement—as the correspondents phrased it—were the peasants on side-earnings in the factories, in the mines and in the towns. As more developed persons, they naturally became the leaders of the movement; in some cases they brought into the countryside—along with the newspapers—news about the agrarian and the workers' movement in other places, and unconsciously propagandized the idea of the agrarian movement.[27]

In the Lakes region peasants working in the towns were said to play an important part as "conductors of new ideas and trends."[28] In Pskov province, where many peasants went to work in St. Petersburg, correspondents wrote: "Those who had been in the factories in the city urged on the movement, and said that only thus could we achieve equal rights with members of the other legal estates,[29] and obtain the land"; "those on side-earnings were insistent that the laws be worked out according to a new system"; and "an important part was played by the distorted rumors and gossip which were brought by those returning from side-work, who had been influenced by the propaganda of the various revolutionary parties."[30]

A similar role to that of the peasant workers was played by the peasant soldiers and sailors returning to their villages from the Russo-Japanese war. Although in many areas the movement in the countryside had begun before the troops in the Far East were demobilized, "with their arrival the movement intensified."[31] In some cases the troops were active conductors of revolutionary agitation, representing the "most liberal and aware" element in the countryside,[32] and "broadening the political consciousness of the peasantry";[33] in other cases, their tales about the military fiasco in the Far East served simply to fuel the existing flames of discontent in the villages. There was a widespread belief among the soldiers that the tsar should reward them for the hardships they had suffered by granting them more land. A hostile report from Riazan claimed:

> The soldiers returning from Manchuria—most of whom were liars—exaggerated their hardships, expressed dissatisfaction with their commanders, talked about various abuses of state funds, and extolled their difficulties, for which they said the state was obliged to reward them by giving them the land for nothing."[34]

The troops often returned to find their farms run down, which gave them an added material incentive for revolt. It was reported from Saratov:

> In some places the soldiers returned from Manchuria during the movement, and intensified the general excitement. They found their economy devastated: "there was nothing for them to eat, and no fuel for them to heat their huts". And then they learned that their wives and families had received no allowances, or had received them only at irregular intervals. The discontented soldiers adhered to the movement and demanded land, saying, "Why have we spilt our blood, if we do not have the land?"[35]

In other cases, however, the soldiers "returned from Manchuria with money, feeling fine, and paid no attention to the entire movement."[36] In one case reported from Novgorod, the soldiers, after an initial expression of support for the movement, thereafter reverted to their traditional repressive role, "turning into watchmen on the invitation of the police; at present they enjoy almost universal hatred from the peasants."[37]

Let us turn now to the question of participation in the movement by the village peasantry themselves.

In most cases the peasants participated in the movement as an entire village or commune,[38] with all socioeconomic strata taking part. A typical report is that from the Lakes, where

the internal stratification of the peasantry in terms of property status did not substantially influence the participation in the movement of the various elements in the village. In the majority of cases, peasants of all strata took part in the movement.[39]

In many individual cases, however, some strata are reported to have been more active than others, and some are more regularly said to have been active rather than passive. The most varied evidence concerns participation by the two extreme categories, the rich and the poor. The evidence suggests that participation by these two strata was determined primarily by local conditions and by the forms assumed by the movement in individual localities.

A considerable proportion of replies depicts the poor and landless peasants as the most active participants in the movement. The reasons for this are usually considered to be self-evident, in that these peasants had nothing to lose and everything to gain from the movement.[40] There were some forms of the movement, however, from which they were barred by virtue of their poverty: a peasant with no cow could not engage in illicit cattle-grazing on the landowner's meadow, and a peasant without a horse was at a disadvantage when it came to carting away timber from the master's forest or plunder from his manor.[41] Even in wage strikes—the form of the movement in which the poor were most likely to participate—they sometimes found themselves restrained. A correspondent from Podoliia reported that

the leaders of the movement were the more prosperous peasants (none are rich); the most timid were the landless, because they cannot exist without their daily earnings, and they were soon compelled to bring the strike to an end, to avoid starvation.[42]

In exceptional cases, however, the poorer peasants were subsidized during a strike by their more prosperous fellows.[43] The poorer peasants, too, were most dependent for their livelihood on the local landowner and therefore the most vulnerable to retaliatory measures. Realization of this could sometimes serve as a deterrent against participation in the movement.

In areas of capitalist farming with an extensive landless agricultural proletariat, solidarity with the local communal peasantry was most noticeable when the laborers were recruited from the neighboring villages; where the work force on the large estates consisted largely of immigrant labor from other areas, as in Novorossiia, conflicts of interest often arose:

> In those cases where the peasants aimed to obtain all the land, they frequently demanded the removal of the immigrant workers, or even made the latter lay off work, so that the landowner could not conduct his enterprise, but sometimes the peasants restricted themselves to demanding that local workers be hired instead of immigrants.[44]

The rich peasants, especially those who had purchased land as their individual private property, and those who employed the labor of others, usually remained aloof from the movement, though it was only in rare cases that individual peasant proprietors were themselves the victims of the movement (see table 10.1). Explanations of the passivity of the richer peasants were usually in terms of their general distrust of attacks on property, which might easily be directed against themselves.[45] More rarely the nonparticipation of the richer peasants was attributed to their very affluence. A correspondent from Pskov, describing a local case of illicit wood-cutting, wrote, "Of course, most of the disturbances were by the land-hungry peasants; they are short not only of land, but also of firewood. As for the rich, why should they take part, if they have enough as it is?"[46] In cases in which the rich peasants participated in the movement, however, their avarice and the fact that they possessed the means of gratifying it were often attributed as an important motive. This was particularly true when the movement assumed the form of pillaging the large estates. A report of an incident of illicit wood-cutting in Penza implies that the rich peasants benefited not only from their ownership of horses and carts to bear away the timber but also from the services of their hired workers: "they had the most horses and the greatest labor force, and therefore enjoyed the greatest advantage."[47]

In some cases in which the rich participated in the movement alongside the other strata of the village, it appears that although they had purchased land, they still felt themselves to have more in common with their fellow-villagers than with the landlord, and shared common grievances against him. A correspondent from Kherson reported:

> Poor, middle and prosperous peasants took part. Their attitudes were identical, because although the prosperous peasants had bought land through the bank, they had paid dearly for it, and it still did not suffice, and therefore they too were obliged to rent land for 15–18 roubles a *desiatina* from the landowners and the big commercial renters.[48]

A correspondent from Volyn' explained that although the local movement had been initiated by the poor and middle peasants, "the rich took part, as they considered that the landowner had unjustly forbidden cattle-grazing in a certain part of the forest."[49] An interesting distinction between private peasant landownership and the landownership of the gentry, serving to justify the alignment of the peasant proprietors with the communal peasantry rather than with the gentry, was provided in a report from Novgorod:

> All took part in the movement, including the prosperous and those with purchased land. The latter had the same attitude as the poor peasants, saying that they alone had worked for the land they had bought, so that it should not be taken away from them, although it could be taken from others.[50]

A similar distinction, based on the "labor principle," was reported from the Central Black Earth region:

> The movement, in the words of a correspondent from Kozlov district, was directed against "those in general who owned or rented land, but did not work it with their own hands, without distinction as to estate or rank." Therefore peasant farms worked by family labor were not included among the objects of the movement.[51]

In a few cases participation in the movement on the part of the richer peasants was the result of pressure exerted by the poorer strata for a demonstration of solidarity. The generally ambivalent position of the prosperous peasantry was exemplified by a report from Saratov:

> The tone of the movement was set by the poor peasants. Sometimes, depending on the circumstances, they would compel the rich to participate in the movement, threatening to deal with them "like with the gentry landowners." At other times they would not permit them to take part in the movement, because they took too much of the landowners' property for themselves. "Sometimes, when the prosperous peasants were away raiding elsewhere, their property would be burned down in their absence."[52]

Finally, in some individual cases factors other than socioeconomic, such as the influence of ideas or generational differences, might impel richer peasants to take part in the movement. From Ekaterinoslav it was reported: "In those villages which did not act with total solidarity, it was the poor and middle peasants who participated, and from the prosperous only individuals for whom the political and social slogans of the epoch served as the impulse."[53] From Tambov the interaction of age and economic factors was noted: "The large landowners amongst the peasants prepared to defend themselves, but the smaller landowners fell into two categories: the older ones protected their property, but the young men joined in with the others."[54]

The middling peasants, who shared all of the advantages and none of the disadvantages of the poor and rich strata for participation in the movement, were the group whose active role was most consistently stressed. According to one report from Chernigov, "The poor peasants could not take part in the wood-cutting movement, because they had no horses, and the prosperous peasants feared repressions, but the middle peasants said that they would be no worse off in prison, so the wood was chopped by the middle peasants."[55] A similar report came from Podolia:

> The rich peasants and the poor peasants did not sympathize with the strikes, although they did not display any energetic opposition. The principal strikers were the middle peasants, who had enough work on their own fields, and could therefore hold out for higher wages without suffering particular losses themselves. The poor peasants were especially in need of earnings, and therefore did not sympathize with the strike.[56]

In other cases, however, the middling peasants were less involved in the strike movement, as in this report from Kiev:

> The strike was conducted with solidarity on the basis of class enmity [toward the gentry landowners]. But all the same, the active elements were the young and the poor. The middle peasants were not particularly interested in the strike, because they do not go to work on the large estate, neither do they hire workers themselves, but manage their own fields.[57]

Clearly it is very difficult to generalize concerning the differential participation in the movement by the various strata of the peasantry, even if it were possible to establish specific criteria for classifying a peasant as "poor," "middling," "prosperous," or "rich"—for it seems that no uniform definitions were applied by the correspondents who contributed to the survey materials. The form of the movement and the extent of social differentiation within the village appear to have been major factors in determining the nature of the alignments in individual localities. Middling, poor, and landless peasants, with the occasional exception of the most destitute, were most likely to take part in wage or rent strikes and boycotts, whereas the prosperous and rich, if they took part at all, were more likely to do so in cases of pillage.[58]

Whether the richer peasants—and especially those with purchased land—participated in the movement, stood aloof, or were themselves the victims appears to have depended on the extent to which the process of social differentiation in the countryside was reflected in the peasants' "class-consciousness."[59] Where the prosperous peasants saw themselves or were seen by their fellow-villagers as representing simply the most fortunate and successful stratum of the communal peasantry, they would be more likely to participate in the movement, to defend common peasant interests against the gentry landowners and other nonpeasant commercial farmers. To the extent that the *kulaks* saw themselves as a distinct socioeconomic group, with similar economic interests to the gentry landowners, from whom they were distinguished only in terms of their ascription to an inferior legal estate, they would be more likely to remain apart from the movement, or be themselves the object of attack. Factors that might influence the categorization of the richer peasant in the social consciousness of the village would include the proportions of his land that were purchased, as opposed to his share in the communal holdings; the degree to which his farm was worked by hired rather than family labor; the extent to which his land was rented to or from others; whether his farmstead was in the village or separate; his commercial interests outside agriculture; and the nature of his life style.

The ambivalent position of the richer strata of the peasantry constituted a major problem for both revolutionary parties in their attempts to define the class nature of the peasant movement—a problem that neither satisfactorily resolved. In Social Democratic theory cases in which the *kulaks* were aligned with the rest of the peasantry represented the first stage of the revolution in the countryside; incidents in which the *kulaks* were themselves the objects of the movement belonged to the second, socialist stage.[60] This analysis, however, failed to account for the fact that most of the attacks reported on *kulaks* came not from the rural proletariat, as the two-stage theory strictly required, but from the same communal peasantry as attacked the gentry landowners.[61] The movement against the *kulaks* was perhaps more adequately explained by the Socialist Revolutionary view of the class struggle in the countryside between the exploited and the exploiters: but the Socialist Revolutionaries in turn faced a problem in explaining those cases in which the *kulaks* displayed solidarity with the rest of the village. They explained such conflicts between the *kulaks* and the gentry landowners as "an enmity purely between legal estates, not a class enmity, not a form of the conflict between labour and capital, but rather a form of the conflict of capital against land-rent and the monopolies of the feudal serf-owner."[62] In other words, the antifeudal bourgeois-democratic character that the Social Democrats attributed to the movement of the peasantry as a whole the Socialist Revolutionaries attributed solely to the *kulaks*; the anticapitalist, prosocialist character that the Socialist Revolutionaries attributed to the "working peasantry" as a whole (excluding the *kulaks*), the Social Democrats attributed solely to the rural proletariat. Overall, the conflicts and confusions in the revolutionary parties' analyses derived from the complexities of the patterns of behavior of the various strata within the peasantry—complexities that the crude generalizations of party political formulas could not easily account for. In a period of transition, when the commune was increasingly under pressure from economic factors leading to greater social differentiation in the countryside, it was hardly surprising that alignments within the peasantry should be in a state of flux.

The question of peasant participation in the movement was further complicated by the influence of other factors that modified the impact of purely socioeconomic characteristics. Of these sociobiological criteria such as age and sex were probably the most important.

As might have been expected, given the generally subordinate position of women in Russian peasant society, women as a rule played a more passive part in the movement than did men, although it was only in isolated cases that they actually acted as a restraining influence. When the women did oppose the movement, this was usually explained in terms of their lack of awareness. From Riazan a correspondent reported that "the general mass of women and girls are so undeveloped that they can hardly understand the meaning and significance of the movement."[63] A similar report came from Tula, where "the majority of the women have difficulty in understanding the movement, and restrain it."[64] More often, however, women shared the attitudes of men. In the words of a peasant correspondent from Novgorod, "the women too sympathized with the movement—they live in the same huts as their husbands."[65] In some cases the women not only participated along with the men but were even "more ardent."[66] Frequently, although the women did not actually participate themselves, they spurred on their menfolk with taunts and reproaches. A correspondent from Voronezh reported: "Anyone who didn't go and pillage was reproved by his mother or his wife, saying that their neighbour was bringing back a lot of goods, whereas he, her husband or son, did not care about his home and family."[67] In the south, where the women were extensively engaged in agricultural wage labor, they took an active part in the strike movement, sometimes acting as initiators of a wider movement, as in this report from Kiev:

> At first the participants in the movement were exclusively women and adolescents, but later the whole village joined in. Because the cultivation of sugar-beet employs predominantly female labour, and both the poor and prosperous women do this work, then of course they found support for their demands from all members of their families.[68]

In other instances in which women and children are reported to have been in the van of the movement, however, it seems that it was not so much a case of the women taking the initiative and setting an example as a tactical device adopted by the peasants to explore the ground by sending ahead an advance party composed of the weakest elements of the community, against whom the authorities would be more reluctant to initiate punitive action. This would appear to be the most likely explanation for reports such as this one from Voronezh: "The course of the raids was almost identical throughout the district: first went the young lads and girls, and the women; they rushed into the orchard to pick the fruit, and later they were joined by the adults, and the pillaging began."[69]

The young men of the village usually took a more active role in the movement than their elders. Where explanations were considered necessary for the militancy of the young, these were often in terms of the greater literacy and general awareness of the generation that had had the advantage of the expansion of primary education at the end of the nineteenth century. The teenage lads, too, were more likely to engage in seasonal wage work in the towns and to be influenced by urban attitudes.[70] Also, a young single man had much less to lose, in case of failure, than men with family responsibilities. According to evidence from Podolia, the last two factors were more important than the first:

> The most active stratum during the movement, according to the majority of correspondents, were the young. However, the reports connect this not with the greater development and education of the young, but rather with their greater fondness for diversions, or with their position as the group which plays the greatest part in hired labour, or which in general has not yet settled down, in contrast to the proper householders.[71]

The old men were usually more passive than the young or middle-aged peasants, but, as with the women, it was only in rare cases that they actively opposed the movement. In Tula province all the peasants took part in the movement, "up to and including the old women of seventy-five years";[72] in other cases, the old sympathized, without taking an active part,[73] and in Tver the old men "moved significantly leftwards" in the course of the movement.[74] Evidence is contradictory concerning the nature of the influence of serfdom on the older generation. A correspondent from Tambov noted that support of the movement came from "the old women in particular, who had experienced the oppression of serfdom."[75] In other cases the hostility of the older peasants was explained in terms of the natural conservatism of the aged. It was reported from Pskov that "the old men are opposed to everything, and say that they lived and were satisfied without all these movements"; further:

> Many of the young sincerely believe in the imminence of a new, more perfect and just system of land use, "but the old men, who are generally sceptical about anything new, did not believe in the possibility of a total transfer of the land into the hands of the peasants, and not only did they not believe in it, but neither did they desire it, feeling that the peasants could not cope with this land."[76]

The survey materials therefore show that participation by the peasantry in the movement was determined primarily by the social structure of the countryside and the immediate economic interests of the various strata; other sociological variables, however, such as age and sex, modified the impact of purely socioeconomic factors. Access to knowledge about revolutionary unrest elsewhere played an important part: hence the role of those groups—such as peasant workers, peasant soldiers, and the literate—who served as intermediaries between the village and the world outside, and contributed to the diffusion of the revolution from the towns and armed forces to the countryside, and from one area to another. External influence on the movement was usually confined to the information function of such marginal groups: in some cases, however, when the outsiders belonged to one or another of the revolutionary parties, their role was more consciously political. We shall therefore turn now to a more detailed study of the parties' attitudes toward the peasantry in 1905–7.

Organizing the Peasants

Before 1905 the Social Democrats had adopted a rather cautious attitude toward the peasantry. Marxist analysis saw the peasantry as petty-bourgeois: in Russian conditions the peasantry as a whole had a stake in the antifeudal bourgeois-democratic revolution, but a revolutionary force for socialism could develop in the countryside only after the peasantry had become differentiated into a class of capitalist farmers on the one hand, and a landless rural proletariat on the other. The attitude of the party toward the aspirations of the peasantry would therefore be different at the two stages of the revolution.

The Second Party Congress of 1903 concentrated on the agrarian program for the first stage and advocated the return to the peasantry of all the lands they had lost at emancipation.[77]

In 1905, however, on Lenin's prompting, the party adopted a more radical policy. The Third (Bolshevik) Congress resolved to support all revolutionary measures undertaken by the peasantry, including confiscation of the lands of the large estates. The congress resolution made it clear that at the same time as the peasantry as a whole was engaged in conflict with the gentry landowners, the Social Democrats should be preparing the way for the second, socialist stage of the revolution by organizing the rural proletariat separately and explaining to them "the irreconcilable contradiction between their interests and the interests of the peasant bourgeoisie."[78] A similar but more cautious resolution, supporting land seizures but condemning agrarian terrorism, was passed by the Menshevik conference in Geneva.[79]

Soviet sources claim that the Third Congress gave the impetus to a wave of intensive propaganda and organizational activity in the countryside by Social Democratic and especially Bolshevik committees, although the documentary evidence for this, as they themselves admit, is slight.[80] Lane's study of local Social Democratic organizations in the 1905 Revolution suggests that their influence on the peasantry was limited.[81] It was spread primarily through the party's contacts with the workers and appears to have been confined to areas closely linked with industry. According to Dubrovskii, the party's rural cadres "were usually formed of urban workers connected with the countryside, workers in enterprises located in the countryside, proletarian and semi-proletarian elements in the countryside, the progressive rural intelligentsia, and so on."[82]

Whereas the Social Democrats' interest in the peasantry appears to have been more theoretical than practical until the spring of 1905, the Socialist Revolutionaries had been consciously devoting their energies to revolutionary agitation in the countryside for several years before the Revolution. They rejected the Social Democratic view of the peasantry as petty-bourgeois, arguing that the economy of the small peasant producer was qualitatively and not merely quantitatively different from that of the bourgeois capitalist. For the Socialist Revolutionaries, class allegiance was determined less by relationship to the means of production (as in the Marxist analysis) than by relations of distribution—that is, by source of income.[83] The Socialist Revolutionaries believed in the socialist potential of the mass of the working peasantry; they argued that the development of capitalist agriculture was not inevitable in the Russian countryside, and that the repartitional commune represented an institutional basis for the transition to socialist agriculture through the "socialization" of the land.[84]

In 1902, after the outbreaks of peasant unrest in Little Russia and of the Volga, the party formed its own Socialist Revolutionary Peasant Union, with the aim of organizing the peasantry on a political basis.[85] The Socialist Revolutionaries believed that the socialization of the land should be achieved by political means, and they saw it as their task to divert the spontaneous, anarchistic, revolutionary energy of the peasantry into conscious and organized political channels. To this end they devoted a considerable proportion of their propaganda effort to the countryside. An analysis of the biographies of over two hundred Socialist Revolutionary activists in the countryside shows that the most important social groups engaged in peasant propaganda were members of the minor professions, such as teachers; workers and artisans; peasants; and students. More than half of the manual and clerical workers were themselves of peasant parentage. The Socialist Revolutionaries found that the rural intelligentsia provided a valuable source of revolutionary cadres in the countryside, and in 1903 the party formed its own Socialist Revolutionary Union of Primary Teachers, one of the stated aims of which was the dissemination of party propaganda among the peasantry.[86] By 1905 the party had established a widespread network of peasant "brotherhoods" belonging to the Socialist Revolutionary Peasant Union, and it had considerable success in recruiting peasant support, especially in the Central Black Earth region and on the Volga.[87]

In 1905 the party was divided on the attitude it should adopt toward the outbreak of the spontaneous peasant movement. The semianarchist faction of Maximalists or agrarian terrorists considered that even the most violent, *jacquerie*-type aspects of the movement should be encouraged because they made a positive contribution to the destruction of the old regime. The official party leadership, however, headed by Chernov, held that the party should endeavor to restrain the more destructive aspects of the movement and impose on it consciousness and organization.[88] Spontaneous land seizures were welcomed as an indication of the revolutionary mood of the peasantry, but the Socialist Revolutionaries emphasized that the socialization of the land would be the result not of land-grabbing, which amounted simply to "the arbitrary seizure of individual parcels of land by individuals," but of an organized process of "revolutionary expropriation" by organized peasant unions, which would hold the land until a democratically elected Constituent Assembly approved legislation for its egalitarian distribution on a national scale.[89]

In the course of 1905 another body claiming the leadership of the peasantry was established. The initiative for the organization of an All-Russia Peasant Union came in May 1905 from a group of *zemstvo* liberals who sought to involve the peasantry in the campaign for the formation of national trades and professional unions which was playing a major role in the revolutionary movement at that time.[90] The Peasant Union held two congresses in July and November 1905, at which about four-fifths of the delegates were peasants, the rest members of the intelligentsia.[91] At the congresses resolutions were passed in favor of the abolition of private property in land, and the declaration of all land to be "the common property of the entire people," with exclusive rights of use for those who worked it with their own labor.[92] In contrast to the demands of the revolutionary parties, however, the majority of delegates to the first congress were prepared to have compensation paid for the alienation of the gentry estates and the purchased lands of the peasantry.[93] Politically the union demanded a constitutional monarchy, with a Constituent Assembly to be elected on the basis of universal suffrage. On the question of the means the peasants should employ to achieve their ends, the Peasant Union congresses were far from explicit. They agreed that the ultimate solution of the land problem must come from a democratically elected Constituent Assembly, but there were bitter debates at the second congress as to whether political freedom should be gained by peaceful means or by violent action. The resolution finally adopted was a compromise that gave priority to peaceful means but reserved the threat of an armed uprising if these should fail.[94]

Between July and November 1905 the Peasant Union succeeded in establishing a network of local organizations throughout most of European Russia.[95] Although the original impetus for the formation of the union had come from the liberals, a major role in the creation of the local organizations was played by the Socialist Revolutionaries, who could work from their own organizational base in the countryside. A recent Soviet study of the local organizations of the Peasant Union shows that the rural intelligentsia played an important part in their creation.[96] The Peasant Union, however, never achieved the significance in the countryside that the workers' soviets attained in the towns, and following the arrest of the leadership soon after the November congress, the organization of the union gradually disintegrated, though its policies continued to find expression, for instance through the Labour Group of peasant deputies in the Dumas.

For all parties the problem of organizing the peasantry for political action proved insurmountable. The task of mobilization over the vast geographical extent of the Russian countryside was beyond their resources; and they had difficulty, too, in making their programs and tactics meaningful to the peasants, who, with some justification, placed greater reliance on their "own means" of local direct action than on preparations for the elusive national armed uprising that was promised by the revolutionaries. The mass of the peasantry apparently still believed in 1905 that "land and liberty" could be achieved within the framework of tsarism; they saw no need for the removal of the autocrat and ignored the socialists' call for a boycott of the elections to the First Duma, in the belief that this body would represent a true "union of Tsar and people," giving the peasants' elected representatives direct access to the tsar without the hostile intervention of the landowners and officials.[97] These hopes, however, were soon disappointed. Largely because of the radical proposals for agrarian reform put forward by the peasant deputies, the First and Second Dumas were dissolved, and the introduction of a new electoral law in June 1907 marked the triumph of counterrevolution. The peasant movement was brutally suppressed by military punitive expeditions, but the government realized the need for concessions to the peasantry if the stability of the countryside was to be preserved. Redemption payments were canceled, certain legal restrictions abolished, and the activity of the Peasant Bank extended. The most significant response by the government to the lessons of 1905, however, came in the legislation of November 9, 1906, which facilitated the peasant's withdrawal from the commune and his establishment as an independent individual smallholder. This was Stolypin's famous "wager on the strong," designed to replace the old communal peasantry, with its dangerously egalitarian notions, by a class of petty capitalist farmers with a healthy respect for the institution of private property. Although they gave greater economic freedom to the more prosperous peasant entrepreneurs, the Stolypin reforms did little to alleviate the problems of the great mass of the Russian peasantry: as the events of 1917 were to prove, the land-hungry communal peasantry remained a major revolutionary force.

Although the events of 1905–7 failed to achieve more than a fraction of the aims of the revolutionary parties, the role of the peasantry was decisive for the attainment of such concessions as were made by the Imperial government in 1905. The forces of law and order, engaged simultaneously on three fronts—the Far Eastern, the urban, and the rural—were severely overextended, and it was only the prompt conclusion of the Japanese war and the return of loyal troops to European Russia after October that restored the upper hand to the government. Yet the weaknesses of the revolutionary forces, too, were considerable. The socioeconomic development of Russia in the postemancipation period was such as to guarantee the simultaneity of revolutionary action by the proletariat and peasantry in 1905; her political and cultural development, however, was insufficient to ensure conscious coordination between town and countryside, or much awareness of common revolutionary goals. In a situation in which the coercive power of the state had already collapsed, as in 1917, this lack of coordination mattered little; in 1905, however, it was a fatal weakness. The peasant movement of 1905–7 was partly related to, partly independent of, the parallel movement in the towns. The peasants pursued their own sectional interests, largely unaware of the broader social and political implications of their actions: the revolutionary significance of their movement derived not from the level of political consciousness of the participants but from the fact that the iniquities against which they rebelled were, in the words of Eric Wolf, but "parochial manifestations of greater social dislocations."[98]

Notes

1.   Cited in S. Iu. Witte, *Vospominaniia*, 2 vols. (Berlin, 1922), 1: 262.

2.   The classic English-language study of the prerevolutionary peasantry is G. T. Robinson, *Rural Russia under the Old Regime* (London, 1932).

3. It is estimated that the gentry sold nearly one-third of all their lands between 1877 and 1905; see Robinson, ibid., 130–31.

4. N. Cherevanin, "Dvizhenie intelligentsii," in *Obshchestvennoe dvizhenie v Rossii v nachale dvadtsatago veka*, ed. L. Martov, P. Maslov, and A. Potresov (St. Petersburg, 1909–14), 1: 259–90; A. Potresov, "Evoliutsiia obshchestvenno-politicheskoi mysli v predrevoliutsionnuiu epokhu," in ibid., 1: 538–640.

5. The difference in peasant attitudes was noted by an old Populist returning to European Russia in 1896 from Siberian exile: E. K. Breshkovskaia, "Vospominaniia i dumy," *Sotsialist-Revoliutsioner* 4 (1912): 117–19.

6. Accounts of peasant receptivity to revolutionary propaganda at the turn of the century can be found in ibid., 123–7; V. M. Chernov, *Zapiski Sotsialista-Revoliutsionera*, (Berlin, 1922), 245–339; S. Nechetnyi, "U zemli," *Vestnik Russkoi Revoliutsii* 2 (1902): sec. 2, 37–82; I. Rakitnikova, "Revolyutsionnaya rabota v krestianstve v Saratovskoi gubernii v 1900–1902 gg.," *Katorga i ssylka* 47 (1928): sec. I, 7–17.

7. P. Maslov, *Agrarnyi vopros v Rossii*, 2 vols. (St. Petersburg, 1905–8), 2: 159–60.

8. Dubrovskii calculates that 50 instances of peasant unrest were reported in 1901; 340 in 1902; 141 in 1903; 91 in 1904; 3,228 in 1905; 2,600 in 1906; and 1,337 in 1907. These figures are based on a study of central archive materials, especially police reports, and the national press, and do not claim to be exhaustive; S. M. Dubrovskii, *Krestianskoe dvizhenie v revoliutsii 1905–1907 gg.* (Moscow, 1956), 38–39.

9. Ibid., 63–66.

10. Ibid., 59–83; A. Shestakov, *Krestianskaia revoliutsiia 1905–1907 gg. v Rossii* (Moscow, 1926), 51–53.

11. For a discussion of the "labor principle" in peasant customary law and in the peasant movement of 1905, see K. R. Kachorovskii, *Narodnoe pravo* (Moscow, 1906).

12. More than three-quarters of all peasant households in 1905 belonged to communes that were at least nominally repartitional; Robinson, *Rural Russia*, 211.

13. Dubrovskii, *Krestianskoe dvizhenie*, 82–83.

14. This analysis is developed in V. I. Lenin, "Agrarnaia programma russkoi sotsial-demokratii," *Polnoe sobranie sochinenii*, 5th ed., 55 vols. (Moscow, 1958–65), 6: 303–48, and in his "Proletariat i krestianstvo," in ibid., 9: 341–46.

15. "Kharakter sovremennago krestianskago dvizheniia," *Revoliutsionnaia Rossiia* 8 (1902): 5.

16. *Agrarnoe dvizhenie v Rossii v 1905–1906 gg.* (*Trudy Imperatorskago Volnago Ekonomicheskago Obshchestva*, 1908, nos. 3, 4–5), 2 vols. (St. Petersburg, 1908), 1: vi.

17. Ibid., 1: xv.

18. The editors included such noted economists as V. G. Groman (Novorossiia), P. P. Maslov (Lower Volga), S. N. Prokopovich (Central Black Earth and Urals), and B. B. Veselovskii (Belorussia).

19. Ibid., 1: 48 (Central Black Earth), 173 (Lakes); 2: 8 (South-West), 289–90 (Little Russia), 418–19 (Novorossiia).

20. Ibid., 2: 417–18.

21. Ibid., 1: 363 (Belorussia).

22. Ibid., 2: 480 (Kherson).

23. In 1905 the peasants themselves came to use the word "student" to refer to anyone, including peasants, with radical or oppositional views. "The term 'student' is losing its academic character and is becoming a political category. Of the inhabitants of a whole number of villages it is said that they 'have gone and turned into students' "; V. G. Tan, *Novoe krestianstvo* (Moscow, 1905), 115.

24. *Agrarnoe dvizhenie*, 1: 217.

25. Ibid., 1: 58 (Kursk).

26. Ibid., 1: 56.

27. Ibid., 1: 49.

28. Ibid., 1: 174.

29. Prerevolutionary Russian society was divided into a number of legal estates (*soslovie*) enjoying various degrees of privilege. The most important were the gentry (*dvoriane*), the townsmen (*meshchane*), and the peasantry (*krestiane*).

30. *Agrarnoe dvizhenie*, 1: 218–19.

31. Ibid., 1: 93 (Mid-Volga).

32. Ibid., 1: 137 (Saratov).

33. Ibid., 2: 336 (Poltava).

34. Ibid., 1: 66.

35. Ibid., 1: 147.

36. Ibid., 2: 371 (Chernigov).

37. Ibid., 1: 298.

38. Ibid., 2: 21 (South-West), 290 (Little Russia).

39. Ibid., 1: 175.

40. Ibid., 1: 120 (Penza).

41. Ibid., 1: 77 (Tambov), 109 (Nizhnii Novgorod); 2: 335 (Poltava).

42. Ibid., 2: 59.

43. Ibid., 2: 23 (South-West).

44. Ibid., 2: 409.

45. Ibid., 1: 58 (Kursk), 398 (Kovno); 2: 306 (Kharkov).

46. Ibid., 1: 220.

47. Ibid., 1: 129.

48. Ibid., 2: 476.

49. Ibid., 1: 144.

50. Ibid., 1: 300.

51. Ibid., 1: 51.

52. Ibid., 1: 146.

53. Ibid., 2: 448.

54. Ibid., 1: 78.

55. Ibid., 2: 371.

56. Ibid., 2: 59.

57. Ibid., 2: 106.

58. These findings correspond in general terms with those of the comparative studies by H. Alavi, "Peasants and Revolution," *Socialist Register* (1965): 241–77, and E. R. Wolf, *Peasant Wars of the Twentieth Century* (London, 1971), 289–93, both of which stress the revolutionary role of the middle peasantry in comparison with the ambivalent position of both the poorer and the richer strata.

59. For a discussion of the manner in which patterns of socioeconomic mobility within the Russian peasantry impeded the crystallization of class consciousness, see Teodor Shanin, *The Awkward Class: Political Sociology of Peasantry in a Developing Society: Russia 1910–1925* (Oxford, 1972), 137–41.

60. This view is still accepted by Soviet historians. See Dubrovskii, *Krestianskoe dvizhenie*, 65.

61. While not denying this, Dubrovskii claims that the movement against the *kulaks* occurred in areas where social differentiation within the peasantry was greatest (ibid., 82–83).

62. "Chto delaetsia v krestianstve," *Revoliutsionnaia Rossiia* 21 (1903): 14.

63. *Agrarnoe dvizhenie*, 1: 66.

64. Ibid., 1: 71.

65. Ibid., 1: 299.

66. Ibid., 2: 61.

67. Ibid., 1: 87.

68. Ibid., 2: 106.

69. Ibid., 1: 87.

70. Ibid., 1: 71 (Tula), 123–24 (Penza), 146 (Ufa).

71. Ibid., 2: 61.

72. Ibid., 1: 71.

73. Ibid., 1: 18 (Vladimir).

74. Ibid., 1: 23.

75. Ibid., 1: 78.

76. Ibid., 1: 219.

77. *Vtoroy sezd RSDRP, Protokoly* (Moscow, 1959), 423–24.

78. *Tretii sezd RSDRP; Protokoly* (Moscow, 1959), 454.

79. *Pervaia obshcherusskaia konferentsiia partiinykh rabotnikov* (Geneva, 1905), 21–23.

80. Dubrovskii, *Krestianskoe dvizhenie*, 163.

81. D. Lane, *The Roots of Russian Communism* (Assen, 1969), 210.

82. Dubrovskii, *Krestianskoe dvizhenie*, 143.

83. "K teorii klassovoy borby," *Revoliutsionnaia Rossiia* 27 (1903): 10–15; 34 (1903): 5–9. The Socialist Revolutionaries argued that their analysis was in fact more "Marxist" than that of the Social Democrats, being derived from the third volume of *Capital*.

84. The party program was published in *Protokoly pervago sezda Partii Sotsialistov-Revoliutsionerov* (n.p., 1906), 355–65.

85. The formation of the Socialist Revolutionary Peasant Union was announced in a special issue of the party newspaper, *Revoliutsionnaia Rossiia* 8 (1902), devoted to the outbreak of the peasant movement in Little Russia. The issue also continued a statement of policy from the Peasant Union.

86. "Iz partiinoy deiatelnosti," *Revoliutsionnaia Rossiia* 30 (1903): 20.

87. *Rapport du Parti Socialiste Révolutionnaire de Russie au Congrès Socialiste International d'Amsterdam* (Paris, 1904), 15.

88. For the debates on this issue at the First Party Congress, see *Protokoly pervago sezda*, 89–96, 314–38.

89. "Reaktsionnaia demagogiia i revoliutsionnii sotsializm," *Revoliutsionnaia Rossiia* 67 (1905): 3.

90. A comprehensive account of the Peasant Union is provided in E. I. Kiriukhina, "Vserossiyskii Krestianskii Soiuz v 1905 g.," *Istoricheskie Zapiski* 1 (1955): 95–141.

91. Ibid., 103, 115.

92. *Protokol uchreditelnago sezda Vserossiiskago Krestianskago Soiuza* (St. Petersburg, 1905), 38; "Postanovleniia delegatskogo sezda Vserossiiskogo Krestianskogo Soiuza," in *Krestianskoe dvizhenie v revoliutsii 1905 goda v dokumentakh*, ed. N. Karpov (Leningrad, 1926), 77–87.

93. The debates on this issue are reported in *Protokol uchreditelnago sezda*, 26–38.

94. The debates are reported in *Materialy k krestianskomu voprosu; otchet o zasedaniiakh delegatskago sezda Vserossiiskago Krestianskago Soiuza 6–10 noiabria 1905 g.* (Rostov, 1905), 55–66. The text of the resolution appears in Karpov, *Krestianskoe dvizhenie*, 78.

95. E. I. Kiriukhina, "Mestnye organizatsii Vserossiiskogo Krestianskogo Soiuza v 1905 godu," *Uchenye Zapiski Kirovskogo Pedagogicheskogo Instituta* 10 (1956): 83–157.

96. Ibid., 138.

97. Maslov, *Agrarnyi vopros*, 2: 266–316.

98. Wolf, *Peasant Wars*, 301.

Bibliography

Afanasyev, Alexander N. *The Bawdy Peasant: A Selection from the Russian Secret Tales*. London, 1970.

Anderson, Barbara A. *Internal Migration during Modernization in Late Nineteenth-Century Russia*. Princeton, 1980.

Anfimov, A. M., and P. N. Zyrianov. "Elements of the Evolution of the Russian Peasant Commune in the Post-Reform Period (1861–1914)." *Soviet Studies in History* 21, 3 (1982–83): 68–96.

Antsiferov, A. N. *Russian Agriculture during the War*. New York, 1930.

Atkinson, Dorothy. "The Statistics on the Russian Land Commune, 1905–1917." *Slavic Review* 32, 4 (1973): 773–87.

——. "The Zemstvo and the Peasantry." In *The Zemstvo in Russia*, ed. Terence Emmons and Wayne Vucinich, 79–132. Cambridge, 1982.

——. *The End of the Russian Land Commune, 1905–1930*. Stanford, 1983.

Aytova, Alla. *The Lubok: Russian Folk Pictures, Seventeenth to Nineteenth Century*. Leningrad, 1984.

Baker, Anita B. "Community and Growth: Muddling through with Russian Credit Cooperatives." *Journal of Economic History* 37, 1 (1977): 139–60.

——. "Deterioration or Development? The Peasant Economy of Moscow Province Prior to 1914." *Russian History* 5, pt. 1 (1978): 1–23.

Beermann, Rene. "Prerevolutionary Russian Peasant Laws." In *Russian Law: Historical and Political Perspectives*, ed. William E. Butler, 179–92. Leyden, 1977.

Benet, Sula, ed. and trans. *The Village of Viriatino*. New York, 1970.

Bensidoun, Sylvain. *L'agitation paysanne en Russie de 1880 à 1902*. Paris, 1975.

Blum, Jerome. *Lord and Peasant in Russia from the Ninth to the Nineteenth Century.* Princeton, 1961.

Bohac, Rodney D. "Peasant Inheritance Strategies in Russia." *Journal of Interdisciplinary History* 16, 1 (1985): 23–42.

Bradley, Joseph. "Patterns of Peasant Migration to Late 19th Century Moscow: How Much Should We Read into Literacy Rates?" *Russian History* 6, pt. 1 (1979): 22–38.

——. *Muzhik and Muscovite: Urbanization in Late Imperial Russia.* Berkeley, 1985.

Brooks, Jeffrey. "Readers and Reading at the End of the Tsarist Era." In *Literature & Society in Imperial Russia, 1800–1914,* ed. William Mills Todd III. Stanford, 1978.

Bushnell, John. *Mutiny Amid Repression: Russian Soldiers in the Revolution of 1905–1906.* Bloomington, 1985.

——. "Peasant Economy and Peasant Revolution at the Turn of the Century: Neither Immiseration nor Autonomy." *Russian Review* 46 (1987): 75–88.

Chayanov, A. V. *The Theory of Peasant Economy.* Madison, WI, 1986.

Christian, David. "Traditional and Modern Drinking Cultures in Russia on the Eve of Emancipation." *Australian Slavonic and East European Studies* 1, 1 (1987): 61–84.

——. "Vodka and Corruption in Russia on the Eve of Emancipation." *Slavic Review* 46 (Fall/Winter 1987): 471–88.

Coale, A., B. A. Anderson, and E. Härm. *Human Fertility in Russia since the Nineteenth Century.* Princeton, 1979.

Confino, Michael. "La politique de tutelle des seigneurs Russes envers leurs paysans vers la fin du XVIIIe siècle." *Revue des études slaves* 37 (1960): 39–69.

——. *Domaines et seigneurs en Russie vers la fin du XVIIIe siècle.* Paris, 1963.

——. *Systèmes agraires et progrès agricole: L'assolement triennal en Russie aux XVIII–XIXe siècles.* Paris, 1969.

——. "Russian Customary Law and the Study of Peasant Mentalities." *The Russian Review* 44, 1 (1985): 35–43.

Coquin, François-Xavier. *La Sibérie: Peuplement et immigration paysanne au XIXe siècle.* Paris, 1975.

Czap, Peter, Jr. "Peasant Class Courts and Peasant Customary Justice in Russia, 1861–1912." *Journal of Social History* 1, 2 (1967): 149–78.

——. "Marriage and the Peasant Joint Family in the Era of Serfdom." In *The Family in Imperial Russia,* ed. David Ransel, 103–23. Urbana, 1978.

Dodge, Robert H. "Peasant Education and Zemstvo Schools in Moscow Province, 1865–1905." *Topic* 27, 1 (1974): 48–61.

——. "The Role of Zemstvo Schools in Advancing Public Health, 1905–1914." *Slavic and East European Education Review* 2 (1979): 1–10.

Druzhinin, D. M. "The Liquidation of the Feudal System in the Russian Manorial Village (1862–1882)." *Soviet Studies in History* 21, 3 (1982–83): 14–67.

Dunn, Stephen, and Ethel Dunn. "The Great Russian Peasant: Culture Change or Cultural Development." *Ethnology* 2 (July 1963): 320–38.

——. *The Peasants of Central Russia.* New York, 1967.

Edelman, Robert. "Rural Proletarians and Peasant Disturbances: The Right Bank Ukraine in the Revolution of 1905." *Journal of Modern History* 57 (June 1985): 248–77.

——. *Proletarian Peasants: The Revolution of 1905 in Russia's Southwest.* Ithaca, 1987.

Eklof, Ben. *Russian Peasant Schools: Officialdom, Village Culture, and Popular Pedagogy, 1861–1914*. Berkeley, 1987.

——. "Ways of Seeing: Recent Anglo-American Studies of the Russian Peasant (1861–1914)." *Jahrbücher für Geschichte Osteuropas* 36, 1 (1988): 57–79.

——. "Kindertempel or Shack? The School Building in Late Imperial Russia (A Case Study of Backwardness)." *Russian Review* 47 (April 1988): 117–43.

Emmons, Terence, ed. *The Emancipation of the Russian Serfs*. New York, 1970.

——, and Wayne Vucinich, eds. *The Zemstvo in Russia: An Experiment in Local Self-Government*. Cambridge, 1982.

Engelstein, Laura. "Morality and the Wooden Spoon: Russian Doctors View Syphilis, Social Class, and Sexual Behavior, 1890–1905." *Representations* 14 (Spring 1981): 169–208.

Farnsworth, Beatrice. "The Litigious Daughter-in-Law: Family Relations in Rural Russia in the Second Half of the 19th Century." *Slavic Review* 45, 1 (1986): 49–64.

Field, Daniel. *The End of Serfdom: Nobility and Bureaucracy in Russia, 1855–1861*. Cambridge, 1976.

——. "A Far-off Abode of Work and Pure Pleasures." *Russian Review* 39 (July 1980): 348–58.

——. "Peasants and Propagandists in the Russian Movement to the People of 1874." *Journal of Modern History* 59 (September 1987): 415–38.

——. *Rebels in the Name of the Tsar*. Boston, 1989.

Figes, Orlando. "The Russian Land Commune and the Agrarian Question, 1905–1930." *Peasant Studies* 11 (Winter 1984): 119–30.

——. "Collective Farming and the 19th-Century Russian Land Commune: A Research Note." *Soviet Studies* 38, 1 (1986): 89–97.

Freeze, Gregory L. *From Supplication to Revolution: A Documentary Social History of Imperial Russia*. New York, 1987.

Frieden, Nancy M. "The Russian Cholera Epidemic, 1892–93, and Medical Professionalization," *Journal of Social History* 10 (June 1977): 538–59.

——. "Child Care: Medical Reform in a Traditionalist Culture." In *The Family in Imperial Russia*, ed. David Ransel, 236–59. Urbana, 1978.

Gatrell, Peter. *The Tsarist Economy 1850–1917*. London, 1986.

Gerschenkron, Alexander. "Agrarian Policies and Industrialization: Russia 1861–1917." In *The Cambridge Economic History of Europe*, vol. 6, pt. 2, 706–800. Cambridge, 1965.

Glickman, Rose. "An Alternative View of the Peasantry: The *Raznochintsy* Writers of the 1860s." *Slavic Review* 32, 4 (1973): 693–704.

Gorer, Geoffrey, and John Rickman. *The People of Great Russia: A Psychological Study*. New York, 1962.

Gorkii, Maksim. "On the Russian Peasantry." *Journal of Peasant Studies* 4 (October 1976): 11–27.

Grant, Steven. "*Obshchina* and *Mir*." *Slavic Review* 35 (December 1976): 636–52.

Gregory, P. R. "Grain Marketing and Peasant Consumption in Russia, 1885–1913." *Explorations in Economic History* 17, 2 (1980): 135–64.

——. *Russian National Income, 1885–1913*. Cambridge: 1982.

Hamburg, G. M. "The Crisis in Russian Agriculture: A Comment." *Slavic Review* 37, 3 (1978): 481–86.

Harrison, Mark. "Resource Allocation and Agrarian Class Formation: The Problem of Social Mobility among Russian Peasant Households, 1880–1930." *Journal of Peasant Studies* 4, 2 (1977): 127–61.

Hennessy, Richard. *The Agrarian Question in Russia 1905–1907. The Inception of the Stolypin Reform.* Giessen, 1977.

Hilton, Alison. "Russian Folk Art and 'High' Art in the Early Nineteenth Century." In *Art and Culture in Nineteenth-Century Russia,* 237–54. Bloomington, 1983.

Hoch, Steven L. "Serf Diet in Nineteenth-Century Russia." *Agricultural History* 56, 2 (1982): 391–414.

———. *Serfdom and Social Control in Russia: Petrovskoe, A Village in Tambov.* Chicago, 1986.

Hourwich, Isaac A. *The Economics of the Russian Village.* New York, 1970. (Reprint of 1892 edition.)

Hussain, Athar, and Keith Tribe. *Marxism and the Agrarian Question.* Vol. 2, *Russian Marxism and the Peasantry 1861–1930.* London, 1981.

Immonen, Hannu. *The Agrarian Program of the Russian Socialist Revolutionary Party, 1900–1914.* Helsinki, 1988.

Ivanits, Linda J. *Russian Folk Belief.* Armonk, NY, 1989.

Johnson, Robert E. "Peasant Migration and the Russian Working Class: Moscow at the End of the Nineteenth Century." *Slavic Review* 35 (December 1976): 652–64.

———. "Family Relations and the Rural-Urban Nexus: Patterns in the Hinterland of Moscow, 1880–1900." In *The Family in Imperial Russia,* ed. David Ransel, 263–79. Urbana, 1978.

Kahan, Arcadius. "Determinants of the Incidence of Literacy in Rural 19th-Century Russia." In *Education and Economic Development,* ed. C. A. Anderson and M. J. Bowman, 298–302. Chicago, 1965.

———. *Russian Economic History: The Nineteenth Century.* Chicago, 1989.

Kennard, Howard P. *The Russian Peasant.* New York, 1980. (Reprint of 1908 edition.)

Kerblay, Basil. "L'Evolution de l'alimentation rurale en Russie 1896–1960." *Annales ESC* 17 (1962): 885–913.

Kingston-Mann, Esther. *Lenin and the Problem of Marxist Peasant Revolution.* New York, 1983.

Kolchin, Peter. *Unfree Labor: American Slavery and Russian Serfdom.* Cambridge, MA, 1987.

Kovalchenko, I. D., and N. B. Selunskaia. "Labor Rental in the Manorial Economy of European Russia at the End of the 19th Century and the Beginning of the 20th." *Explorations in Economic History* 18, (January 1981): 1–20.

Krug, Peter F. "The Debate over the Delivery of Health Care in Rural Russia: The Moscow Zemstvo, 1864–1878." *Bulletin of the History of Medicine* 50, 2 (1976): 226–41.

Krukones, James H. *To the People: The Russian Government and the Newspaper "Selskii Vestnik" ("Village Herald"), 1881–1917.* New York, 1987.

Lewin, Moshe. "Rural Society in Twentieth-Century Russia: An Introduction." *Social History* 9, 2 (1984): 171–80.

———. "Customary Law and Russian Rural Society in the Post-Reform Era." *The Russian Review* 44, 1 (1985): 1–19.

Macey, David A. *Government and Peasant in Russia, 1861–1906: The Pre-History of the Stolypin Reforms.* DeKalb, 1987.

Manning, Roberta. *The Crisis of the Old Order in Russia: Gentry and Government.* Princeton, 1982.

Martynova, Antonina. "Life of the Pre-Revolutionary Village as Reflected in Popular Lullabies." In *The Family in Imperial Russia*, ed. David Ransel, 171–85. Urbana, 1978.

Matossian, Mary. "The Peasant Way of Life." In *The Peasant in Nineteenth Century Russia*, ed. W. S. Vucinich, 1–40. Stanford, 1968.

——. "Climate, Crops and Natural Increase in Rural Russia, 1861–1913." *Slavic Review* 45 (Fall 1986): 457–69.

Melton, Edgar. "Proto-Industrialization, Serf Agriculture and Agrarian Social Structure: Two Estates in Nineteenth-Century Russia." *Past & Present*, no. 115 (May 1987): 69–106.

Minenko, N. A. "Traditional Forms of Investigation and Trial among the Russian Peasants of Western Siberia in the 18th and the First Half of the 19th Century." *Soviet Anthropology and Archeology* 21, 3 (1982–83): 55–79.

Mixter, Timothy. "Of Grandfather Beaters and Fat-Heeled Pacifists: Perceptions of Agricultural Labor and Hiring Market Disturbances in Saratov, 1872–1905." *Russian History* 7, pts. 1–2 (1980): 139–68.

Moore, M. P., Teodor Shanin, and Eugene D. Vinogradoff. "Horses, Households, and Villages in Peasant Russia." *Peasant Studies Newsletter* 5, 2 (1976): 18–25.

Mosse, W. E. "Stolypin's Villages." *Slavonic and East European Review* 43 (June 1965): 257–74.

Munting, R. "Outside Earnings in the Russian Peasant Farm: Tula Province, 1900–1917." *Journal of Peasant Studies* 3, 4 (1976): 428–46.

——. "Mechanization and Dualism in Russian Agriculture." *Journal of European Economic History* 8 (1979): 743–60.

Nosova, G. A. "Mapping of Russian Shrovetide Ritual (from Materials of the 19th and early 20th Centuries)." *Soviet Anthropology and Archaeology* 14, 1–2 (1975): 50–70.

Onias, Felix J., and Stephen Soudakoff, eds. *The Study of Russian Folklore.* The Hague, 1975.

Owen, Launcelot A. *The Russian Peasant Movement 1906–1917.* New York, 1963.

Pallot, Judith. "Open Fields and Individual Farms: Land Reform in Pre-Revolutionary Russia." *Tijdscrift voor Economische en Sociale* 5 (1983).

——. "The Development of Peasant Land Holding from Emancipation to the Revolution." In *Studies in Russian Historical Geography*, vol. 1, ed. James Bater and R. A. French, 83–108. London, 1983.

——. "Agrarian Modernization on Peasant Farms in the Era of Capitalism." In *Studies in Russian Historical Geography*, vol. 2, ed. James Bater and R. A. French, 423–49. London, 1983.

——. "*Khutora* and *Otruba* in Stolypin's Program of Farm Individualization." *Slavic Review* 43 (Summer 1984): 242–56.

——. and Denis J. B. Shaw. *Landscape and Settlement in Romanov Russia.* New York, 1989.

Pape, Carsten. "The 'Peasant Zemstva': Popular Education in Vjatka Gubernija, 1867–1905." *Jahrbücher für Geschichte Osteuropas* 27, 4 (1979): 498–519.

Pearson, Thomas S. "The Origins of Alexander III's Land Captains: A Reinterpretation." *Slavic Review* 40 (Fall 1981): 384–403.

——. "Russian Law and Rural Justice: Activity and Problems of the Russian Justices of the Peace, 1865–1889." *Jahrbücher für Geschichte Osteuropas* 32, 1 (1984): 52–71.

Perrie, Maureen. "Document: The Russian Peasantry in 1907–1908: A Survey by the Socialist Revolutionary Party." *History Workshop Journal* 4 (1977): 171–91.

Poggio, Pier Paolo. *Commune contadina e rivoluzione in Russia: L'Obščina*. Milano, 1976.

Pushkarev, S. G. "The Russian Peasants' Reaction to the Emancipation of 1861." *The Russian Review* 27 (1968): 199–214.

Ramer, Samuel C. "Childbirth and Culture: Midwifery in the Nineteenth-Century Russian Countryside." In *The Family in Imperial Russia*, ed. David Ransel, 218–35. Urbana, 1978.

Ransel, David. *The Family in Imperial Russia: New Lines of Historical Research*. Urbana, 1978.

——. *Mothers of Misery: Child Abandonment in Russia*. Princeton, 1988.

Rayfield, Donald. "The Soldier's Lament: World War One Folk Poetry in the Russian Empire." *Slavonic and East European Review* 66, 1 (1988): 66–90.

Robbins, Richard G., Jr. *Famine in Russia, 1891–1892*. New York: 1975.

Robinson, G. T. *Rural Russia under the Old Regime*. New York, 1932.

Sadovnikov, D. *Riddles of the Russian People: A Collection of Riddles, Parables and Puzzles*, trans. A. C. Bigalow. Ann Arbor, 1986.

Sanders, John T. "'Once More into the Breach, Dear Friends': A Closer Look at Indirect Tax Receipts and the Condition of the Russian Peasantry, 1881–1899." *Slavic Review* 43 (Winter 1984): 657–66.

Seregny, Scott J. "Politics and the Rural Intelligentsia in Russia: A Biographical Sketch of Stepan Anikin, 1869–1919." *Russian History* 7, 1–2 (1980): 169–200.

——. "A Different Type of Peasant Movement: The Peasant Unions in the Russian Revolution of 1905." *Slavic Review* 47 (Spring 1988): 51–67.

——. *Russian Teachers and Peasant Revolution: The Politics of Education in 1905*. Bloomington, 1989.

Shanin, Teodor. "Socio-Economic Mobility and the Rural History of Russia, 1905–1930." *Soviet Studies* 23, 2 (1971): 222–35.

——. *The Awkward Class: Political Sociology of Peasantry in a Developing Society: Russia 1910–1925*. Oxford, 1972.

——. *Late Marx and the Russian Road: Marx and 'the Peripheries of Capitalism.'* New York, 1983.

——. *The Roots of Otherness: Russia's Turn of the Century*. Vol. 1, *Russia as a 'Developing Society'*; Vol. 2, *Russia 1905–07: Revolution as a Moment of Truth*. New Haven, 1985.

Shimkin, Dmitri B. "National Forces and Ecological Adaptations in the Development of Russian Peasant Societies." In *Process and Pattern in Culture*, ed. R. A. Manners, 237–47. Chicago, 1964.

Shimkin, Dmitri B., and Sanjuan, Pedro. "Culture and World View: A Method of Analysis Applied to Rural Russia." *American Anthropologist* 55, 3 (1953): 329–48.

Shinn, William T., Jr. "The Law of the Russian Peasant Household." *Slavic Review* 20, 4 (1961): 601–21.

Simms, James Y., Jr. "The Crisis in Russian Agriculture at the End of the Nineteenth Century: A Different View." *Slavic Review* 36, 3 (1977): 377–98.
——. "The Crop Failure of 1891: Soil Exhaustion, Technological Backwardness, and Russia's 'Agrarian Crisis.'" *Slavic Review* 41, 2 (1982): 236–50.
——. "The Economic Impact of the Russian Famine of 1891–92." *Slavonic and East European Review* 60 (January 1982): 63–74.
Smith, R. E. F., and David Christian. *Bread and Salt: A Social and Economic History of Food and Drink in Russia.* New York, 1984.

Thurston, Gary. "The Impact of Russian Popular Theater, 1886–1915." *Journal of Modern History* 55 (June 1983): 237–67.
Treadgold, Donald W. *The Great Siberian Migration: Government and Peasant in Resettlement from Emancipation to the First World War.* Princeton, 1957.
Tultseva, L. A. "Calendrical Religious Festivals in the Life of the Contemporary Peasantry (Based on Materials from Riazan Oblast)." *Soviet Anthropology and Archaeology* 13, 1 (1974): 38–54.

Vasudevan, H. S. "Peasant Land and Peasant Society in Late Imperial Russia." *Historical Journal* 31 (March 1988): 207–22.
Vinogradoff, Eugene D. "The 'Invisible Hand' and the Russian Peasant." *Peasant Studies Newsletter* 4, 3 (July 1975): 6–19.
——. "The Russian Peasantry and the Elections to the Fourth State Duma." In *The Politics of Rural Russia 1905–1914*, ed. Leopold H. Haimson, 219–60. Bloomington, 1979.
Von Laue, Theodore H. "Russian Peasants in the Factory." *Journal of Economic History* 26 (1961): 61–80.
Vucinich, Wayne S., ed. *The Peasant in Nineteenth-Century Russia.* Stanford, 1968.

Wada, Haruki. "The Inner World of Russian Peasants." *Annals of the Institute of Social Science* 20 (Tokyo, 1979): 61–94.
Weissman, Neil. "Rural Crime in Tsarist Russia: The Question of Hooliganism, 1905–1914." *Slavic Review* 37 (June 1978): 228–40.
Wilbur, Elvira M. "Was Russian Peasant Agriculture Really That Impoverished? New Evidence from a Case Study from the 'Impoverished Center' at the End of the 19th Century." *Journal of Economic History* 43, 1 (1983): 137–44.
Worobec, Christine. "Customary Law and Property Devolution among Russian Peasants in the 1870s." *Canadian Slavonic Papers* 26, 2–3 (1984): 220–34.
——. "Reflections on Customary Law and Post-Reform Peasant Russia." *The Russian Review* 44, 1 (1985): 21–25.
——. "Horse Thieves and Peasant Justice in Post-Emancipation Imperial Russia." *Journal of Social History* 21 (Winter 1987): 281–93.

Yaney, George L. *The Urge to Mobilize: Agrarian Reform in Russia, 1861–1930.* Urbana, 1982.

About the Contributors

John Bushnell is associate professor of history at Northwestern University. His publications include *Mutiny amid Repression: Russian Soldiers in the Revolution of 1905–1906* (1985) and *Moscow Graffiti: Language and Subculture* (1990).

Ben Eklof is associate professor of history at Indiana University. In addition to several articles on education and the peasantry in rural Russia, he is the author of *Russian Peasant Schools: Officialdom, Village Culture, and Popular Pedagogy, 1861–1914* (1986) and *Soviet Briefing* (1989).

Barbara Engel is associate professor of history at the University of Colorado, Boulder. She is the author of *Mothers and Daughters: Women of the Intelligentsia in Nineteenth-Century Russia* (1983) and co-editor, with Clifford Rosenthal, of *Five Sisters: Women Against the Tsar* (1975, 1987).

Stephen P. Frank is assistant professor of history at Boston University. He is the author of *Cultural Conflict, Law, and Criminality in Rural Russia, 1861–1907* (forthcoming).

Rose Glickman is the author of numerous articles on Russian women and of *Russian Factory Women: Workplace and Society, 1880–1914* (1984). Her current research involves rural peasant women.

Robert E. Johnson is associate professor of history at Erindale College, University of Toronto. He is the author of *Peasant and Proletarian: The Working Class of Moscow in the Late Nineteenth Century* (1979).

Moshe Lewin is professor of history at the University of Pennsylvania. His numerous publications include *Russian Peasants and Soviet Power: A Study of Collectivization* (1968), *Lenin's Last Struggle* (1968), *The Making of the Soviet System: Essays in the Social History of Interwar Russia* (1985), and *The Gorbachev Phenomenon* (1988).

Boris Mironov is senior research fellow at the Leningrad Section of the Institute of History, USSR Academy of Sciences. Among his many publications are *Vnutrennii rynok Rossii vo vtoroi polovine XVIII — pervoi polovine XIX v.* (Leningrad, 1981) and *Khlebnye tseny v Rossii za dva stoletiia (XVIII–XIX vv.)*, as well as articles on the rural economy and peasantry in imperial Russia.

Maureen Perrie is lecturer in Russian history at the Centre for Russian and East European Studies at the University of Birmingham. Her publications include *The Agrarian Policy of the Russian Soviet–Revolutionary Party, From its Origins Through the Revolution of 1905–1907* (1976) and *The Image of Ivan the Terrible in Russian Folklore* (1987).

Index

Agitation, revolutionary 200–2, 211–12
Agrarian crisis. *See* Peasant movement of 1905–7
Agrarian reforms 7–8, 23, 28–31, 41, 214
Agriculture
   collectivization of 32, 76, 173
   demographics and productivity of 21, 89–90
   division of labor in 47–9, 52–4, 56, 71
   land utilization systems 32, 42
   post-reform decline in 28–31, 194–9
Ancestor cults 159–60, 162–3, 166
Army the tsarist
   battle performance of 111, 193
   cultural modernization and 101–3, 110–11, 210
   economic functions of 103–9
   1874 reform of 22–3
   military conscription and rejection 22–3, 28–9
   officer roles in 106–9
   peasant recruitment into 22–3, 28–9, 68, 109
Art peasant
   bird and horse motifs 176–82
   cultural assimilation by 179–80, 185–8
   female figures in 163–4, 169, 176–80
   life of traditional images in 169–74, 179–80
   rural religion and 186–8
   sun and homage motifs 174–5, 182–5
Arteli. See under Work
Artisanal collective (*artel*) 24, 93–5, 109, 201

Bast-matting industry 82, 92–3
Belorussia 23, 197–8
Black earth provinces 54–6, 62, 73, 196–8, 201
Black repartition 197
Bourgeoisie 20–1, 23, 26, 28, 32–3
Brandt, A. F. 138
Brickmaking industry 91–2
Bunakov, Nicholas 128
Bushnell, John 4, 119, 227

Capitalism 21, 28, 70, 76, 81, 83, 194, 203, 211
Catholicism 156, 166
Central Industrial Region 50–3, 67–72, 198
Character education (*vospitanie*) 117–18
Charity, rural 10, 22, 148
Charivaris. See under Crime and punishment
Chekhov, Anton Pavlovich 185
Children
   primary education of 115–30
   raising of 70, 76, 82–4, 87–9

spirits of 162–3
survival rates of 71–2
work by 76, 82, 87–9, 91
Christianity, peasant 157–60, 166–8, 186–7
Chukhloma district 67–77
Church Slavonic 125–7
Cities, growth of. *See* Urbanization
Class consciousness 206–8, 211
Common law, peasant
   community justice and 133–5
   rural communes and 11–13
   women's status under 45–6
   See also Crime and punishment
Communes, rural peasant
   conformity and 13, 19–20, 22, 25–6, 140–1
   durability of 31–3, 167–8
   functions of 8–13
   norms of life in 25–7
   post-reform directions of 32–3, 214
   principles of 25–7, 29
   repartitional 28–31, 197, 211
   socialization by 18–20, 29
   See also Village assembly
Communication
   revolutionary unrest and 200–2, 210
   zemliak networks and 91–2, 94–5
Composite communes 8–9
Conformity. *See under* Human behavior
Courting. *See under* Marriage
Crafts needlework
   embroidery 170, 182
   lace-making 52, 58
   See also Kustar production work
Crime and punishment
   collective community actions (*vozhdeniia*) 138, 150
   community violence and 133–5, 144–5, 148–9
   horse theft 144–7, 150
   murder 74, 135, 145, 148
   official *vs.* peasant 147–9
   rough music (*charivaris*) 134–5, 137–44, 149
   self-adjudication (*samosud*) 134–7, 144–9
   theft, petty 138–41
   witchcraft 133–4, 147–50
   within marriage 48, 73–4, 142–3
Cults. *See* Popular religion
Cultural life, peasant
   army service and 109–11
   charivaris and 134–5, 137–44, 149
   city-living and 95–6

Cultural life, peasant (*cont.*)
  elite attitudes toward 57–9, 115, 117, 129–30, 155, 171, 185
  festivals and holidays 155, 157, 159–60, 164
  juridical beliefs of 134–7, 148–50
  official culture transmisson and 115, 117, 120–1, 124–30, 148–50
  reading patterns and 126
  revolutionaries' views of 197, 199
  rural communes and 10, 167
  social groups within 197–8
  waning of 173

Dementev, E. M. 87
Demonology 160–2, 166
Denisov, Andrei 187
Deviant behavior. *See under* Human behavior
Distaffs, tower-house (*teremkovye*) 172–5
District councils. *See Zvemstva* councils
Dragomirov 103, 106
Dress and clothing
  factory hand-made 50–3, 55–8
  fashionable and city 19, 28, 52, 71–2, 185–6
  wife-made 47, 55

Economic status, peasant 148, 202–8
  leveling mechanisms of 21–3, 27, 197
Education, peasant
  by official (*zemstvo*) schools 115, 117, 120–1
  by peasant free schools (*volnye shkoly*) 117–19, 121
  costs of 120–1
  elite attitudes on 115, 117, 129–30
  literacy without socialization 124–30
  peasant uses of 117, 123–4, 126–7, 129–30
  school attendance and 123–4
  schools expansion movement 115–18, 121–2
Efimenko, Petr 135–6
Eklof, Ben 4–5, 227
Elders, peasant (*stariki*) 15–16, 18–19, 46, 93–4, 195
Elite culture. *See* Official culture
Emancipation of the serfs. *See under* Serfdom
Engel, Barbara 4, 227
Engelgardt, A. N. 27
Erikson, Erik 172
Estates (*sosloviia*) 25, 197, 207
Europe, Western 81, 85, 89, 127, 134, 137–8, 156
European Russia 21, 24–5, 29–30, 198, 213–14

Factory work
  internal 87–9

See also Kustar production work
Family income
  communal assistance and 20–2, 27, 148
  household inheritance and 23, 82
  outmigration and 67–72, 75–6, 84–6
Family landholding 23, 29, 81
Family life
  city factory workers and 82–5, 87–9, 93–6
  hereditary factory workers 87–9
  household mythology and 159–62, 167–8
Family structure
  bifurcated 49, 53, 66–7, 71–4, 76, 84–90
  multiple-family household 46–8, 89–90
  nuclear 48, 73
  working/consuming households 20–1
Famine of 1891–92 117
Farmakovskii, V. 121–2
Feudalism. *See* Serfdom
Folk art. *See* Art, peasant
Folk songs. *See* Oral traditions
Fragmented communes 9
France 127
Frank, Stephen P. 5, 227

Galich district 67, 73
Generational continuity 18, 209–10
Gentry, landowner
  peasant movement against 195–9, 202–8, 212
  taxation of 120
Girls, attitudes towards 2–3, 59, 116, 118, 124, 141, 144
Glickman, Rose 4, 228
Gogol, Nikolai Vasilyevich 164

Hajnal, J. 84
Hand-made clothing. *See* Dress and clothing
Handmade products 50
See also Kustar production work
Health
  illness and 161
  migrants' families and 71–3
  of unfit army recruits 28–9
Historical theories 1–3, 200
Holy Synod schools 125
Homes, peasant 72, 177, 180
Horizontal mobility. *See under* Social mobility
Human behavior
  conformity and non-conformity 13, 19–20, 22, 25–6, 140–1
  individualism 20, 29, 32
Human rights equality 21, 26

Icon veneration 158, 164, 166
Icons, folk. *See* Art, peasant

Imperial Free Economic Society 7, 29, 199–210
Individualism. *See under* Human behavior
Industrial society characteristics 31–3, 77
Industrialization policy 193–4
Information sources
   attitudes and biases in 1, 57–9
   Free Economic Society surveys 7, 29, 199–210
   school census 121–2
   zvemstva studies 2, 49, 56–7, 59, 67, 86, 120, 128–30
Inheritance 23, 45, 48, 81–2
Intelligentsia, rural 194, 201, 211–13
Islam 167

Johnson, Robert 69, 228
Justice, popular. *See* Crime and punishment

Kapterev, P. F. 120–1
Kartsev, E. 135
Knitting work 50–1, 54
Korolenko, Vladimir G. 22
Kostroma province 67–77
Kulaks 27, 196–7, 204–7
Kulomzin, A. N. 120
Kustar production work
   factory putting-out 50–3, 55–8
   participants in 50, 58–9

Labor
   household units of 20–1
   work crews (*arteli*) 24, 93–5, 109
   See also Migration; Work
Labor principle and peasant movement
   exemption 205
Land allotments
   communal holding of 18, 26, 29–30, 81
   redemption payments and 29–30, 68, 72, 194, 213
   retention and renunciation of 84, 88
   seizure by peasants 23, 195–9, 204–5, 212
Land distribution movement 29–31, 41
   See also Peasant movement of 1905–7
Land ownership
   communal *vs.* private 23, 29, 212
   household *vs.* communal 23, 29, 81
   types of 12
Language skills 126–7
Leadership, communal 15–19, 46, 93–4, 195
Leather crafts and industry 51–2, 58
Legal system, state
   rural communes and 9, 147, 149–50
   township courts (*volost*) 136, 142–3
   See also Common law, peasant

Lenin Vladimir Ilich Ulyanov 87, 126, 156, 210
Lerner, Daniel 101–2
Lewin, Moshe 2, 5, 228
Libraries 126, 129
Literacy
   in the army 102, 119
   peasant illiteracy and 15, 29, 32, 58, 201
   peasant-sponsored 118–19, 121–2
   of women 72, 74, 118
Livestock ownership 68, 203–4
   horses 144–7, 150, 180–2, 203

Magic and sorcery 156–7, 164–5
   witchcraft 133–4, 147–50
Marriage
   city and country patterns of 81–2, 84–6, 95–6
   courtship and 69, 71, 96, 184
   disapproved 138, 141
   patrilocal 45–7
   rates of 69, 85–6
   traditional 45–9, 81–2
   urban-rural economics 65–72, 75–6, 83–6, 94–5
Material culture 19, 169–74, 179–80
Math skills and numeracy 126, 132
Men's roles
   domestic violence and 48, 73–4, 142–4
   as patriarchs 45–8, 60
   as workers without families 83–4
Men's work 45, 47, 53–4, 56, 68, 71, 75–6, 179
   in the army 104–9
Middlemen (*khoziaiki*) 59
Migration
   divided households and 67–72
   female wage labor 52, 55, 70–1, 75, 83, 86, 90
   hiring agents and 93–4
   men's wage labor 49, 55, 63, 66–7
   1905–7 peasant movement and 194, 201–2, 204
   regional loyalties and 90–6, 204
   seasonal 71, 75–7, 88, 93, 104–6, 110, 201–2
   soldiers' civilian work and 104–7
   stable patterns of 75–7
   women's lives and 71–4
   See also Social mobility
Military life. *See* Army, the tsarist
Miliutin, Dmitrii 102, 108, 119
Mining-metallurgical industries 93
Mironov, Boris 4, 228
Modernization 85, 124, 195
   military service and 101–3, 110–11
Moiseenko, Petr A. 94–5
Morality
   ethical relativity and 12–13

Morality (*cont.*)
  marriage and 74, 138, 141
  rural communes and 12–13, 69, 136
  See also Crime and punishment
Moscow 82–7, 90–1, 95
Music. *See under* Oral traditions
Mutinies, army 110–11
Mythology. *See* Popular religion

Names and nicknames 18, 129
Netting, Anthony 4–5
Nonagricultural communes 8–9
North America 90–1, 134, 137–8

Official culture
  peasant conflicts with 148–50
  peasant views of 184–6
Officials, elected communal
  functions and duties 13–14, 22
  informal roles of 14
  selection of 14–15, 35
Old Believer movement 168, 187
Oral traditions 15–16, 18
  folk songs 71, 73, 95
  proverbs 17, 23, 46, 145, 162
  rough music (*paramusique*) 137–44
Outmigration. *See* Migration
Outside views of peasant life 3, 57–9, 197, 199

Pascal, Blaise 156
Passports and migration 55, 62, 68–71, 95
Patriarchy and patrilocalism 45–6, 59–60, 66–7, 76, 183, 195
Pay
  army 105
  men's *vs.* women's 52–3, 56
Peasant movement of 1905–7
  development and forms of 194–9
  external influences on 200–2
  revolutionary parties and 205, 210–14
  sociobiological participation factors 205, 208–10
  socioeconomic participation factors and 202–8
  studies of 199–210
Peasant Union, All-Russia 200, 212–13
Peasant Union, Socialist Revolutionary 211–12
Permagore 179
Perrie, Maureen 5, 228
Peskov, P. A. 88
Piatnitskii, M. E. 95
Pokrovskii district 53
Politics, communal 13–17, 74
Poor and landless peasants 203–4, 206

Popular religion
  characteristics of rural 10, 155–7, 160–2, 166–8, 186–8
  demonology and 160–2
  magic and sorcery and 156–7, 164–5
  outcast souls beliefs 162–4
  peasant Christianity as 157–60, 186–7
  rural Christianity and 166–8
Population growth
  birthrates 71
  mortality rates and 71–3
  urban 24–5, 54, 81–4
Populist movement of the 1870s 194–5
Priests and clergy 16–17, 159, 201
Produce selling by women 53–4
Prokopovich, S. N. 75–6
Proletariat groups 20–1, 23, 65, 75–6, 87–90, 207–8, 211, 214
Property ownership
  private 45, 212
  See also Land ownership
Provincial councils. *See Zvemstva* councils
Public opinion
  humiliation and ostracism 137–44
  influence of 13, 18–20, 29
  revolutionary ideas and 200–2, 205, 208
  See also Intelligentsia, rural

Rashin, A. G. 83
Reading and language skills 127–30
Reforms
  1906 Stolypin agrarian 23, 214
  1917 orthographic 126–7
  agrarian 7–8, 23, 28–31, 41, 214
  land distribution movement 29–31, 41
  Miliutin army 102, 108
  See also Serfdom
Regional loyalties 90–6
Religion. *See* Popular religion
Remeslo work 56
Revolts, peasant 110–11, 168, 187
  See also Peasant movement of 1905–7
Revolution of 1917 33, 75–6
Revolutionary parties
  peasant movement theories of 207–8, 211–12
  Social Democrats 197, 199–200, 207, 210–11
  Socialist Revolutionaries 199–200, 207, 211–13
Rich peasants. *See Kulaks*
Rittikh, A. 101, 103
Rituals, community. *See* Cultural life, peasant
Robinson, G. T. 1, 122
Robinson, Richard D. 101–2
Rural communes. *See* Communes, rural peasant

Russian Geographical Society survey 7
Russo-Japanese War 193, 202, 214
Rybakov, B. A. 169

St Petersburg 53–4, 95, 195
   male peasant migrants and 66, 68–9, 71, 75–6, 94, 172, 201
Saints, cults of the 157–9
Samosud. See under Crime and punishment
Samovars 170, 186
Saratov province 54–5
Schools. *See* Education, peasant
Sects. *See* Popular religion
Serfdom 29, 209
   1861Emancipation Act and 23, 28–31, 54, 66, 68, 193–4
   post-reform parallels to 88, 103–11, 148–9
Sexual roles and customs 46, 57, 77, 163, 184
   community control over 74, 138, 141–4
Shanin, Teodor 2, 66
Shelley, Percy Bysshe 175–6
Shuiskii district 52
Shuster, Iu. A. 66
Simmel, Georg 19
Sirin images 176–80
Social Democrats. *See under* Revolutionary parties
Social mobility, peasant 10, 24–5, 32
   horizontal 24, 88–9
   vertical 24–5
   See also Migration
Socialist Revolutionaries. *See under* Revolutionary parties
Socialist Revolutionary Union of Primary Teachers 212
Soligalich district 67–77
Spinning occupations 51, 55
State authority 13–16, 213–14
   See also Zvemstva councils
State religion, Orthodox, and anti-Orthodox beliefs 155–7, 166, 186–7
Statistics
   army rejects 28–9
   1905–7 peasant movement 196–8
   primary education 116
   school admissions 122
Status, homogeneity of socio-economic 20–3
Stereotypes. *See* Outsider views of peasant life
Stolypin reforms of 1906 23, 214
Strikes and strikers 195–7, 201, 203, 206, 208
Suicide 19, 162

Taxation
   arrears 21, 28, 72

communal proportionality of 9, 27
refusal to pay 195
rural communes and 9, 12, 21, 27–8, 120
Teachers 115, 119–21, 124, 194, 201, 211–12
Tenishev, Vlacheslav V. 136
Testing, schooling retention 124–30
Textile industries 51, 83, 92
Third World countries and internal migration 86, 90–1
Thompson, Edward 137
Training
   military 102, 104, 119
   occupational 58, 68
   See also Education, peasant
Tugan-Baranovskii 87
Turkish army 101–2

Ukraine 23
Urban culture, peasant migrants and 24–5, 33, 69, 82–4, 87–9, 95–6, 110
Urban living conditions, peasant migrant 73, 82–4, 94–6
Urban-rural nexus
   family economy and 65–72, 75–6, 83–6, 94–5
   revolutionary ideas and the 194, 200–2
Urbanization 24–5, 33, 54, 81–4, 86, 110–11

Vacation area jobs 54
Vannovskii 102
Village assembly
   functions of 8, 16–17, 19
   justice of 136, 139–41
   women in the 17, 74
Vilnius province 23
Violence
   community or mob 133–5, 139–40
   domestic 48, 73, 142–3
   internal army 106
Vladimir district 52–3, 88
Vodka 28, 139–41, 144
Volnye raboty. See under Work
Voronezh province 124–5, 128

Water maidens (*rusalki*) 163–4, 177–80
Weaving for factories. *See Kustar* production work
Weber, Max 156, 164
Wife-beating 48, 73, 142–3
Witchcraft. *See* Magic and sorcery
Witte, Sergey Yulyevich 2, 193
Women, peasant
   observer views of 57, 59–60, 208

Women, peasant (*cont.*)
  oppression and exploitation of 48, 59–60,
    73–4, 139, 141–4
  quality of life of 57–60, 71–4
Women's roles
  as in-laws 46–7, 66
  as migrants to cities 52, 55, 83, 86
  in peasant art images 163–4, 169, 176–80
  political 17, 74, 208–10
  rural Christianity and 167
  as teachers 124
  as widows and spinsters 73, 84, 90
  witchcraft and 133–4, 147–50
  See also Marriage
Women's work
  city and factory 52, 55, 83, 86
  dairy and produce selling 53–4
  domestic household, city 70
  domestic household, country 45–9, 184
  domestic service 83, 90
  domestic wage-earning 49–57
  expectations about 45–9, 59–60, 66, 69, 142
  fieldwork 47–52, 54, 56–7, 71
  geographical distribution of 52–7
  Kustar production 50–3, 55–8
  middlemen and 50, 58–9
  rural family share of 49, 52, 56–7

Wool industry 60–1
Work
  agricultural 45, 47–9, 52–4, 56, 71
  family domestic 45–8
  gender-differentiated 45, 47, 49, 52–4, 56, 62,
    68, 71, 75–6, 179
  hereditary factory 87–9
  regional concentrations of 58, 91–2
  regional networking (*zemliakchestvo*) and
    91–2, 94–5, 109
  soldier's civilian (*volnye raboty*) 104–7,
    109
  wage labor 49, 52–3, 56, 70, 75–6
  work crews (*arteli*) 24, 93–5, 109
  See also Men's work; Women's work

Young militancy 209–10

Zelenin, D. K. 162
Zemliachestvo. See Regional loyalties
Zhbankov, D. N. 67, 73, 75–6, 96
Zvemstva councils
  definition of 61
  education and the 115, 117, 120–1
  employees of 194, 201, 212
  studies and reports 49, 56–7, 59, 67, 86, 120,
    128–30